Edited by Nick Pulford

Contributors

David Baxter	David Jennings	James Pugh
Richard Birch	Paul Kealy	Dave Randall
Matt Boyle	Andrew King	Stuart Riley
Marcus Buckland	Jon Lees	Colin Russell
James Burn	Richard Lowther	Alan Sweetman
Tom Collins	Kevin Morley	James Thomas
Dave Edwards	Tony O'Hehir	Sam Walker
Nick Freedman	Dave Orton	Kevin Walsh
Jack Haynes	Bryan Pugh	Nick Watts

Designed by David Dew
Cover artwork by Jay Vincent
Inside artwork by David Cramphorn, Nigel Jones and Stefan Searle

Published in 2017 by Racing Post Books, Raceform Ltd, 27 Kingfisher Court, Hambridge Road, Newbury, RG14 5SJ
Copyright © Racing Post 2017

ISBN 978-1910497067

Printed by Henry Stone Ltd

WELCOME to the Racing Post Cheltenham Festival Guide 2017, which we hope will once again prove to be the most comprehensive preview of jump racing's showpiece meeting.

Compiling this book always give me plenty of food for thought as I digest the various opinions of the Racing Post's experts and put together the many strands of festival form, and I hope every reader will feel the same as they make their way through the 208 pages.

We start with Racing Post tipsters, who pick their fancies and debate some of the burning issues, before the bookmakers do the same in our traditional Q & A.

Then we move on to the specialist scrutiny of Racing Post Ratings, Topspeed and the Racing Post analysts, who highlight the strengths and weaknesses shown by the leading protagonists in the build-up to the festival.

We also hear from champion trainers Willie Mullins and Paul Nicholls, who between them had ten of the 28 winners last year, and focus on the Irish challenge, trainer analysis and jockeys to watch.

Along the way, we look at the horses most likely to grab the headlines, course specialists, up-and-coming jockeys and trainers, things we learned from last year's festival, pedigree pointers and other talking points.

And that's just the first half of the book. In the second half, Racing Post betting editor Paul Kealy provides his extensive race-by-race guide with forthright opinions and profiles of more than 100 of the top runners, along with key trends.

And there are so many exciting names to talk about – Douvan, Altior, Thistlecrack, Unowhatimeanharry, Death Duty, Finian's Oscar, Melon, Defi Du Seuil . . .

We hope the Racing Post Cheltenham Festival Guide will help to cement your views about who will be the bankers and blowouts on March 14-17, those much-anticipated four days that have long been circled in red on the calendar.

Not long to go now.

Nick Pulford
Editor

Views from the specialists

The Racing Post's team of experts reveal their festival fancies and the major bookmakers discuss the big issues in our Q & A

Native River's power can make the difference

By Richard Birch

SHEER class, in theory at least, should be the main prerequisite for a Timico Cheltenham Gold Cup winner, but that has often not been the case.

Even without looking up past results, names like Lord Windermere, Synchronised, Cool Dawn, Cool Ground and Master Smudge come readily to mind as far from top-class winners. It isn't always pure ability that wins Gold Cups, it is bottomless stamina.

Colin Tizzard's King George hero Thistlecrack is a wonderfully talented horse, but the way he stands off his fences worries me. If he takes off two strides before the tricky downhill fence at Cheltenham, he will be on the floor.

His stable companion **Native River** stays four miles (he was an excellent second over the trip at last year's festival), improves with every run, jumps superbly and warmed up for the blue riband with a tremendously impressive Newbury victory. As soon as he crossed the line at the Berkshire track I muttered to myself, "that's the Gold Cup winner".

Some will argue Native River isn't quick enough to win a Gold Cup, but he didn't look slow in a three-runner Newbury field over just short of three miles.

With further progress to come, I can see him grinding away at the head of affairs and eventually breaking the hearts of his challengers up the straight.

The Stan James Champion Hurdle lacks overall quality this year and **Yanworth** should prove difficult to beat.

I recommended him as my 2017 festival fancy in the Racing Post just days after the conclusion of last year's meeting and his odds have contracted sharply as a host of possible rivals have been sidelined.

Yanworth stayed on strongly to win the Christmas Hurdle at Kempton and his potent combination of class, speed and stamina can prove decisive.

He is another with proven festival form, the single most important factor when it comes to assessing races at this great meeting.

Moon Racer, winner of the Champion Bumper in 2015, has long been a strong fancy for the Sky Bet Supreme Novices' Hurdle.

David Pipe has never made any secret of the regard in which he holds the son of Saffron Walden and Moon Racer's early-season victories over Ballyandy were franked by that rival's pulsating success in the Betfair Hurdle in February.

The eight-year-old clearly hasn't been easy to train – his racecourse appearances have been restricted to six starts (five wins) – and it's no surprise that Pipe put him away for this race after scoring at Cheltenham in November.

Moon Racer has always given the impression there is a massive race in him, and the temptation to go for the Champion Hurdle must be hard to resist.

However, every top stable is judged on number of Cheltenham winners and, with Pond House hardly packed with star names at present, it would be surprising if Pipe put a festival win in jeopardy by risking all for Champion glory.

Assuming Pipe opts for the calmer waters of

the Supreme, Moon Racer rates an excellent bet.

Some people consider Paul Nicholls to be lacking Cheltenham dynamite this year, but three of his team are firmly on my radar.

Wonderful Charm, who boasts a BHA rating of 153, must have a huge chance of landing the St James's Place Foxhunter if the ground rides good.

Sent off 5-1 third favourite for the JLT Novices' Chase three years ago, Wonderful Charm finished a highly creditable fifth behind Taquin Du Seuil, Uxizandre, Double Ross and Felix Yonger.

Quietly fancied for the Grand National last April until a pre-race downpour turned underfoot conditions against him, Wonderful Charm possesses real class at hunter-chase level and will prove hard to beat.

Cliffs Of Dover has been a revelation this campaign, winning six of his seven starts over hurdles.

The manner in which he skipped away from Nietzsche at Wetherby in October was that of a potentially high-class performer and, if he turns up for the JCB Triumph Hurdle after a recent training setback, my money will be down.

Movewiththetimes has multiple Cheltenham entries and it's all about second guessing where he will end up.

I thought he ran an absolute blinder in the Betfair Hurdle to make Ballyandy pull out all the stops and he will take plenty of beating if he lines up for the County Hurdle.

Movewiththetimes arrived at Newbury on the back of just four starts – three over hurdles and one in a bumper. He boasts abundant scope for improvement, possesses the cruising speed that will be required for a big-field Cheltenham test and gained valuable experience from Newbury.

Take Ballyandy out of the Betfair Hurdle and Movewiththetimes would have beaten Clyne, who had run The New One close at Haydock, by six lengths. What's not to like about him?

Wonderful Charm: the Foxhunter could be his for the taking

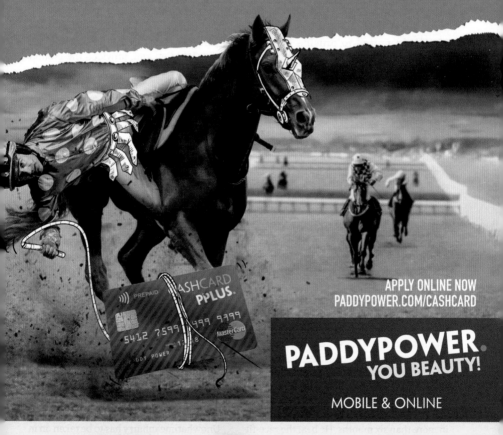

Mullins to turn up lots of aces despite losses

By David Jennings

WILLIE MULLINS and Rich Ricci have been dealt some horrible hands in the run-up to Cheltenham but they still have strong cards to play and chief among them is **Djakadam**, who looks poised to provide Ireland's champion trainer with his first Timico Cheltenham Gold Cup triumph.

Many believe Djakadam has missed his chance – twice, in fact. They were two glorious opportunities, but perhaps his best chance of glory is his third try in the race. Hear me out.

Rewind to the 2015 race. Djakadam was trying to do something that has not been achieved since Mill House back in 1963 – win the race as a six-year-old. He almost managed that remarkable feat but could not reel in the mud-loving Coneygree, who may have been a novice but was two years his elder.

Last year Djakadam was simply not himself and Ruby Walsh has admitted as much. He was runner-up again, this time to Don Cossack, but it was a more laboured effort on ground that was a little too lively. Why the flat performance? I'm convinced it was because he had fallen in the Cotswold Chase on the second-last day of January.

Djakadam's best performance, to these eyes anyway, was in the 2015 John Durkan Chase when he hammered Valseur Lido by a dozen lengths and was given an RPR of 175. It was significant that it was his first outing in more than six months. He beat the race-fit pair Outlander and Sub Lieutenant in this season's race, again after returning from a lengthy absence.

Djakadam has not been seen since finishing third to Outlander in the Lexus. Forget that run, as it was only 17 days after his John Durkan triumph. He needs to be fresh to show what he is made of.

Mullins has had the best part of three months to get him tuned up for another crack at the Gold Cup and, provided the ground does not turn quick by the Friday, Djakadam can make it third time lucky. He has posted RPRs of 176 and 177 in the last two runnings of the race and perhaps that could be good enough this time around.

Plenty of punters will place their faith in Melon to get their week off to a winning start but it is another Mullins representative, **Bunk Off Early**, who appeals more in the Sky Bet Supreme Novices' Hurdle.

The grey son of Zebedee was an 82-rated performer on the Flat for Andy Oliver and he appears to adore jumping hurdles, attacking them with relish. Having been so keen off a slowish pace in the Deloitte Novice Hurdle at Leopardstown over 2m2f, he did remarkably well to finish a close second (traded at a low of 1.1 in running).

The Supreme should suit him better as there will be an increased early tempo with a greater emphasis on jumping – his trump card. There was some 16-1 available straight after the Deloitte. Sadly that has long gone but 8-1 is still a fair price and he looks the most likely winner.

Unowhatimeanharry has to be taken on in the Sun Bets Stayers' Hurdle and **Shaneshill**, runner-up at the last three festivals, looks the one for the job at 12-1. He loves Cheltenham, comes alive in the spring and arrives on the back of a Grade 2 win at Gowran Park.

Mullins might have had high-profile defections in recent weeks, but he still has a top team heading to the Cotswolds and perhaps the mare **Let's Dance** is his best novice. She has looked a star this season and her experience as a second-season novice could prove paramount in the Trull House Stud Mares' Novice Hurdle.

Alpha Des Obeaux (below) burst a blood vessel on his latest outing at Leopardstown but reports suggest he is back to himself now and he has to be backed at 12-1 for what looks a weak renewal of the RSA Chase.

I am not convinced Cheltenham is Might Bite's track, Bellshill has blotted his copybook, Our Duke is not even entered and Disko is going for the JLT, so it looks a pretty poor race at this stage. Alpha Des Obeaux chased home Thistlecrack in last year's World Hurdle and has loads of experience over fences. Trust Mouse Morris to have him in peak condition for a race that has been his ultimate aim all season.

Master Blueyes has long been my idea of the Fred Winter winner and, needless to say, I was devastated when he bolted up by 18 lengths at Ludlow last time. However, to my amazement the handicapper put him up only 1lb to a mark of 133. Bizarre. What's more, there is still some 16-1 available with Betfair. That has to be taken as he could start favourite on the day. He has been crying out for better ground.

Noel Meade won the Albert Bartlett with a big-priced outsider in 2014 when Very Wood scored at 33-1 and he could so again, this time with **Mouin A Vent**, who does not deserve to be 50-1 given how close he got to Death Duty at Navan having jumped deplorably throughout. His schooling has gone swimmingly since according to his trainer and he is on course for the race.

Brain Power can solve Champion conundrum

By Nick Watts

THE Champion Hurdle market has never really had a solid look all season and now we have a favourite, Buveur D'Air, who started the season over fences.

He looked good when winning at Sandown last time out and beat Petit Mouchoir at Aintree last season, so he obviously has a chance but it is hard to see his price changing much before the festival.

I prefer instead the claims of his stablemate **Brain Power**. He has only been winning handicaps but he has been doing it with elan and an official mark of 162 puts him bang there, particularly when there must be more to come.

Reading between the lines, he has been a bit slow to cotton on to racing, but the evidence of his last two starts suggests he has got there now. Although we could not see much of his win at Ascot before Christmas, he finished on the bridle and he looks to have plenty of pace, an important asset for the sharp nature of the Champion Hurdle course.

His trainer, Nicky Henderson, has one of the most likeable horses in training in **Top Notch**, who finished fifth in last season's Champion Hurdle and now finds himself among the favourites for the JLT Novices' Chase.

Rightly so, too, as he has taken to fences amazingly well (he is not the biggest), winning four in a row culminating in a Grade 1 win in the Scilly Isles at Sandown in early February.

Critics may point to Clan Des Obeaux underperforming there, but that does a disservice to Top Notch's pinpoint jumping and the way he travelled through the race. He is clearly full of confidence and good ground should not unduly bother him. Indeed, as a small horse, it may even help him in the jumping department as it will make it easier when he takes off.

He has Yorkhill to beat – unless that rival is switched to the Champion Hurdle – but last year's Neptune Novices' Hurdle winner has not been overly impressive in his two chase outings and has won soft races. He won't find this as easy.

Prior to the Cotswold Chase, the Cheltenham Gold Cup looked a done deal and it still might be. But Thistlecrack's defeat by Many Clouds has left the door ajar for his rivals and the festival showpiece looks more open now.

Colin Tizzard hasn't done much wrong this season, but maybe running Thistlecrack in the Cotswold was a mistake. It is invariably a tough race and, with Many Clouds and Smad Place in this year's renewal, it took on a gruelling dimension, self-evident after the race following the sad demise of the winner.

Thistlecrack stayed all right, but he must have endured an awfully tough race too and it might have left a mark.

If that is the case, the obvious one to beat him is **Djakadam**. He is not everyone's favourite chaser and he gets beaten more often than not, but what should not be forgotten is his age. He is still only eight, and to have been placed in two Gold Cups already is no mean achievement. Add to that a brace of John Durkan wins and a romp in the Thyestes, and you can turn the question round and say he has achieved an awful lot for a still young chaser.

His two efforts in defeat at Cheltenham have been hard to crab – he was only just done by Coneygree in 2015 (as a six-year-old) and last year he was the only one to give Don Cossack any kind of race.

He arrives fresh this year having not raced since the Lexus, which should help him, and despite what some pundits say there has never been a stamina question about him. Remember it took The Fellow four attempts to win a Gold Cup, so there is plenty of time for Djakadam yet.

For a solid favourite, look no further than **Cantlow** in the Glenfarclas Chase. He has been a revelation for Enda Bolger and has been supremely consistent since switching to banks races (form figures of 202112).

He won at Cheltenham in December and, although he failed to follow up last time out over the same course and distance, he was conceding more than a stone to the winner, Urgent De Gregaine, and was ridden more prominently than may have been ideal.

He seems to get on well with Mark Walsh, so it would be nice to see him back in the saddle at the festival, and I don't feel his January defeat diminished his chances at all.

As a lover of fast ground, he is suited by the cross-country track at Cheltenham, which doesn't get as much water as the other two tracks, and a dry spring would increase confidence.

Cantlow: well suited by the demands of the cross-country course

Jon Lees on five horses who could be big stories of this year's festival

Thistlecrack

He has been the most talked-about jumps horse this season and victory as a first-season novice in the Cheltenham Gold Cup would set the seal on his rise to superstardom and create a buzz beyond the confines of the racing world.

He has had the X-factor ever since his devastating performance last year in what is now the Stayers' Hurdle, and only two months after starting his chasing career he added a mightily impressive victory in the King George.

His head defeat by Many Clouds on Festival Trials Day was overshadowed by the winner's unfortunate death but that has only added to the fascinating 'will he? won't he?' debate that will rage right up to race time on March 17.

Altior (right)

In Nicky Henderson's estimation, Altior possesses all the attributes to be the heir to the great Sprinter Sacre. The seven-year-old has some way to go yet but he is unbeaten over jumps, with five hurdles wins culminating in last year's Supreme Novices' Hurdle (Sprinter Sacre, remember, was third in that race in 2011) and four over fences this season.

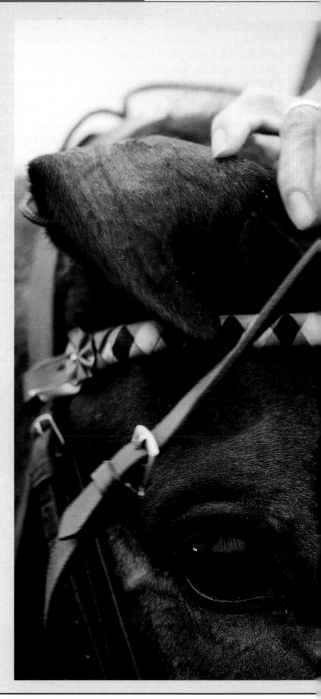

Altior "has the raw talent to be everything" according to Henderson and has been untroubled in those four appearances over fences, winning by a cumulative distance of 100 lengths. He is rated 4lb ahead of Sprinter Sacre at the same stage of his career and 5lb better than Douvan before last year's Racing Post Arkle success.

Douvan

Douvan v Altior is a clash to savour but, although both have entries for the Queen Mother Champion Chase, Nicky Henderson is likely to keep his fast-rising star on the novice route this season.

That will leave us to marvel again at the superb athleticism and effortless cruising speed of Douvan, who is heavy odds-on favourite for the Champion Chase after crushing all opposition since joining Willie Mullins as a novice hurdler in 2014.

He is unbeaten in 13 starts for the Irish champion trainer, including two at the festival (2015 Supreme Novices' Hurdle and 2016 Arkle Chase), and over fences his smallest winning margin is six and a half lengths.

If he wins again on March 15 – and any doubter is hard to find – comparison with the greats awaits him.

Unowhatimeanharry

We all know how much JP McManus stakes on having a festival winner and his early-season purchase of last season's Albert Bartlett Novices' Hurdle winner Unowhatimeanharry has turned out to be one of his wisest investments.

The nine-year-old's three starts in the green and gold silks have yielded a Grade 1 victory in the Long Walk Hurdle and two Grade 2 races in which Unowhatimeanharry consolidated the view he is one of the festival bankers.

He has proved so dominant that McManus was persuaded to take Yanworth off the Stayers' Hurdle trail and if that horse lands him the Champion Hurdle the owner will be doubly delighted.

Wholestone

Searching for a new star among the novice hurdlers is one of the fascinating aspects of every festival and there will be many opinions about this year's crop, which includes Melon, Finian's Oscar, Death Duty and Defi Du Seuil.

But don't discount Wholestone, whose trainer Nigel Twiston-Davies regularly punches above his weight at his local track. The six year-old's Graded victories at 2m4f and 3m give him a choice of options but unless it is very soft the Albert Bartlett Novices' Hurdle is the likely destination.

Few novice hurdlers will be better equipped for Cheltenham after his four appearances there this season and three wins.

'Thistlecrack may have left his race behind in Cotswold'

Will Thistlecrack add the Gold Cup to his King George victory?

Kevin Walsh Yes, if he can go out and bully his opponents from the front as he did with that power-packed Kempton display. An ever-improving Native River is the obvious danger, but Thistlecrack will be hard to stop if he gets a lead of any kind as the race hots up.

David Jennings He could, but he doesn't appeal at current odds. He certainly needs to be ridden more aggressively than he was in the Cotswold Chase. I expect Tom Scudamore to take it up with a circuit to race and try to do what Sam Thomas did on Denman in 2008. At the prices Djakadam appeals as a cracking each-way play at 7-1. He has posted RPRs of 176 and 177 in the last two years and arrives fresh having not run since the Lexus in December.

Paul Kealy My big concern with Thistlecrack is how much effort he puts into jumping fences as that takes its toll. The all-out figure he ran to in the Cotswold Chase was the sort he could run to on the bridle over hurdles and I think jumping fences takes it out of him, at least at Cheltenham. Djakadam looks rock solid to me and he can make it third time lucky.

Nick Watts I have a serious concern that Thistlecrack may have left his race behind in the Cotswold Chase. That was a gruelling contest – we know because of what happened to Many Clouds – yet Thistlecrack was fighting it out with him all the way up the home straight and must have endured an awfully tough race. I'm going for Djakadam, who comes into the race fresh having not raced since Christmas.

*Thistlecrack:
mixed opinions
on his chance
in Gold Cup*

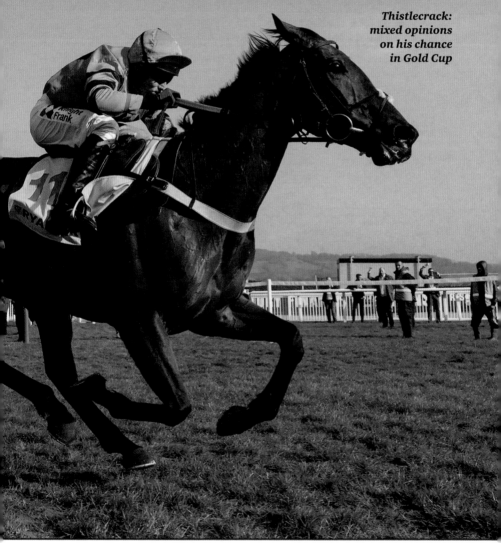

Richard Birch Thistlecrack's relative inexperience is a concern and I can't forget some of his over-extravagant leaps at Kempton. Cheltenham's steeplechase course – particularly in a Gold Cup – is unforgiving and I could see him ending up on the floor. His hard-as-nails stablemate Native River is less flashy but he will devour the final hill and looks perfectly equipped to rise to the biggest challenge of his career.

Who is your pick for an open-looking Champion Hurdle?

David Jennings Buveur D'Air. He might have had an unorthodox preparation for a Champion Hurdle but he is a slick jumper with speed and his Aintree victory over Petit Mouchoir now looks the strongest piece of form on offer.

Paul Kealy I have a feeling it could be between last year's Aintree one-two Buveur D'Air and Petit Mouchoir. The latter has got to get the fractions right and not do too much in front, while Buveur D'Air will be the closer. The softer the ground on day one, the stronger a fancy Buveur D'Air would be.

Kevin Walsh Events have transpired to

Buveur D'Air: popular choice for the Champion Hurdle

present Buveur D'Air with a huge opportunity and he should be able to take it. The recent exploits of both Altior and Min – albeit over fences – mean last year's Supreme is starting to look very strong and it's comfortably the best piece of form on offer here.

Nick Watts This is far from straightforward. Although he has yet to run in a trial I'm intrigued by Brain Power. He's been described as lacking some brainpower in the past by Nicky Henderson, but the evidence of his two runs this season (albeit limited by fog in one instance) suggests he has grown up and, if his official rating is to be believed, it puts him bang in contention.

Richard Birch It is the worst Champion Hurdle I can recall in terms of overall quality. Yanworth possesses the ability and staying power to take the crown. Petit Mouchoir rates a significant threat. I cannot understand why Buveur D'Air, who beat Rayvin Black only narrowly at Sandown, is favourite. Surely he is one to lay at current odds.

Is there any stopping Douvan in the Champion Chase?

Kevin Walsh In a word, no. If he completes the round he is highly likely to put up the best performance of the week. Fox Norton was firmly put in his place by the extraordinary Altior at Newbury recently but ran a solid trial for this and can complete the forecast.

Nick Watts Nothing except the fences or injury will stop Douvan. It'll be a struggle to find something to line up against him, with Colin Tizzard floating the idea of a Ryanair challenge with Fox Norton. Maybe Garde La Victoire could finish in the frame but it'll be at a respectful distance.

Paul Kealy Douvan wins, it's that simple. He's head and shoulders above the rest and only has to get round. In 'betting without' I'd take a chance on Garde La Victoire at a price if he gets the go-ahead. He's getting his act together and the rest are nothing special.

Richard Birch Douvan rates a special talent and odds of 1-3 seem spot on. He will win with his head in his chest and then the world of jump racing will hope and pray that a clash with the similarly superb Altior, who trades at the same price for the Racing Post Arkle, can materialise in the near future. What a duel that would be for everyone to look forward to.

David Jennings Douvan is flawless. Everything comes so easy to him and it is hard to envisage anything other than a straightforward success. What chases him home? Well, that's a very open race but my slight preference would be Garde Le Victoire as the likely small field might enable him to jump better than he has done at previous festivals.

Is Unowhatimeanharry one of the big bankers in the Stayers' Hurdle?

Richard Birch Not to the extent of Douvan or Altior, but he has enhanced his standing in the stayers' ranks with every outing this season and it's hard to see one of the British-trained contingent lowering his colours. There are one or two Irish possibles who could throw down a serious challenge, but at this stage Unowhatimeanharry is clearly the one to beat.

Nick Watts It all depends what JP McManus runs. If he is happy to sling a horse of Jezki's class into the Champion Hurdle and just run the favourite, I would think Unowhatimeanharry is bordering on a certainty. If Jezki did happen to run here, then a horse who has won eight Grade 1s, stays three miles, and who is a previous festival winner, might be the one they all have to beat.

Paul Kealy There's no doubting Unowhatimeanharry is rock solid as he keeps on winning and knows how to dig deep. However, I did like Cole Harden's run in the Cleeve on ground he doesn't like. He was getting weight, but if it's good ground on the Thursday I'd expect him to go close and he looks fair each-way value.

LIVE STREAM <u>ALL</u>

RACES AT THE CHELTENHAM FESTIVAL

(EVEN THE ONES NOT ON TV)

PADDYPOWER.
YOU BEAUTY!

MOBILE & ONLINE

David Jennings Unowhatimeanharry is a winning machine and has done very little wrong in the last two seasons but he has been beating moderate animals. He might win but he is plenty short enough. Far more appealing is Shaneshill, given that he has been second at the last three festivals and has been laid out for the race.

Kevin Walsh Beaten yardsticks such as Cole Harden and Lil Rockerfeller leave nagging doubts about what Unowhatimeanharry has achieved. Perennial bridesmaid Shaneshill loves this time of year, loves this festival and increasingly seems to love a scrap as he gets older. He could spring a minor surprise.

What do you fancy for the novice hurdles?

Nick Watts I hope Ballyandy runs in the Supreme. He's a very good horse who maybe isn't looked upon as such because he happened to win a handicap last time out. Melon is an awful price. William Henry is interesting each-way in the Neptune, while West Approach must have a shout in the Albert Bartlett after his placed effort in the Cleeve Hurdle last time.

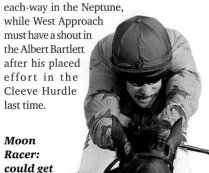

Moon Racer: could get meeting off to a flyer

Paul Kealy I've backed both Ballyandy and Movewiththetimes on a non-runner no bet basis for the Supreme and Neptune. They are simply too big based on their perfomances in the Betfair Hurdle, the hottest handicap run this year. In the Albert Bartlett I've backed West Approach and I'm beginning to get interested in Monalee, who is by Milan and may relish quicker ground than he's been running on.

David Jennings Bunk Off Early and Moon Racer look the two to concentrate on in the Supreme, although Charli Parcs could be a bit special and would be a major danger if he showed up. Let's Dance is my idea of the Neptune winner, while quotes of 50-1 about Moulin A Vent for the Albert Bartlett are ludicrous.

Richard Birch I'm a huge fan of Moon Racer and it will be a mighty expensive start to the meeting if he fails to justify ante-post support in the Supreme. His old rival Ballyandy could pose the biggest threat. I prefer Neon Wolf to Finian's Oscar in the Neptune, can't see Wholestone finishing out of the first three in the Albert Bartlett and fancy Cliffs Of Dover in the Triumph if Paul Nicholls wins his race against time to get him there.

Kevin Walsh Finian's Oscar has done very little to merit Neptune favouritism and Augusta Kate will be a fascinating contender if she turns up. The remorseless Death Duty is the bet of the week in the Albert Bartlett.

Which novice chasers stand out?

Paul Kealy Altior for the Arkle and you really don't need to ask why. The JLT is much more competitive, notwithstanding Yorkhill's price. Politologue jumps really well, though, and I was delighted to see a hood fitted at Kempton last time. He'll take some stopping if he keeps calm. In the RSA I've got Might Bite down as a flat-track bully and I'll take him on even though he is the standout on form.

RUBY WALSH, MICK FITZGERALD,
HENRY DE BROMHEAD AND CHARLIE AUSTIN

THE PADDY POWER
BLOG

YOUR BEST BET FOR THE CHELTENHAM FESTIVAL

VISIT BLOG.PADDYPOWER.COM

PADDYPOWER.
YOU BEAUTY!

Royal Vacation was a long way behind him at Kempton before being gifted the race, but he improved again at Cheltenham on Trials Day and is just the sort who wins this race, which often doesn't go to the best horse.

Kevin Walsh Altior cannot be beaten in the Arkle. Waiting Patiently is a smooth traveller with an excellent attitude and if he was trained by Willie Mullins he'd be half his current price for JLT glory. Might Bite oozes class and will be hard to beat in what looks a poor RSA.

Nick Watts Altior will win the Arkle and I hope his stablemate Top Notch wins the JLT. His jumping for a small horse is unbelievable and he has plenty of class, having run well in the Champion Hurdle last year. The RSA is very tricky, but Whisper would be interesting

each-way if Nicky Henderson decided to run him here rather than in the JLT.

Richard Birch Altior took the breath away at Newbury, wonderfully reminiscent of Sprinter Sacre in so many ways. Victory in the Racing Post Arkle looks a formality. Yorkhill simply oozes class and it's hard to forget his Neptune victory over Yanworth at this meeting last year. He should justify favouritism in the JLT.

David Jennings The Racing Post Arkle is a done deal – Altior wins that by daylight. If Yorkhill sticks to the JLT it's hard to see anything troubling him. Alpha Des Obeaux has had a stop-start season but I trust Mouse Morris to have him at the peak of his powers on the big day and he should take some stopping in the RSA.

Full house: all of our experts can't see anything other than Altior storming up the Cheltenham hill again

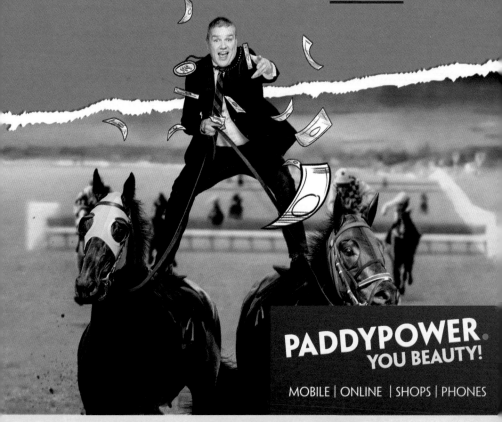

PADDY'S GOT YOU COVERED

BEST ODDS
GUARANTEED
ALL CHELTENHAM BETS

ON THE APP, ONLINE, PHONES AND IN SHOPS!

PADDYPOWER.
YOU BEAUTY!

MOBILE | ONLINE | SHOPS | PHONES

WHEN THE  STOPS

gambleaware.co.uk

ITV the new companion for armchair viewers

THE Cheltenham Festival returns to a prime slot on terrestrial television for the first time in more than two decades with ITV Racing having taken over as broadcaster from Channel 4.

The new rights-holder has scheduled much of the build-up coverage on ITV4 but the Cheltenham Festival – like other big events such as the Grand National meeting and Royal Ascot – will be shown on the main ITV channel, which should lead to a much bigger audience than Channel 4 was able to deliver.

The last time the festival was on one of the two showpiece terrestrial channels was in 1994, which was the final year of BBC coverage before Channel 4 poached the contract.

Like Channel 4, ITV is permitted by Racecourse Media Group to show only the first five races across the four days of the festival before RMG's own channel Racing UK (which covers every race) becomes the sole broadcaster of the final two events on each day. In addition, ITV will have The Opening Show (its version of The Morning Line) on air every morning of the festival.

Old title returns

A familiar name returns to the festival line-up with the Stayers' Hurdle reverting to its original title, having been known as the World Hurdle since 2004.

The Grade 1 race, one of the feature events of day three along with the Ryanair Chase, was first run with its current race conditions in 1972 and has been won by high-class stayers such as Big Buck's (four-time winner in 2009-12), Inglis Drever (2005, 2007, 2008), Baracouda (2002-03) and Thistlecrack last year.

The race has a new sponsor in a three-year deal and will be run as the Sun Bets Stayers' Hurdle.

Name dropped

Another new sponsor has brought a change of name for the County Handicap Hurdle on the final day.

Randox Health, also the new sponsor of the Grand National, will back the 2m1f Grade 3 contest but their involvement means Vincent O'Brien's name has been dropped from the race title.

O'Brien, who made his name at the festival with

A quick guide to festival betting

In the shops Most betting shops open earlier during the festival, usually at 8.30-9am

Free bets Many bookmakers offer free bets for new customers during the festival, but remember to check the terms and conditions. For a great range of free bets, go to racingpost.com

Compare the odds Find the best odds on your selections from a range of bookmakers by using the odds comparison table at racingpost.com

Early prices Be quick if you want to take an advertised price on the morning of the race – most firms hold their prices for a maximum of 15 minutes when their shops open and some offer no guarantee

Each-way Bookmakers often extend their place terms during the festival. In the big handicaps, it can pay to look for firms offering a quarter the odds for the first five places, or paying out on six places. The standard each-way terms are a quarter the odds for the first four places

Best odds Several firms offer 'best odds guaranteed', which means they will match the SP if you have taken an early price and your selection wins at bigger odds

Non-runner no bet Most bookmakers offer this concession from early March – some earlier on the bigger races. In this case, your stake is returned if your selection doesn't run

Specials A vast range of special bets is available at the festival, including perennial favourites such as top trainer, top jockey and the number of Irish winners

McNamara honoured

The National Hunt Chase on the opening day will be run in honour of the late JT McNamara. He died last year at the age of 41, having suffered life-changing injuries in a fall in the Fulke Walwyn Kim Muir Handicap Chase at the 2013 festival.

McNamara, acknowledged as the leading amateur rider of his generation, had four festival victories, including two in the National Hunt Chase on Rith Dubh (2002) and Teaforthree (2012).

McNamara's wife Caroline said: "John Thomas was never one for the limelight during his career but I'm sure he would want his life remembered for his achievements and success. The race being run in his name at the festival is a huge honour in his memory."

The JT McNamara National Hunt Novices' Chase for amateur riders is the sixth race on day one.

hat-trick scorers Cottage Rake (Cheltenham Gold Cup 1948-50) and Hatton's Grace (Champion Hurdle 1949-51) before switching to the Flat, had been honoured in the race title for the past 20 years.

'He's lost his air of invincibility . . . he has chinks in his armour'

Will Thistlecrack add the Gold Cup to his King George victory?

Bet365 Pat Cooney No. Much has changed since Boxing Day – Thistlecrack has been beaten, Native River has impressed again, Sizing John is now a player and Cue Card runs here instead of the Ryanair. All these new factors make him beatable. I still think Colin Tizzard will win it, but with Native River.

Betfair Niall O'Reilly It's a race that has really divided the race room in recent weeks, with many feeling Native River will have his measure. I personally think Thistlecrack will win, though I wouldn't really have any interest in backing him at current odds.

Betfred Matt Hulmes In what could now turn out to be a bigger field than originally anticipated, he will need to jump much slicker than on his last two course attempts. The twice Gold Cup-placed Djakadam still rates a solid each-way alternative.

Betway Alan Alger He's still the one they all have to beat, but he's lost his air of invincibility. Native River is the obvious alternative, but plenty will go there with a live chance.

BoyleSports Liam Glynn It looked likely that Thistlecrack would be hard to oppose in the Gold Cup until his defeat at Cheltenham, which then saw the market come alive again. Sizing John was very good at Leopardstown

and any horse who was runner-up to Douvan on several occasions cannot be ignored. Native River was very good at Newbury and he's the biggest danger to his stablemate.

Coral Andrew Lobo The experience of defeat will certainly help Thistlecrack, as will a return to better ground. All his chase runs have been in single-figure fields and the hustle and bustle of more runners could catch him out. That won't be a problem for Native River and Djakadam, who look the obvious dangers.

Ladbrokes Matt Trounce I don't think he's as clear on form as the market suggests. I'm not the biggest fan of Native River either, so Djakadam is an obvious alternative. I wouldn't be surprised if something at a bigger price improved to get involved, with an obvious type being Minella Rocco. His season has been more stop than start but his trainer is a master at producing them for the big day.

Paddy Power Feidhlim Cunningham He was immense in the King George and, although he was beaten in the Cotswold Chase by the ill-fated Many Clouds, they were 17 lengths clear of the rest and he'll have learned plenty from that. We know he has a big engine and, although the heart can skip a beat at some of his jumps, he seems efficient over them. Native River is the danger to him but will likely play second fiddle to his classier stablemate.

Sky Bet Ken Dickson Thistlecrack is still the worthy favourite, despite meeting his first defeat over fences in the Cotswold Chase, and I expect him to add the Gold Cup to his impressive King George victory. I think the experience in the Cotswold will have done him more good than bad, although it does prove he is beatable, which didn't look the case before that race. Of the challengers, Native River has improved in leaps and bounds and has done nothing wrong, but I'd prefer to take a chance on Sizing John at a price if he goes the Gold Cup route.

Sporting Index John O'Connell After his defeat on Trials Day there will be plenty willing to take on Thistlecrack and Native River looks a rock-solid contender with his jumping and stamina so assured.

William Hill Jamie McBride He showed last time there are chinks in his armour and he looks plenty short enough at current odds. At the prices I would side with Sizing John.

Who is your pick for an open-looking Champion Hurdle?

Bet365 None of the market leaders appeals at current odds, so I'd prefer to look for value at the bigger prices and Moon Racer appeals. It's a concern that he hasn't run since November but he's unbeaten at Cheltenham and is certainly talented enough to figure.

Betfair I quite like Buveur D'Air. His novice hurdle form from last year entitles him to be towards the head of the market and he's the one they all have to beat. The only other I'd have any interest in backing is Moon Racer non-runner no bet at 20-1 just in case he shows up here.

Betfred JP McManus holds the key. With impressive Betfred Contenders Hurdle winner Buveur D'Air being rerouted to hurdling, it doesn't appear there is much faith in Yanworth, while 2014 winner Jezki showed he still possesses a turn of foot on his comeback at Navan. I would like to see Sutton

Petit Mouchoir: will again be the centre of attention if he lands the Champion Hurdle

Place supplemented as he still has plenty of improvement to come.

Betway Yanworth. The only time he's been beaten over hurdles was in last year's Neptune when Alan King was going through a lean spell. He's done everything right this season and could be hard to beat.

BoyleSports I'm very keen on Petit Mouchoir and he has certainly impressed me this season. He looks a solid each-way bet in a wide-open race.

Coral Although late to the party, Buveur D'Air must have a strong chance and it's interesting that connections decided to switch from fences in a weak year. His Supreme run is looking better all the time and there is every reason to think he can better it. He has to go well. Yanworth looks more of a stayer, while many of the others still need to improve.

Ladbrokes Buveur D'Air is a deserving favourite. He was only third in the Supreme last year but that form is strong and he looks like the type who wouldn't have been hard trained for that race. Sprinter Sacre filled the same position in the race for Nicky Henderson before going on to much better things.

Paddy Power It has become an intriguing betting contest. I wasn't overly impressed with Yanworth's effort at Wincanton and I'm not sure who Barry Geraghty will pick between him and Buveur D'Air. That choice will decide the favourite on the day. Footpad is too big at 25-1 in places; if they go as quick as in previous years, he could easily run into contention up the hill.

Sky Bet Buveur D'Air. Last season's Sky Bet Supreme Novices' Hurdle third looked impressive, albeit at short odds, on his return to hurdles and it must be noted he finished in front of the current second favourite Petit Mouchoir on two occasions last season. Of the rest, Brain Power needs to improve after contesting handicaps this season and Jezki may be better suited to the Stayers' Hurdle nowadays.

Sporting Index 'Messy' would be a better description for this race. Brain Power is no longer under the radar but his Ascot win before Christmas was a smart effort and maybe he doesn't need to improve too much more.

William Hill Those at the front end of the market hardly look unbeatable. I would take a chance with Sceau Royal, who can probably be forgiven his Newcastle run and looked very progressive prior to that.

Is there any stopping Douvan in the Champion Chase?

Bet365 He should win by daylight. The betting 'without Douvan' market on the day may throw up some value, potentially with God's Own.

Betfair I can't see anything getting close to him. He's potentially one of the best ever on what we've seen so far. The only one I think is value each-way is God's Own, who looks a likely runner and should get his preferred conditions on the day.

Betfred He can't be taken on and a completed round will see him victorious. He has to be up there with the best of them. Apart from a couple of errors at Cork his jumping has been faultless and he should be a joy to watch. It's hard to choose a forecast selection, fresh air will be second, but if pushed perhaps Sir Valentino can cap a fine season and take the runner-up spot.

Betway Douvan looks unbeatable. Sizing John's recent form just goes to show how good he is. God's Own could be the one to chase him home.

BoyleSports Nothing can stop Douvan and we'll be hoping to welcome him to our sponsored Champion Chase at the Punchestown festival in April as the Champion Chase winner. I suppose God's Own could be the one to enter the placings at a double-figure price.

Coral He looks impossible to oppose and I

BECAUSE INSTINCTIVELY YOU KNOW YOU DON'T WANT TO MISS IT

EVERY SINGLE DAY - RELENTLESS - POWERFUL

You don't want to miss it
www.irishferriesfreight.com

IRISH FERRIES
FREIGHT

+353 (0) 818 22 15 60 E: dublinfreight@irishferries.com Skype: irishferriesfreight

just hope he takes on Altior at some point down the line. Fox Norton looks the obvious one for a well-beaten second.

Ladbrokes He's an outstanding horse in an otherwise poor renewal. God's Own is very solid for a place and I would have him ahead of Fox Norton for second best.

Paddy Power He's every inch a superstar. We've been blessed with a great generation of two-mile chasers and he's another joy to behold. The rest are racing for second, but God's Own would be the one to take in the 'without' market. He looks a definite runner, he beat Vautour in the Irish Champion Chase at Punchestown at the backend of last season and he ran a fine race in the Tingle Creek.

Sky Bet I can't see any horse troubling Douvan, who has always looked a superstar of the game. It would have been fascinating to see Altior take him on but I guess we'll have to wait a while longer for that. Opposition looks thin on the ground and Garde La Victoire, at double-figure prices, is the selection in the betting 'without Douvan' non-runner no bet market.

Sporting Index He's a superb two-mile chaser who will scare off plenty of others. It's conceivable God's Own could be ridden to pick up the pieces for a place.

William Hill I'm not Douvan's biggest fan. He has proved very little this season and wasn't that impressive in winning the Arkle, but sadly opposition looks thin on the ground. God's Own could be the one to chase him home.

Is Unowhatimeanharry one of the big bankers in the Stayers' Hurdle?

Bet365 I'm still not convinced by him despite the form book. He's hard to read as he idles in front, but he'll have to work harder in March. It's easy to make an each-way case for Cole Harden at double-figure odds. Spring ground will be ideal for him.

Betfair His form looks a fair way clear of the opposition he's likely to face and it's hard to oppose him strongly. Shaneshill looks a decent each-way alternative given how well he seems to go at Cheltenham.

Betfred He has handsomely beaten all British challengers and was super impressive in the best trial last time. The only one certain to turn up from Ireland at this point looks to be Shaneshill and he could prove the main danger.

Betway Unowhatimeanharry always does just enough, but you get the impression he would keep finding more if required up the hill. He seems to have all the British challengers covered, so if he does get beaten chances are it will be by an Irish raider.

BoyleSports Our traders have been very impressed with him and he's one of the top six ante-post losers for the firm. However, if Jezki is aimed at the race he could well put it up to him.

Coral He looked beatable on his last two runs but he seems to have stepped up on last year's form again this season and has to go well. Jezki could still be a big danger if connections decide to go down the three-mile route with him.

Ladbrokes I would have nagging doubts about him at a short price on fast ground. He looked a bit slow at stages in last season's Albert Bartlett and if the ground is like it is at a typical festival, I'm not sure it would suit him. Lil Rockerfeller seems somewhat forgotten after one poor run but his close second to Yanworth, giving 4lb, at the beginning of the season is arguably the best bit of form in the book.

Paddy Power Unowhatimeanharry is one of the leading fancies I'd be keen to take on. He often just does enough and could be vulnerable. Jezki is the each-way bet and don't be put off by his effort in the Red Mills on ground he doesn't like over a trip that may be a touch sharp for him these days. He's all class, loves spring ground and it would be fantastic to see him add a Stayers' Hurdle to the trophy cabinet.

Sky Bet It's fair to say as a popular horse Unowhatimeanharry will be many people's idea of a festival banker and a terrible result for the bookmakers. He has beaten everything put in front of him this season. However, the Irish might have a say and Jezki could be a real contender over a trip he hasn't had many goes at.

Sporting Index He has never looked like being beaten this season and has won on all four visits to the track. Shaneshill could be an each-way player as we know he's being aimed there.

William Hill Unowhatimeanharry looks a solid favourite and will be hard to beat. Shaneshill has a good record at the festival and could finish in the places again.

What do you fancy for the novice hurdles?

Bet365 Melon seems short enough in the Supreme market. It looks a strong race this year and he's had just the one run over hurdles, so his inexperience is a negative. Ballyandy is better value. I'm with Finian's

Oscar in the Neptune, West Approach in the Albert Bartlett and Mega Fortune in the Triumph.

Betfair I'm a big Moon Racer fan and if he shows up in the Supreme I think he's a certainty, with Ballyandy giving his form a strong boost in the Betfair Hurdle. I'd like to see Ballyandy go for the Neptune, where he'd have a strong chance, while Peregrine Run looks a big price in the Albert Bartlett given his form with Wholestone and West Approach, particularly if the ground comes up good. I think Melon is an awful price on what he's done so far.

Jezki: could serve it up to Unowhatimeanharry if sent down Stayers' route

Betfred I'm a big fan of Charli Parcs and he can win whichever race he's declared for, while Neon Wolf looks a smart type too and he can land the Neptune. Melon has to be the one who's in a false position in the market, priced up on his connections rather than evidence. Defi Du Seuil clearly has an engine but his jumping will need to be better in a good-ground, big-field Triumph Hurdle.

Betway Melon looks too short in the Supreme on all known form. I like Bunk Off Early as he ran a great race in the Deloitte with early keenness probably costing him. It's hard to form a view in the Neptune until nearer the time, while West Approach has to go very close in the Albert Bartlett. He's been running with great credit outside of novice company and was beaten only three lengths by Unowhatimeanharry in the Cleeve. Defi Du Seuil looks one of the most solid favourites of the week in the Triumph and will be hard to beat.

BoyleSports Melon has been the ante-post gamble for the Supreme and that result will set the tone for us for the week. Bunk Off Early was eyecatching at Leopardstown in the Deloitte and he could be the one to cause an upset. Finian's Oscar will be hard to oppose in the Neptune and is at present number three in our top six losers. Death Duty is all the rage for the Albert Bartlett. The Triumph is turning out to be an exciting betting heat and my money will be going on the Gordon Elliott-trained Mega Fortune.

Coral I'd expect people to chase after Melon – the price is very much based on connections rather than form. Bunk Off Early for the same yard ran a lovely trial in the Deloitte and that could be a key bit of form as I'd be keen on Bacardys in whichever of the staying races they decide to run him in. Augusta Kate seems a forgotten horse, favourite for last year's Champion Bumper, and she had every chance when falling behind strong Albert Bartlett favourite Death Duty. If she were to run in one of the staying novice races I would

side with her, getting the allowance. Defi Du Seuil is a favourite I'd be keen to oppose on the day in the Triumph as I'm not sure there is much substance to his form and I expect one of the Irish juveniles to improve past him.

Ladbrokes The Supreme is definitely open for a shock as I don't particularly like anything at the top of the market. I was impressed by Bacardys last time in Ireland and would support him wherever he turns up. Finian's Oscar is another market leader who hasn't impressed me. Other novice hurdlers on my radar are Neon Wolf (Neptune), Any Drama (Albert Bartlett) and Coeur De Lion (Triumph).

Paddy Power Bunk Off Early is the one at the prices in the Supreme. If you stopped the video on the home turn in the Deloitte, he looked the winner and was just run out of it on ground a touch too soft for him. With better underfoot conditions he should play a part. You have to respect Melon's chances but he's skinny enough for a maiden hurdle winner. Finian's Oscar won nicely on his debut with a big reputation and has increased that by showing he was versatile enough to drop back to two miles. He's open to any amount of improvement and the Neptune trip looks ideal. Gordon Elliott earmarked the Albert Bartlett from an early stage for Death Duty and he's done everything asked of him. I could see him gaining real momentum in the market in the coming weeks. I'm mad about Defi Du Seuil for the Triumph and he could progress to be a real Champion Hurdle contender next year.

Sky Bet The Sky Bet Supreme Novices' Hurdle looks open this year if the market is anything to go by. Melon has a big reputation/connections but you can't help thinking his price looks too short based on what he's achieved so far. I prefer Ben Pauling's High Bridge, who is improving all the time and could represent some value. Death Duty will be hard to beat in the Albert Bartlett, which looks like the race he'll contest, but I also like West Approach. He could only manage 11th in the race last year but has improved since

GO WHERE CHAMPIONS GO IN APRIL 2017

The Punchestown Festival hosts the grand finale of the national hunt season with 12 Grade 1 championship races over five fun filled days.

Easy to get to, worth the trip, great value and a unique racing experience.

PUNCHESTOWN

WWW.PUNCHESTOWN.COM

FESTIVAL 2017
25TH – 29TH APRIL

Visit www.punchestown.com • Call +353 (0)45 897704

CONTACT US **t** +353 (0)45 897704 **e** info@punchestown.com **w** www.punchestown.com

Alpha Des Obeaux: has plenty of supporters for the RSA Chase

and his form in the Long Walk and Cleeve this season must give him every chance.

Sporting Index High Bridge could run a big race in the Supreme as he brings a deal of experience to the table. Neon Wolf looked a class act at Haydock and I would fancy him strongly wherever he turned up. Death Duty promises to be even better over three miles and has the look of a good thing in the Albert Bartlett, while in the Triumph Defi Du Seuil stands out in a race that could cut up.

William Hill I like Bunk Off Early in the Supreme and would be respectful of Let's Dance in the Neptune or Albert Bartlett, in which Death Duty looks plenty short enough. Rather boringly I think Defi Du Seuil will be hard to beat in the Triumph.

Which novice chasers stand out?

Bet365 Altior is 'bar a fall' in the Arkle, Yorkhill is no value at all in the JLT and I prefer Disko here after his strong Leopardstown win, with Coney Island my idea of the RSA winner.

Betfair The opposition to Altior and Yorkhill in the Arkle and the JLT looks quite weak. In the RSA I'm very sweet on Alpha Des Obeaux, who is sure to be primed for the race by Mouse Morris.

Betfred Altior is clearly the obvious one but I will put up Charbel each-way in the Arkle as he beat Top Notch at Uttoxeter on his chasing debut and was fifth in a Supreme. Yorkhill will be many people's banker if going for the JLT as now seems likely, while Alpha Des Obeaux has been supported by some shrewd judges in the RSA. He was second in a World Hurdle.

Betway It's impossible to see past Altior in the Arkle. In the JLT there's no doubting Yorkhill's ability but he has his quirks and I wasn't overly impressed last time. Disko seemed to relish the drop in trip at Leopardstown and must go close. Might Bite's Kempton form looks outstanding. If his jumping holds up, he should win the RSA, but it's quite a big if.

BoyleSports Altior is the new aeroplane in Nicky Henderson's yard and, judging by the way he polished off his rivals at Newbury, his opponents in the Arkle will be running for pride and place money. Yorkhill is one of our top six losers in the Cheltenham ante-post books and it's hard to find anything that can upset him in the JLT. He seemed to have plenty in the tank when he was eased down at Leopardstown last time out. The RSA has seen the momentum of support build up for Might Bite over the past few weeks but I like Alpha Des Obeaux as a solid each-way bet.

Coral Altior looks unbeatable if he stands up. Yorkhill will have to show more than he has done so far over fences, which is entirely possible, but Politologue looks to have a decent chance in the JLT and the course should suit him well. The RSA looks very open with Might Bite having the standout bit of form in the book but slight doubts as to whether Cheltenham really is his track – his win there was in a weak novice hurdle.

Ladbrokes The Arkle is Altior's to lose, whereas the other two look more open. Might Bite has the best form in the RSA but his jumping isn't foot-perfect and there's a suspicion he could be a bit of a flat-track bully. Belami Des Pictons has crept under the radar but posted a big figure at Warwick last time and is now four from five for the Venetia Williams yard. Yorkhill is opposable at a short price in the JLT and Flying Angel looks an interesting each-way play at big prices.

Paddy Power The Arkle is a one-horse race. I think Eddie Harty will go for the JLT with

Coney Island after his Leopardstown defeat and he has lots of upside at 10-1. The RSA is a tough one but American dismissed Champers On Ice in good style at Warwick and he looks a solid each-way alternative to Might Bite.

Sky Bet You couldn't fail to be impressed with Altior when he won at Newbury and he looks nailed on for a weak Arkle. Nicky Henderson also has two strong contenders in Top Notch for the JLT and Might Bite for the RSA. Both have been visually impressive this season but at a bigger price Charbel looked a horse worth following when second to Altior in December. He is fresh for this time of year and is open to any amount of improvement after just two starts over fences.

Sporting Index Nicky Henderson has sound claims of pulling off a big treble with Altior, Top Notch and Might Bite. Throw in Beware The Bear in the four-miler and he could be looking at a clean sweep in the novice chases.

William Hill The Arkle should be a procession for Altior. I'm less convinced by the claims of Yorkhill and Might Bite in the JLT and RSA respectively and if there's cut in the ground I would be a fan of Waiting Patiently and American in those races.

What are the biggest losers in your book?

Bet365 We laid plenty of 10-1 about Thistlecrack to win the Gold Cup soon after last year's World Hurdle win, he's our biggest position so far, with Melon in the Supreme not far behind, but we're in good shape on the other races. It could be worse.

Betfair Melon is our biggest loser at the moment as we laid him at big prices prior to his maiden hurdle win. We've also been best price Thistlecrack since his defeat by Many Clouds and it's fair to say he won't be a great result for us.

Betfred It has not been a huge ante-post frenzy this season due to the issues surrounding so many leading contenders and previous defections and late changes. The biggest liability is on Thistlecrack and there have been plenty of multiples including both Douvan and Altior. The biggest move elsewhere is for A Genie In Abottle in the National Hunt Chase.

Betway Unowhatimeanharry and Thistlecrack would be our two biggest losers at the moment. Douvan's too short for most punters and we've laid a fair bit of Fox Norton each-way.

BoyleSports Our ante-post liabilities will all depend on how Melon gets on in the Supreme. He's the worst ante-post loser for the firm and if he wins the multiples will start to grow. The absence of Faugheen, Annie Power and Min has eased the pressure a little bit but the result of the Supreme will determine the liabilities for the week. Thistlecrack is the second-worst result for us in the Gold Cup and the liability for Yorkhill in the JLT continues to grow.

Coral Thistlecrack is by far the worst loser currently and probably of the last few years. A rather more unique one in the Pertemps is that we've seen plenty of Tobefair in our Welsh shops. He's won seven on the bounce and we can never get back what we've paid out on him and the eight-timer at the festival really would be the straw that breaks the camel's back. Best of luck to them, though, it's a great story.

Ladbrokes Thistlecrack is by far the biggest loser and one horse we definitely want beaten. We also have a significant liability on Defi Du Seuil and will be hoping faster ground catches him out.

Paddy Power The Irish punters love a dark unraced one and Melon is one we laid for plenty before his Irish debut. Unowhatimeanharry would be another poor result.

Sky Bet Thistlecrack is by far the biggest loser in our ante-post markets, having been available at 10-1 at the end of last year's Cheltenham Festival, and he'll also be a terrible result on the day. Other notable losers are Moon Racer in the Sky Bet Supreme Novices' Hurdle, Yanworth in the Champion Hurdle and Unowhatimeanharry in the Stayers' Hurdle. JP McManus looks to have a strong hand this year and his market leaders could run up significant liabilities.

Sporting Index As a spread betting company we don't have ante-post liabilities, but come the week we'll be against favourites and big distances.

William Hill Altior in the Arkle looks one for the punters but we can be more hopeful of getting Thistlecrack (Gold Cup), Death Duty (Albert Bartlett) and Moon Racer (Supreme) beaten.

Who are the ones to watch from Ireland?

Bet365 A Genie In Abottle looks just the type for the National Hunt Chase, while On The Fringe is my idea of the odds-against Irish banker in the Foxhunter after his excellent comeback run.

Betfair Death Duty looks to have a really strong chance having done nothing wrong all season. I also like the look of Battleford in the Martin Pipe at 10-1. Willie Mullins has a very good recent record in this race and I get the feeling it may have been the plan for Battleford all along.

Betfred Other than Douvan, I expect the Irish to latch on to Cantlow in the cross-country, On The Fringe in the Foxhunter and they will also land the Mares' Hurdle, probably courtesy of Apple's Jade. Carter McKay's bumper form is working out really well but I'll be against Melon in the traditional Irish banker stakes, the Supreme Novices'.

Betway There aren't as many Irish bankers as in recent years, with Willie Mullins having a weakened hand. A Genie In Abottle has been heavily backed in the four-miler, with Jamie Codd set to take the ride, and On The Fringe has been backed as though defeat is out of

the question in the Foxhunter. Death Duty looks short enough in the Albert Bartlett, as does Yorkhill in the JLT.

BoyleSports Yorkhill will be hard to oppose in the JLT and I'd be wary about getting stuck into Carter McKay in the Champion Bumper. The Irish banker of the festival for me is On The Fringe in the Foxhunter, having impressed on his return to the racecourse at Leopardstown to finish a close second to Foxrock.

Coral Airlie Beach in the mares' novice hurdle has been favourite for a while but, if Let's Dance runs, I'd prefer her of the two Mullins runners. The Deloitte one-two of Bacardys and Bunk Off Early look good and I'll follow that form line at the festival. With Douvan looking short enough for your average punter, Death Duty in the Albert Bartlett could be one of the Irish bankers of the week.

Ladbrokes They'll have more than their share of handicap winners and Squouateur looks to have been laid out to try to be one of them. He has started slowly over fences but as a consequence he should get a mark in the mid-130s. There was more sign of life last time over an inadequate trip and it shouldn't be forgotten he was sent off 9-4 favourite at last year's festival off 141. Bacardys would be my Irish banker at a price wherever he turns up.

Paddy Power It will be interesting to see what marks Phil Smith allocates some of the Irish raiders and I'll be looking out for Tony Martin's Long Call in the Fred Winter. Gordon Elliott's The Storyteller looked extremely well treated on his initial British mark but that may now change. I think Monalee will outrun his odds whichever novice engagement he takes up.

Sky Bet A couple of likely Irish raiders who appear to have slipped under the radar somewhat are Red Jack for the Champion Bumper and Kemboy in the Albert Bartlett. Red Jack had subsequent impressive winner Debuchet behind when landing a Naas bumper on his debut, impressing with how quickly he saw off that rival having moved smoothly into things in the straight. He's entitled to improve

for the experience, comes from a yard that does well in this sphere and looks overpriced.

Sporting Index Apple's Jade has the look of a good thing in the Mares' Hurdle and Cantlow likewise in the cross-country chase, but Melon could be worth taking on in the opener.

William Hill I like Bunk Off Early, Let's Dance and Sizing John. Sub Lieutenant can go close in the Ryanair and in the handicaps Isleofhopendreams and The Storyteller could be interesting.

Give us a value bet for the festival

Bet365 Gigginstown House Stud to be the top owner. The biggest armies usually win the wars, they'll be competitive in most races throughout the meeting and 3-1 looks very fair.

Betfair Romain De Senam at 20-1 in the Close Brothers Novices' Handicap Chase on day one. He was second in the Fred Winter last year off a mark of 136 and should just sneak into this race off 137, which would suggest he's well handicapped, particularly as he looks potentially a much better chaser than he was a hurdler.

Betfred Martello Tower in the National Hunt Chase. He's an Albert Bartlett winner and has run fairly well in Graded novice company this season. The four-mile trip will serve him well.

Betway More Of That each-way in the Gold Cup. He had every chance when falling at the last in the Irish Gold Cup and if he's regained his old sparkle he could cause a bit of an upset.

BoyleSports Royal Caviar in the Arkle. This horse caught my eye as a real prospect to follow way back when he won a point-to-point at Castletown Geoghegan. He was unlucky in the Irish Arkle when falling at the last and, although I can't see him upsetting Altior, he looks each-way value at his current price.

Coral Augusta Kate if she's declared to run in the Neptune or Albert Bartlett.

Ladbrokes I think Auvergnat shouldn't be far off favourite in the cross-country and rates a

solid each-way bet. There aren't that many contenders this year and he should continue to improve as he gets more experience of the unique course.

Paddy Power Quick Jack in the County Hurdle. He has had one spin this winter when an eyecatching fifth in the old Ladbroke at Ascot. He could pitch up with serious prospects for previous winning connections Tony Martin and John Breslin.

Sky Bet Not many Willie Mullins novices head into the festival appealing as a value selection, but there is reason to think Kemboy can offer more than his current price of 25-1 suggests in the Albert Bartlett. He may have finished a long way behind stablemate Let's Dance at Leopardstown last time but he was value for a good deal better behind a more experienced rival, doing well to get as close as he did after a mistake two out and being short of room turning in.

Sporting Index One who seems sure to have just the one target in a handicap is Presenting Percy in the Pertemps Final. He has few miles on the clock and must have claims of giving his trainer another win in the race following Mall Dini last year.

William Hill Sceau Royal can run well in an open renewal of the Champion Hurdle.

What's your best bet of the festival?

Bet365 I'd love to see Heartbreak City run in the Coral Cup or County Hurdle. He's very well handicapped over hurdles, but of course has many other options on the Flat as well. If he runs at the festival he'll be carrying my money as well as most of Ireland's.

Betfair I like Alpha Des Obeaux for the RSA at 10-1 in what looks a weak renewal. He boasts strong festival form from last year and I have plenty of faith in his trainer having him in top form for Cheltenham.

Betfred Charli Parcs to win the Supreme or the Triumph Hurdle.

Betway Uxizandre in the Ryanair. He ran a blinder, staying on behind Un De Sceaux, when having his first run in almost two years. He's entitled to come on for that run and could easily reverse the form over the extra half-mile to take this prize again.

BoyleSports I'm a sucker for each-way value and I have to go with Bacardys in the Albert Bartlett. Patrick Mullins put him to sleep at the start of the Deloitte at Leopardstown and gradually snuck him into the race. He will relish the step up in trip and at 10-1 he looks a solid each-way bet.

Coral Buveur D'Air to confirm his eyecatching Supreme run in the Champion Hurdle in what looks a weak year, with his Aintree defeat of Petit Mouchoir, Limini, North Hill Harvey and Agrapart looking all the better now.

Ladbrokes Bacardys wherever he turns up. He holds the strongest form in the novice hurdle book and he can only improve with Ruby Walsh back on.

Paddy Power Defi Du Seuil in the Triumph. He looks a class above his rivals.

Sky Bet Uxizandre in the Ryanair Chase. Alan King's nine-year-old has an excellent record at Cheltenham, with his last victory coming in this race at the 2015 festival. Although he's had his problems with being off the track until January, he showed the ability still remains behind Un De Sceaux in the Clarence House Chase. Understandably he wasn't given a hard time that day and I'd expect him to beat that rival on the likely better ground back up in trip when he meets him again at the festival.

Sporting Index Having mentioned Nicky Henderson's strong hand for the novice chases, he may be able to nick a handicap or two as well, which would make him a big runner for the top trainer award.

William Hill With many horses who had looked like Ryanair contenders switching their attention to the Gold Cup after Thistlecrack's defeat, the shorter race could cut up and Sub Lieutenant must go close.

Marcus Buckland highlights some key lessons from last year's meeting

Don't ignore the obvious

It was a year to forget for bookmakers with ten successful favourites in the 28 races. A further seven races were won by the second favourite and another by the third choice in the market.

The biggest-priced winner came in the 28th and final race, Solar Impulse (28-1) in the Grand Annual Handicap Chase. There were only eight double-figure winners across the four days, and seven of them were in handicaps.

In a year of few upsets, the four championship races were won by Annie Power (5-2), Sprinter Sacre (5-1, *main picture*), Thistlecrack (evens) and Don Cossack (9-4).

Headgear angle

Headgear changes are always worth noting and four of last year's winners were wearing a certain type of headgear for the first time, all of them in handicaps. These were Ballyalton (12-1, first-time cheekpieces) in the Close Brothers Novices' Handicap Chase, Diego Du Charmil (13-2, first-time tongue-tie) in the Fred Winter Juvenile Handicap Hurdle, Mall Dini (14-1, first-time tongue-tie) in the Pertemps Final and Solar Impulse (28-1, first-time

blinkers) in the Grand Annual.

Any Currency's win at 11-1 in the Glenfarclas Chase cannot be included in this statistic as he was later disqualified, although it is worth noting he was running only in cheekpieces as opposed to the hood and cheekpieces he had worn on his three previous starts.

Experience is key

Experience at Cheltenham again proved important with 19 of the 28 winners having already run at the course. Fifteen of the 19 had won at the track before, seven of them over the same course and distance. Five of them were winning at the festival for at least the second time.

Champion Hurdle), both on the freshest ground on day one and both ridden by Ruby Walsh.

In the 14 Grade 1 races, two winners were front-runners, six tracked leaders, four came from midfield and two from the rear.

A much clearer pattern developed in the five handicap hurdles, all won by horses ridden in midfield.

Three of the five handicap-chase winners were hold-up horses (plus one who tracked the leaders and one who raced in midfield).

Old boys' network

Handicap hurdle races at the festival have tended to be a happy hunting ground for five- and six-year-olds in recent seasons but last year's Coral Cup was a different story with three eight-year-olds dominating the finish.

Watch out for Russell in handicaps

Davy Russell *(left)* has a tremendous record in festival handicap hurdles and he made it three Coral Cup victories since 2008 when steering 12-1 shot Diamond King home in front last March. His two previous winners of the race were Naiad Du Misselot (7-1) and Carlito Brigante (16-1). The Irishman added the Pertemps Final to his CV with 14-1 chance Mall Dini, making it a hugely profitable meeting for his supporters.

Stay off the pace

Horses ridden in midfield had the best record at last year's festival (11 winners), followed by those who tracked the early lead (nine) and those held up at the rear of the field (six). Out of the 28 races, only two of the winners made the running (Douvan in the Arkle and Annie Power in the

Now is the time for Petit Mouchoir and De Bromhead

By Sam Walker

CHAMPION HURDLE This race blew wide open when Faugheen and Annie Power were ruled out. Buveur D'Air took up the favourite's mantle after being rerouted from a novice chase campaign, but he still has plenty to find on RPRs and I'm happy to take him on.

The ten-year average RPR for Champion Hurdle winners stands at 169, with a high of 173 (Hurricane Fly) and a low of 162 (Annie Power).

Buveur D'Air has a peak rating of 156 and, while he's open to improvement, only one Champion Hurdle winner in the last ten years arrived with a lower RPR than 162, so there's plenty of speculation built into his current price of 7-2 – particularly considering he prefers soft ground.

Petit Mouchoir (166) would be a more realistic favourite and he leads the Irish challenge after winning Grade 1s at Leopardstown on his last two starts.

He has stepped forward a lot from his novice form and trainer Henry de Bromhead is having a great season, so he could be the now horse for the now trainer.

Yanworth looked a superstar in the making before getting chinned by Yorkhill in the Neptune last year. He bounced back from that defeat with a couple more wins and improved his RPR to 165 in the Christmas Hurdle at Kempton, which puts him right in the mix.

Apple's Jade (169, including her mares' allowance) would be an intriguing contender if she turned up as she leads the RPRs judged on last year's form (once you factor in her allowance) but she may go elsewhere.

Footpad caught the eye last time when staying on late and closing down Petit Mouchoir to a length in the Irish Champion Hurdle. He can hit the frame at 25-1.

GOLD CUP It's easy to come down on either side of the Thistlecrack debate but the truth probably lies somewhere in the middle.

You could take the view Colin Tizzard's nine-year-old was always destined to be a chaser and that he's so classy he managed to dominate the staying hurdle division en route to what could be an even better career over fences.

Or you could argue the novice still has questions to answer over his jumping and stamina as far as the Gold Cup in concerned and that his defeat in the Cotswold Chase proved he is eminently beatable.

He made Cue Card look second-rate when powering off the bend in the King George VI Chase, which makes him potentially the class act in the Gold Cup field. But is an extended 3m2f around Cheltenham at a fast pace the best place to showcase that talent?

On the ratings he's right up there with the ten-year average RPR for Gold Cup winners judged on his King George performance,

CHAMPION HURDLE

This year's top rated	RPR
Apple's Jade (right)	*169
Nichols Canyon	166
Petit Mouchoir	166
The New One	165
Yanworth	165
Vroum Vroum Mag	*164
Brain Power	162
Footpad	162
My Tent Or Yours	160
Sceau Royal	159
*Includes 7lb mares' allowance	

How the past ten winners rated

Year Winner	Win RPR	Pre-race RPR
2016 Annie Power	162	164
2015 Faugheen	170	169
2014 Jezki	173	167
2013 Hurricane Fly	173	173
2012 Rock On Ruby	171	166
2011 Hurricane Fly	171	169
2010 Binocular	172	172
2009 Punjabi	165	164
2008 Katchit	165	162
2007 Sublimity	167	148

10yr winning average RPR: 169

GOLD CUP

This year's top rated	RPR
Cue Card	180
Thistlecrack	178
Djakadam	177
Bristol De Mai	173
Native River	171
Champagne West (right)	170
Outlander	170
Road To Riches	169
Don Poli	168
Sizing John	168
Smad Place	168

How the past ten winners rated

Year Winner	Win RPR	Pre-race RPR
2016 Don Cossack	182	181
2015 Coneygree	178	168
2014 Lord Windermere	170	157
2013 Bobs Worth	181	174
2012 Synchronised	173	171
2011 Long Run	181	181
2010 Imperial Commander	182	177
2009 Kauto Star	185	184
2008 Denman	184	183
2007 Kauto Star	175	184

10yr winning average RPR: 179

worth a mark of 178. But he ran below that level (174) in the Cotswold Chase, where he didn't travel with such fluency and his jumping came under a bit more pressure.

He still looks the most likely winner and ranks a fair favourite, but if the extra furlong and hotter pace in the Gold Cup shaves another couple of pounds off his rating his class advantage could dwindle away.

When you get down to the low 170s there are a host of challengers ready to upset the favourite, but there's also Cue Card (180), who has the edge over Thistlecrack on RPRs.

Also trained by Tizzard, Cue Card is another live player if you overlook his defeat in the King George. He was a 15-length winner over Coneygree in the Betfair Chase and scored by the same margin at Ascot last time. Both those performances were of Gold Cup-winning standard.

He fell when going well in last year's Gold Cup and has a great record at the festival, having won the Champion Bumper and Ryanair Chase, as well as finishing second in an Arkle. Judged on his best form it would be no surprise to see the old boy win.

Champagne West would be a bit more of a surprise package if he went in but it's not out of the question for the Thyestes Chase winner to step up on the big day.

He posted an RPR of 170 when winning the Thyestes under a big weight last time and he has won round Cheltenham before. He has every chance of hitting the frame at a nice price.

CHAMPION CHASE Douvan, Douvan, Douvan. Will we ever get to the bottom of him? He has won all nine starts over fences with effortless ease and nothing has ever finished within six lengths of him.

CHAMPION CHASE

This year's top rated	RPR
Douvan	178
Altior	175
Un De Sceaux	174
Fox Norton	170
God's Own (right)	170
Sir Valentino	170
Sire De Grugy	170
Special Tiara	170
Uxizandre	168
Garde La Victoire	164

How the past ten winners rated

Year	Winner	Win RPR	Pre-race RPR
2016	Sprinter Sacre	176	173
2015	Dodging Bullets	169	173
2014	Sire De Grugy	173	174
2013	Sprinter Sacre	190	178
2012	Finian's Rainbow	175	167
2011	Sizing Europe	176	166
2010	Big Zeb	172	171
2009	Master Minded	169	186
2008	Master Minded	186	168
2007	Voy Por Ustedes	167	167

10yr winning average RPR: 175

STAYERS' HURDLE

This year's top rated	RPR
Apple's Jade	*169
Unowhatimeanharry (right)	167
Nichols Canyon	166
Jezki	165
The New One	165
Yanworth	165
Vroum Vroum Mag	*164
Ballyoptic	162
Footpad	162
Lil Rockerfeller	162
Agrapart	161
Clondaw Warrior	159
Shaneshill	159

*Includes 7lb mares' allowance

How the past ten winners rated

Year	Winner	Win RPR	Pre-race RPR
2016	Thistlecrack	178	172
2015	Cole Harden	168	158
2014	More Of That	172	161
2013	Solwhit	166	165
2012	Big Buck's	170	175
2011	Big Buck's	162	176
2010	Big Buck's	174	176
2009	Big Buck's	176	166
2008	Inglis Drever	174	170
2007	Inglis Drever	169	167

10yr winning average RPR: 171

A peak RPR of 178 ranks him among the best horses in training and there's every chance he can break the 180 barrier when he finds a rival to push him that high, although he may have to wait for a clash with Altior to hit those heights.

His best rating last season did not come in his Arkle success and there's a chance this race will not provide the highlight of his season, but he shouldn't have to get close to his best to win.

The bookies are understandably taking no chances and he's been odds-on in the ante-post lists all season. He should win at a short price, so the place market is a bit more interesting.

Garde La Victoire looks the best bet to hit the frame at a tasty price of 33-1. A Grade 2 winner over course and distance, he was a top novice last season and went off co-favourite for the JLT Novices' Chase, where he fell when still going well.

His latest RPR of 164 is good enough to make the top three in a typical year and that might not be his limit

STAYERS' HURDLE The favourite Unowhatimeanharry has enjoyed a miraculous turnaround in his career. He hadn't won from 11 attempts over hurdles just two years ago and since then he has won eight in a row, bagging a string of top races including last year's Albert Bartlett.

He is the clear pick of the British contingent, having run to RPRs of 167 for wins at Newbury, Ascot and Cheltenham this season, which puts him just 4lb shy of the ten-year average for winners of this race (171).

A repeat of that level may be enough but he's short enough in the ante-post lists and

GO RACING
IN IRELAND 2017

Wherever you are in Ireland, you're never far from a race meeting and if you want to ...derstand one of our country's great passions, choose from over 300 race meetings at any ...the 26 racecourses around the country. Play the odds, raise a glass and enjoy good times ...with friends – you'll have a day out you'll always remember. So what are you waiting for?

It's time to go racing... because nothing else feels like this.

...017 RACING FESTIVALS

...RK
...ter Festival
...1 - 17th April

...RYHOUSE
...ter Festival
...1 - 18th April

...NCHESTOWN
...ional Hunt Festival
...1 - 29th April

...LARNEY
...ing Festival
...1 - 16th May

...RRAGH
...neas Festival
...1 - 28th May

DOWN ROYAL
Ulster Derby
23rd - 24th June

CURRAGH
Irish Derby Festival
30th June - 2nd July

BELLEWSTOWN
Summer Festival
6th - 8th July

CURRAGH
Irish Oaks Weekend
15th - 16th July

KILLARNEY
July Festival
17th - 20th July

GALWAY
Summer Festival
31st July - 6th August

TRAMORE
August Festival
17th - 20th August

KILLARNEY
August Festival
23rd - 26th August

LAYTOWN
September Festival
5th September

LEOPARDSTOWN
& CURRAGH Longines
Irish Champions
Weekend
9th - 10th September

LISTOWEL
Harvest Festival
10th - 16th September

DOWN ROYAL
Festival of Racing
3rd - 4th November

PUNCHESTOWN
November Winter
Racing
18th - 19th November

FAIRYHOUSE
Winter Festival
2nd - 3rd December

LEOPARDSTOWN
Christmas Festival
26th - 29th December

LIMERICK
Christmas Festival
26th - 29th December

HORSE RACING
IRELAND

...plan your day at the races or for a FREE racing information pack, please call the Marketing Team on
+353 45 455 455 or visit **www.goracing.ie**

facebook.com/goracing   **twitter.com/@goracing**   **@horse_racing_ireland**

Nichols Canyon: has the ability to put in a big effort in the Stayers'

RYANAIR CHASE

This year's top rated	RPR
Djakadam	177
Un De Sceaux	174
Fox Norton	170
God's Own	170
Outlander	170
Road To Riches	169
Sizing John	168
Smad Place	168
Uxizandre	168
10yr winning average RPR: 170	

remains vulnerable to a smart second-season hurdler. It's a pity Yanworth is heading to the Champion Hurdle, as there is every chance he will rate higher than Unowhatimeanharry at some stage and he has never looked short of stamina.

Nichols Canyon deserves his chance to shine after finishing third in a Neptune and third in a Champion Hurdle and the step up to 3m might be the making of him. He was a Listed winner over 1m7½f on the Flat and excelled over 2m4f as a novice, and Graham Wylie has always wanted a replacement for Inglis Drever, his triple winner of this race. On a good day Nichols Canyon can hit 166 and that should put him right up there.

RYANAIR CHASE It's hard to pick a runner in the Ryanair let alone a winner but Empire Of Dirt (167) or Outlander (170) should turn up, as they represent sponsor Michael O'Leary's Gigginstown House Stud.

O'Leary always likes to have runners here and Outlander would

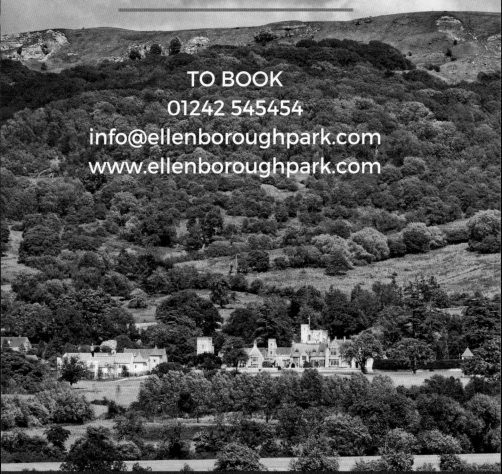

ARKLE CHASE		RSA CHASE	
This year's top rated	RPR	This year's top rated	RPR
Altior	175	Might Bite	165
Top Notch	160	Whisper	160
Waiting Patiently	158	Disko	157
Politologue	158	Briery Belle	*157
Flying Angel	157	Coney Island	156
Bellshill	155	Tiger Roll	156
Le Prezien	155	American	155
Some Plan	153	Bellshill	155
Charbel	153	Royal Vacation	155
Knockgraffon	153	O O Seven	154
Buveur D'Air	152	Emerging Force	152
Gino Trail	152	Shantou Village	152
Listen Dear	*152	A Toi Phil	152
		Our Kaempfer	152

*Includes 7lb mares' allowance

10yr winning average RPR: 166

*Includes 7lb mares' allowance

10yr winning average RPR: 163

SUPREME		NEPTUNE	
This year's top rated	RPR	This year's top rated	RPR
Defi Du Seuil	*158	Let's Dance	*153
Let's Dance	*153	Airlie Beach	*151
Airlie Beach	*151	Ballyandy	151
Ballyandy	151	Movewiththetimes	151
Movewiththetimes	151	Death Duty	150
Neon Wolf	149	Neon Wolf	149
Shattered Love	*149	Shattered Love	*149
Bacardys	147	Livelovelaugh	148
Finian's Oscar	147	Bacardys	147
Charli Parcs	*147	Finian's Oscar	147
Saturnas	147	Landofhopeandglory	*147
Asthuria	*146	Saturnas	147
Augusta Kate	*146	Willoughby Court	147
Landofhopeandglory	*146	Augusta Kate	*146
Messire Des Obeaux	146	Messire Des Obeaux	146
		Peregrine Run	146

*Includes age/sex allowance

10yr winning average RPR: 156

*Includes age/sex allowance

10yr winning average RPR: 155

be just about good enough to win an average renewal.

Uxizandre (168) is another likely to turn up, having won the race two years ago. He finished second to Un De Sceaux over 2m on his return from nearly two years off and can improve on that over this trip.

Un De Sceaux (174) has never run beyond 2m2f over fences and looks a beatable favourite.

NOVICE CHASES Altior is the banker of the meeting. He's the only horse capable of giving Douvan a run for his money and in the novice division he looks completely untouchable.

He posted a massive RPR of 175 when demolishing Fox Norton and Dodging Bullets at Newbury last time and that figure puts him 15lb clear of all his potential rivals in the Arkle Chase.

The seven-year-old has a similar profile to four of the last five winners of the race: Sprinter Sacre, Simonsig, Un De Sceaux and Douvan. They all arrived with peak RPRs of 167 to 171, went off favourite and won by margins of six to seven lengths.

Altior rates even higher than they did at the same stage and, barring accident, he should add his name to that illustrious roll

Defi Du Seuil (right): class act in the Triumph Hurdle

of honour before finally meeting the mighty Douvan next season.

With the Arkle odds as they are, you are probably better avoiding the favourite and looking at something like Charbel to place or in the 'without favourite' market.

Charbel was a decent hurdler but Kim Bailey has always seen him as a chaser and given the way he jumps it is easy to see why. An RPR of 153 puts him right in the mix for minor honours and with just two chase runs on the board there is probably better to come.

Might Bite (165) makes the odd mistake but if he gets round he will be the one to beat in the RSA Chase.

He was miles clear and staying on strongly at Kempton on Boxing Day before falling at the last. If he had stood up he would have clocked a faster time than Thistlecrack achieved in the King George over the same course and distance.

At longer odds Shantou Village is interesting. He was favourite for the Albert Bartlett last year and looks at least as good over fences, having posted RPRs of 152 on his last two starts.

Disko (157) and Coney Island (156) represent the leading Irish form. The JLT has been mentioned for Disko, while Coney Island could be heading to the RSA. Both are rated high enough to be considered a possible winner in an average year.

NOVICE HURDLES Defi Du Seuil is the class choice for the Triumph Hurdle. His peak RPR of 150 is above the pre-race best of any of the last ten winners and it is better than five of the last ten winners achieved on the day.

He won Graded races by wide margins on his last two starts and if he handles the hustle and bustle he could be simply too good.

Mega Fortune looks the pick of the Irish after posting an RPR of 143 for his three-and-a-half-length success over Bapaume (140) in the Spring Juvenile Hurdle at Leopardstown.

Like a lot of Gordon Elliott's youngsters, Mega Fortune has improved his RPR on every start and there is a chance he will progress again on the big day.

Supreme Novices' Hurdle favourite Melon was impressive on his debut for Willie Mullins, winning a Leopardstown maiden by an easy ten lengths and posting an RPR of 138+.

However, his short price has an awful lot of speculation built into it, as he will need to find another 18lb to match the ten-year winning average for this race (156). He also lacks experience with just one run over hurdles.

Ballyandy looks a far more solid proposition. He had the class to win the Champion Bumper last year and proved he handles a big field and fast pace by landing the Betfair Hurdle at Newbury in February.

His RPR of 151 is better than most Supreme winners arrive with and the way he travelled at Newbury suggests he might have a bit more in the locker. He looks the one to back against the favourite.

Willie Mullins and the Riccis haven't had the best of luck this season but they still have plenty of arrows to fire at Cheltenham and Let's Dance can hit the target for them in the Neptune.

Let's Dance is currently a shorter price for the Mares' Hurdle but, with her connections having Vroum Vroum Mag for that one, this one may well end up in the novice race and 16-1 looks a good price.

As a mare she gets a 7lb weight concession from the geldings, which means her peak RPR of 146 puts her at the head of the ratings.

Neon Wolf (149) has been on a clear upward curve this season and can be expected to improve again. The ten-year average for Neptune winners stands at 155, which could be in range.

Gordon Elliott's Death Duty (150) heads what is potentially a strong Irish team in the Albert Bartlett Novices' Hurdle. He is short enough at 2-1 but he is unbeaten from four starts over hurdles and could develop into a top-class stayer.

At the odds it might be worth taking him on with the Willie Mullins-trained Penhill (148), who relished the step up to 3m to win a Grade 2 at Limerick in December.

Colin Tizzard's West Approach (157) tops the ratings after finishing close to Unowhatimeanharry and Cole Harden in the Cleeve Hurdle last time, but his strike-rate of one win from 11 starts doesn't inspire confidence.

Any Drama (150) could be a bit of a wildcard for Harry Fry after dotting up at Market Rasen last time.

Penhill: Willie Mullins' Grade 2 winner could be the value call in the Albert Bartlett

TRIUMPH	
This year's top rated	RPR
Defi Du Seuil	150
Mega Fortune	143
Bapaume	140
Evening Hush	*140
Charli Parcs	139
Landofhopeandglory	138
Cliffs Of Dover	138
Dinaria Des Obeaux	*137
Magie Du Ma	*137
Domperignon Du Lys	130
Forth Bridge	130
Project Bluebook	130
*Includes 7lb fillies' allowance	
10yr winning average RPR: 152	

PALACE HOUSE

NEWMARKET

Frankie Dettori meets Our Vic

The King's Yard

The Rothschild Yard

Much More Than a Museum

A unique attraction on a five acre site in the heart of Newmarket, all in the royal setting of Charles II's sporting palace and stables.

National Horseracing Museum
A much expanded Museum where the latest audio visual technology charts the history of the sport from its origins to the global sport it is today.

Fred Packard Galleries
The National Gallery of British Sporting Art with loans from Tate Britain and the V&A featuring artists as diverse as Stubbs to Blake and Munnings to Wallinger.

Rothschild Yard
The opportunity to meet racing's equine heroes, for the first time former racehorses can be seen seven days a week with daily demonstrations in the Peter O'Sullevan Arena.

King's Yard
Enjoy a relaxing meal in The Tack Room Restaurant and take home unique gifts from the Palace House Shop.

For more information T: 01638 667 314, E: info@palacehousenewmarket.co.uk
Daily opening times 10am -5pm.

National Heritage Centre, Palace House, Palace Street, Newmarket, Suffolk, CB8 8EP

palacehousenewmarket.co.uk

Charity No: **283656**

Gold clock suggests time is still on Djakadam's side

By Dave Edwards

GOLD CUP In the past decade a Topspeed figure of at least 157 has been needed to land the race on seven occasions and six winners achieved 164 or above, which makes clear that the ability to jump fluently and at speed in a pressure-cooker environment is essential.

Nine winners boasted a pre-race figure above 150 but the ability to go much higher is a tremendous asset, with six of them having reached at least 164.

This year all those listed in the table opposite have a career-best rating of 150-plus and around half have achieved that benchmark in the current season.

The two most recent winners, Coneygree and Don Cossack, are missing but they were the 'quickest' winners since 2010 and on that evidence Djakadam, who was second both times, richly deserves to make it third time lucky. Figures in defeat of 167 and 162 highlight his chance, with Cue Card being the only other leading contender who has a career-best figure above 160.

Djakadam ran a fine race in unfavourable circumstances last year, as he did not have the ideal preparation and the ground was quicker than he would like.

Cue Card, a faller three out when bang in contention last year, has an excellent overall profile and an enviable timeline at the festival since winning the Champion Bumper in 2010. He was below par when beaten by Thistlecrack in a moderately paced King George at Kempton but looked back to his best at Ascot and it would be no surprise to see him prove the pick of Colin Tizzard's strong team.

Thistlecrack just crept on to the list when beaten by Many Clouds at Cheltenham in January. While he will have benefited from the experience against battle-hardened rivals in a truly run race, he may still come up short.

CHAMPION HURDLE Brain Power has got his act together this season and in a wide-open year he may prove the best option. Beaten on his first start this winter, he won a moderately paced Sandown handicap under top weight in December and followed up in fine style at Ascot two weeks later, showing his true colours in a strongly run handicap.

A pre-race best above 150 has been the benchmark in the past decade but failure to get there did not stop Sublimity, Faugheen and Annie Power from winning. Brain Power is within touching distance on 148 and he boasts the highest figure of any runner this season, an extremely positive pointer.

Another yet to reach 150 is Brain Power's stablemate Buveur D'Air, who has been switched back from chasing. He was third in the Supreme Novices' Hurdle 12 months ago and claimed the scalp of Petit Mouchoir at Aintree in April.

GOLD CUP

Topspeed figures	Career best	Season best
Djakadam	167	144
Road To Riches	165	121
Cue Card	161	156
Native River	154	154
Smad Place	153	153
Don Poli	152	142
Thistlecrack	151	151
Champagne West	150	150
Sizing John	147	146
Saphir Du Rheu	146	146
Bristol De Mai	145	145

How the past ten winners rated

Year Winner	Win TS	Pre-race TS
2016 Don Cossack	167	165
2015 Coneygree	169	152
2014 Lord Windermere	144	123
2013 Bobs Worth	144	164
2012 Synchronised	164	151
2011 Long Run	157	163
2010 Imperial Commander	180	173
2009 Kauto Star	172	176
2008 Denman	178	157
2007 Kauto Star	144	168

CHAMPION HURDLE

Topspeed figures	Career best	Season best
Jezki	160	136
My Tent Or Yours	159	133
Nichols Canyon	156	135
The New One	156	139
Brain Power	148	148
Diakali	144	-
Buveur D'Air	143	127
Petit Mouchoir	144	144
Sceau Royal	143	143
Apple's Jade	*142	130
Yanworth	142	142
Footpad	140	140
Superb Story	139	139

*Includes 7lb mares' allowance

How the past ten winners rated

Year Winner	Win TS	Pre-race TS
2016 Annie Power	154	139
2015 Faugheen	132	141
2014 Jezki	160	151
2013 Hurricane Fly	135	161
2012 Rock On Ruby	167	160
2011 Hurricane Fly	149	153
2010 Binocular	163	158
2009 Punjabi	155	160
2008 Katchit	157	157
2007 Sublimity	145	139

Brain Power: could prove best option in wide-open Champion Hurdle

All those with a figure above 150 have something to prove. The New One has had three bites at the cherry without success but deserves to take his chance again. Jezki, winner of the race three years ago, returned from a lengthy absence to score at Navan in January but he was favoured by the race conditions and disappointed at Gowran next time. Nichols Canyon, third last year, shaped as though he needed further when falling in the Irish Champion won by Petit Mouchoir in January but along with My Tent Or Yours he cannot be entirely ruled out.

Yanworth lost his unbeaten record over hurdles when outpointed by Yorkhill in the Neptune last term but that race has proved a decent pointer to the Champion in the past and he recorded a career-best Topspeed of 142 when he won the Christmas Hurdle, although he was only workmanlike at Wincanton last time. Yorkhill could be supplemented for the Champion but his best Topspeed of 128 leaves him with plenty to find on the clock.

On the figures Superb Story needs to improve but he won the County Hurdle last season and could punch above his weight.

CHAMPION CHASE

Topspeed figures	Career best	Season best
Uxizandre	163	149
Douvan	159	155
Un De Sceaux	155	155
Special Tiara	156	144
Sire De Grugy	154	154
God's Own	150	150
Sir Valentino	149	149
Simply Ned	148	138
L'Ami Serge	144	84

How the past ten winners rated

Year Winner	Win TS	Pre-race TS
2016 Sprinter Sacre	159	165
2015 Dodging Bullets	144	159
2014 Sire De Grugy	152	158
2013 Sprinter Sacre	153	165
2012 Finian's Rainbow	159	154
2011 Sizing Europe	146	166
2010 Big Zeb	168	159
2009 Master Minded	161	185
2008 Master Minded	185	143
2007 Voy Por Ustedes	159	160

CHAMPION CHASE A measure of the quality of this race is that the average winning Topspeed rating in the past decade is 160 and a figure above 150 has been required to win all but once in that period. Just two of the last ten winners went to post with a pre-race rating of less than 150.

This year's renewal looks at the mercy of Douvan, who has been almost flawless in winning all nine starts over fences. Willie Mullins' spring-heeled seven-year-old won the Supreme Novices' Hurdle in 2015 and was imperious in the Arkle last year. He underlined his finesse with a clear-cut success at Punchestown in February and the rest are seemingly playing for places.

The 2014 winner Sire De Grugy has been in fine form this season, recording figures of 154 and 151, and will have his supporters each-way at least.

Special Tiara was a creditable third behind Sprinter Sacre 12 months ago and on decent ground could run well again.

STAYERS' HURDLE

Topspeed figures	Career best	Season best
Jezki	160	136
Zarkandar	159	110
The New One	156	139
Nichols Canyon	156	135
Cole Harden	151	130
Diakali	144	-
Shaneshill	143	96
Yanworth	142	142
Apple's Jade	*142	130
Un Temps Pour Tout	141	135
Unowhatimeanharry	140	140
Footpad	140	140
Camping Ground	140	92
Lil Rockerfeller	139	123
Wicklow Brave	139	-
Old Guard	138	130
Supasundae	137	104
Clondaw Warrior	136	95

*Includes 7lb mares' allowance

How the past ten winners rated

Year Winner	Win TS	Pre-race TS
2016 Thistlecrack	158	133
2015 Cole Harden	151	135
2014 More Of That	135	118
2013 Solwhit	31	167
2012 Big Buck's	161	154
2011 Big Buck's	119	147
2010 Big Buck's	139	147
2009 Big Buck's	131	147
2008 Inglis Drever	175	162
2007 Inglis Drever	141	162

God's Own produced a lifetime best on the stopwatch when a close third behind Un De Sceaux and Sire De Grugy in the Tingle Creek and, while Douvan is in a different league, Tom George's consistent nine-year-old could improve on his fourth in the race last year.

STAYERS' HURDLE Despite the race title a test of stamina does not materialise too often. Only four of the past ten winners broke the 150 mark and the rest were well below what could be expected for a championship race. An average winning mark of 134 suggests there are plenty with chances even with Unowhatimeanharry as warm favourite.

RYANAIR CHASE

Topspeed figures	Career best	Season best
Djakadam	167	144
Road To Riches	165	121
Uxizandre	163	149
Un De Sceaux	155	155
Smad Place	153	153
Taquin Du Seuil	150	145
God's Own	150	150
Sizing John	147	146
Saphir Du Rheu	146	146
Village Vic	144	144
Irish Cavalier	144	130

How the past ten winners rated

Year Winner	Win TS	Pre-race TS
2016 Vautour	163	150
2015 Uxizandre	163	130
2014 Dynaste	160	127
2013 Cue Card	151	156
2012 Riverside Theatre	162	160
2011 Albertas Run	157	152
2010 Albertas Run	152	148
2009 Imperial Commander	159	160
2008 Our Vic	158	162
2007 Taranis	154	151

fourth last season, hinted at a return to form when chasing home Unowhatimeanharry at Cheltenham in January and better ground will be in his favour.

Unowhatimeanharry is eight from eight since joining Harry Fry and has gone from strength to strength. His timeline suggests he will not be inconvenienced whichever way the race is run but this looks by far his stiffest task.

RYANAIR CHASE Topspeed ratings illustrate how this contest has grown in stature as a championship race. A figure above 150 has been needed to win the race every year since 2007 and four of the last five have raised the bar above 160. Seven of the past ten winners had a pre-race best above 150.

Uxizandre *(below)*, winner of the race two years ago, has plenty in his favour. He was never headed when he won and his Topspeed figure of 163 was one of the best at the 2015 festival. He bettered standard time by almost six seconds, underlining just what searching fractions he had set.

He had been sidelined since that sparkling triumph until he reappeared at Cheltenham in January and was an excellent second behind Un De Sceaux in the rescheduled Clarence House Chase. Alan King's nine-year-old exceeded expectations and with improvement anticipated he has solid credentials. He has five lengths to find with his Clarence House conqueror but the longer trip is in his favour.

Prospective rivals are hard to predict, with many holding alternative engagements, but if Taquin Du Seuil makes the line-up his chance would have to be respected. Sixth behind Vautour last year, he proved a neck too good for Village Vic at Cheltenham in November and has a decent record at the course.

Jezki appears to have better prospects than most. The 2014 Champion Hurdle winner defeated Hurricane Fly on his only attempt at three miles at Punchestown in 2015 and was having his first run since then when successful at Navan in January, although he was slightly disappointing at Gowran next time. If the race develops into its customary 'crawl' his finishing speed could prove decisive.

The New One has been as good as ever this season and invariably acquits himself well in the Champion Hurdle. He has yet to race beyond 2m5f but would be of great interest here if connections decided to swerve the Champion.

Cole Harden, winner two years ago and

Seven horses with good form at Cheltenham

Holywell

The Jonjo O'Neill-trained ten-year-old has an outstanding festival record and even his last-time-out 11th of 14 in the Sky Bet Handicap Chase should not act as too much of a deterrent. Last year he was pulled up in the same race and then finished second in the Ultima Handicap Chase. That took his festival record to 1142 (the wins were in the 2013 Pertemps Final and what is now the Ultima in 2014).

Uxizandre

The 2015 Ryanair Chase victor has a place in history as Sir Anthony McCoy's final Cheltenham Festival winner but he was off for 22 months after that success until returning to action in January with a fine five-length second to Un De Sceaux in the Clarence House Chase, which set him up for another crack at the Ryanair. The Alan King-trained nine-year-old now has two wins and two seconds from four starts at Cheltenham and has recorded his three best Racing Post Ratings at the course.

Shaneshill

The Willie Mullins-trained eight-year-old is set for a fourth crack at the festival, where he has finished second

Whisper: two victories over fences at Cheltenham

for the past three years across all spheres – the Champion Bumper, the Supreme Novices' Hurdle and the RSA Chase. He was switched back to hurdling after last year's half-length defeat by Blaklion in the RSA and has improved in that sphere this season, winning the Grade 2 Galmoy Hurdle on his latest start. His best performance of each season has been at the festival and any more improvement would give him

bring out the best in More Of That, who was pulled up there on his seasonal debut in November but before that had four wins and a third (in last year's RSA Chase) from five runs at the track. He would be an outsider in the Gold Cup but could switch back to hurdles for the Stayers'.

Moon Racer

Three of Moon Racer's five starts for David Pipe have been at Cheltenham and he has won all three, including the 2015 Champion Bumper and a Grade 2 novice hurdle in November. The form of the hurdles win is pretty good, as he had Betfair Hurdle one-two Ballyandy and Movewiththetimes behind him in third and fifth, and he has long been a leading fancy for the Supreme Novices' Hurdle.

Bless The Wings

(main picture)
A novice handicap chase winner at Cheltenham for Alan King in 2012, he switched to Gordon Elliott two years later and has put together a good string of results at the track for his new yard. He was second to The Package in the 2015 Kim Muir and then took up cross-country racing, finishing 3422 in that sphere at Cheltenham. His latest effort in December was a nine-length second to Glenfarclas Chase favourite Cantlow but he was conceding 10lb and the festival race is run at level weights.

a good shout in the Stayers' Hurdle.

Whisper

Nine of Whisper's 20 races have been at Cheltenham and he clearly loves the place, with his only two poor performances at the track coming in last season's lacklustre campaign. The Nicky Henderson-trained nine-year-old has been back on song this season with wins at Cheltenham on his two runs over fences, including the Grade 2 Dipper on New Year's Day. His Cheltenham record now reads 41315P811 (including Coral Cup victory at the 2014 festival) and he looks set to go for the JLT Novices' Chase (probably) or the RSA Chase.

More Of That

This season has not gone to plan for the 2014 World (now Stayers') Hurdle winner, although he was running a big race in the Irish Gold Cup last time out when he unseated at the last. Trainer Jonjo O'Neill has the knack of getting his horses right for the festival and Cheltenham should

Three festival winners of 2016 who are set to come back

Vroum Vroum Mag

Is there a better jumper in training with the range of skills of Vroum Vroum Mag? In the build-up to the festival, the Willie Mullins-trained mare has featured prominently in betting for the Champion Hurdle, Champion Chase, Ryanair Chase, Stayers' Hurdle, Gold Cup and of course the OLBG Mares' Hurdle she won a year ago.

The wellbeing of other horses in the Susannah Ricci colours may decide her ultimate destination but she has not featured in a chase since November 2015, so it could be a coin toss between the Mares' and the Stayers' Hurdle if she is not drafted in as a supersub for Faugheen and Annie Power in the Champion.

Beaten only once in 13 starts for Mullins, she will have to be respected whichever race she contests.

Yorkhill

This is another Willie Mullins contender with a wide range of talents, having beaten Yanworth in last year's Neptune Novices' Hurdle before

switching to chasing this year. The Champion Hurdle was considered the likely target immediately after last year's festival and re-emerged as a possibility in February after Mullins was forced to rule out Faugheen and Annie Power through injury.

That also had something to do with Yorkhill's not entirely convincing display in a Grade 3 novice chase at Leopardstown in January, when he jumped noticeably left. That made him two out of two over fences but he has not had a major examination and the JLT Novices' Chase – his most likely target all winter – would be the acid test.

Ballyandy (left)

Last year's Champion Bumper winner was beaten on his first three starts over hurdles this season before delivering on the big occasion as 3-1 favourite in the Betfair Hurdle with an impressive victory over Movewiththetimes.

That opened up more handicap possibilities at the festival, as well as the novice options in the Neptune and the Supreme. Trainer Nigel Twiston-Davies would favour the longer trip of the Neptune on good ground but the Supreme if the going is more testing.

Proven at Cheltenham and off a strong gallop in the Betfair Hurdle, he has a lot going for him.

Native River and Brain Power can claim vacant crowns

Racing Post analysts Richard Lowther and Dave Orton assess the big winter action

GOLD CUP Colin Tizzard's Venn Farm yard houses three of the top four in the Timico Cheltenham Gold Cup betting, and two of them clashed in a memorable King George VI Chase on Boxing Day. The Kempton showpiece has been contested by half the Gold Cup winners in the past decade, and three of them were successful in both races.

Cue Card, a faller three out in last year's Gold Cup, had not been at his best behind Irish Cavalier in Wetherby's Charlie Hall Chase first time out, perhaps finding himself in front too soon. However, suggestions that he was on the downgrade proved premature when he slammed Conygree by 15 lengths to win his third Betfair Chase at Haydock.

Stablemate Thistlecrack went to Kempton after swatting aside the opposition in novice chases at Chepstow, Cheltenham and Newbury, and announced his arrival at the top table with a breathtaking display. Cue Card could not live with Thistlecrack from the home turn and the younger horse's margin of victory could have been extended considerably. However, Cue Card was a stone or so off his best, only just holding second, and probably prefers softer ground nowadays. His run at Ascot in February was much better.

It was a surprise when Thistlecrack lost his unbeaten status over fences in the BetBright Cotswold Chase at Cheltenham a month later, when Many Clouds beat him a head in a titanic battle with the rest well adrift. Thistlecrack's jumping wasn't quite as slick as it had been previously and he met an opponent who fought to the last. His defeat didn't appear to be a case of him failing to stay, but the Gold Cup is run over an additional furlong with a larger field assured, and his natural ebullience will ask questions of his stamina in March.

Tizzard's third serious contender is Native River, who put himself right in the mix when landing the Hennessy Gold Cup at Newbury off a BHA rating of 155, before adding the Welsh National at Chepstow from the same mark. Those victories were posted in similar style, as he forged clear after racing prominently all the way. He faced just two rivals in the Denman Chase back at Newbury, and chief opponent Bristol De Mai finished lame, but Native River impressed in coming away on the run-in after waiting in front, showing unexpected pace. He possesses all the necessary qualities for Cheltenham, with stamina and guts to go with his obvious class. Denman and Bobs Worth both won the Hennessy in their Gold Cup-winning seasons.

Runner-up in the last two Gold Cups behind Coneygree and Don Cossack, both of whom are absent this year, Djakadam beat Outlander in the John Durkan Punchestown Chase over

2m4f in December. The runner-up exacted revenge in the Lexus at Leopardstown over Christmas, where Don Poli split the pair. Djakadam would appreciate soft ground on Gold Cup day but should be near his peak now at the age of eight.

After a string of consistent efforts in defeat, Outlander richly deserved that win in the Lexus, a race that has supplied three Gold Cup winners in the past decade. It was only Outlander's second try at 3m over fences and the extra quarter-mile could tease out more improvement from him at Cheltenham. Don Poli, beaten over 14 lengths into third in last season's Gold Cup, followed up his rejuvenated Lexus run with another solid effort in the Irish Gold Cup over the same distance, finishing third to Sizing John and Empire Of Dirt. Good ground would surely scupper his chances on the big day.

Victory salute: Aidan Coleman wins the BetVictor Gold Cup on Taquin Du Seuil

Vital statistics

Races with the 'festival factor'

BetVictor Gold Cup
Cheltenham, November 12, 2016
2m4½f, good to soft

1 **Taquin Du Seuil** 9 11-11 A Coleman 8-1
2 **Village Vic** 9 11-10 R Johnson 20-1
3 **Buywise** 9 11-5 P Moloney 12-1
4 **Aso** 6 10-8 C Deutsch 14-1
Trainer: Jonjo O'Neill
Distances: nk, 2l, 3l; 17 ran

Festival pointer This has been one of the better races for finding a festival winner, though none has emerged in the past two years. Four of the first five Ryanair winners came out of this race (and the other was a former winner of this race) but it has not had the same influence in recent years

🐎*Five festival winners have come out of this race in the past ten years*

Betfair Chase
Haydock, November 19, 2016, 3m, heavy

1 **Cue Card** 10 11-7 P Brennan 15-8f
2 **Coneygree** 9 11-7 R Johnson 2-1
3 **Vezelay** 7 11-7 F de Giles 50-1
Trainer: Colin Tizzard
Distances: 15l, 13l; 6 ran

Festival pointer Betfair Chase winners to run in the Gold Cup had finishing positions of 012P3PPF7F (only Kauto Star in 2006-07 has won both in the same season)

🐎*Four festival winners in the past ten years*

Races with the 'festival factor'

Stanjames.com Fighting Fifth Hurdle
Newcastle, November 26, 2016, 2m½f, soft
1 **Irving** 8 11-7 H Cobden 6-1
2 **Apple's Jade** 4 11-0 J Kennedy 15-8f
3 **Hidden Cyclone** 11 11-7 Danny Mullins 12-1
Trainer: Paul Nicholls
Distances: nose, 2½l; 6 ran
Festival pointer The key British trial for the Champion Hurdle in recent years, featuring the winners of 2008, 2009 and 2010, the runner-up in 2011, 2012, 2014 and 2015 and the third in 2013 (their respective finishing positions in the Fighting Fifth were 31511113). Only Punjabi (2008-09) has done the Fighting Fifth-Champion double in the past 20 years
Three festival winners in the past ten years (all in Champion Hurdle)

Hennessy Gold Cup
Newbury, November 26, 2016, 3m2f, good to soft
1 **Native River** 6 11-1 R Johnson 7-2f
2 **Carole's Destrier** 8 10-8 N Fehily 25-1
3 **Double Ross** 10 10-6 J Bargary 50-1
4 **Hadrian's Approach** 9 10-0 P Moloney 33-1
Trainer: Colin Tizzard
Distances: ½l, 5l, 1¼l; 19 ran
Festival pointer Last year's festival was the first since 2011 without a winner who had run in this often informative race. The 2014 Gold Cup winner Lord Windermere had finished eighth here that season; before that Denman (2007-08) and Bobs Worth (2012-13) completed the Hennessy-Gold Cup double and the 2011, 2012 and 2015 Gold Cup runners-up came from this race
Six festival winners in the past ten years

Sizing John saw out 3m well at Leopardstown on his first attempt at the trip, booking his Gold Cup spot, but they went a steady gallop and the six remaining runners were still tightly clustered on the home turn. One of those, former World Hurdle winner More Of That, was bang there when unseating Mark Walsh at the last, following a respectable run in the Lexus. His stablemate Minella Rocco was a casualty in the Irish Gold Cup too, but he holds a verdict over Native River from last season's festival and could yet enter the equation.

Verdict Native River has the make-up of a Gold Cup winner and can get the better of stablemate Thistlecrack. Djakadam should be involved
(Richard Lowther)

CHAMPION HURDLE Opportunity knocks in the Stan James Champion Hurdle with the last two winners, Faugheen and Annie Power, missing through injury. Their trainer Willie Mullins may yet field an able deputy if Yorkhill's burgeoning chase career is put on hold in favour of a Champion Hurdle bid. Mullins could also call upon Vroum Vroum Mag, but the versatile mare has no fewer than five festival alternatives. The best clue to her Champion prospects is the Hatton's Grace Hurdle at Fairyhouse, where she succumbed by a short head to Apple's

Native River leads the field before going on to strike in the Hennessy Gold Cup

Jade, her only defeat since joining Mullins. Vroum Vroum Mag got back on track, but lacked her usual sparkle, when reverting to 2m in a mares' hurdle at Doncaster.

JP McManus owns the two principal British contenders, Buveur D'Air and Yanworth. Runner-up to Yorkhill in the 2016 Neptune, Yanworth won the Ascot Hurdle in November before dropping back in trip to see off The New One in the Christmas Hurdle at Kempton and then having his final prep in the Kingwell at Wincanton, wearing first-time cheekpieces. A true gallop will bring his stamina into play at Cheltenham.

Yanworth was pencilled in for the Contenders Hurdle at Sandown but missed the race with a muscle injury and Buveur D'Air deputised. Buveur D'Air, two from two in novice chases in December, could scarcely have won the Contenders any more easily. That said, a length-and-a-half defeat of Rayvin Black is some way shy of Champion Hurdle form.

Faugheen's defection left the way clear for Petit Mouchoir in the Irish Champion Hurdle at Leopardstown and he added to his victory over course and distance in the Ryanair Hurdle at Christmas. Both wins came when he was allowed to set his own pace, something that will prove trickier in a larger field at Cheltenham. The grey might well have three Grade 1s to his name had he not fallen when in contention in the Fighting Fifth at Newcastle. Now with Henry de Bromhead, Petit Mouchoir was trained by Willie Mullins last season, when he went down by just a neck to Buveur D'Air in a novice hurdle at Aintree.

Nicky Henderson, trainer of Buveur D'Air, has another challenger at single-figure prices in Brain Power, who landed valuable and classy handicaps at Sandown and Ascot before Christmas. The second win, in the race best known as the Ladbroke, was gained in a quick time and Brain Power has 7-8lb in hand of Buveur D'Air on the figures. Rooster Booster in 2002-03, however, was the last Champion Hurdle winner to have contested handicaps that season.

The New One stayed on too strongly for old foe My Tent Or Yours in Cheltenham's International Hurdle and had to dig deep again to secure the Haydock Champion Hurdle Trial in January. In between those victories The New One proved no match for Yanworth in the Christmas Hurdle and, admirable though he is, it is hard to see him proving quite good enough in his fourth crack at the major prize. Neither the International nor the Haydock Trial has had much influence on the Champion Hurdle in recent years.

Verdict In an open year perhaps Brain Power can find the necessary improvement. Yanworth is sure to run well *(Richard Lowther)*

Races with the 'festival factor'

Betfair Tingle Creek Chase

Sandown, December 3, 2016, 1m7½f, good to soft

1 **Un De Sceaux** 8 11-7 R Walsh 5-4f
2 **Sire De Grugy** 10 11-7 Jamie Moore 5-1
3 **God's Own** 8 11-7 A Heskin 7-2
Trainer: Willie Mullins
Distances: 1l, nk; 6 ran

Festival pointer The key guide to the Champion Chase. Seven of the 19 to try have won both races since the Tingle Creek became a Grade 1 and the Champion Chase winner had run in the Tingle Creek in 11 of the past 16 years

🐎*Seven festival winners in the past ten years*

Caspian Caviar Gold Cup

Cheltenham, December 10, 2016, 2m5f, soft

1 **Frodon** 4 10-10 S Twiston-Davies 14-1
2 **Aso** 6 10-7 C Deutsch 13-2
3 **Village Vic** 9 11-12 R Johnson 6-1jf
4 **Quite By Chance** 7 11-1 T O'Brien 20-1
Trainer: Paul Nicholls
Distances: 1½l, hd, ½l; 16 ran

Festival pointer None of the festival scorers to come out of this race in the past ten years had won here, with the latest example being 2015 fifth Darna, who went on to land the Brown Advisory & Merriebelle Stable Plate. The first three Ryanair Chase winners ran in this race (form figures of 2B3) but none has since and nowadays it is more likely to be a guide to the handicap chases

🐎*Five festival winners in the past ten years*

CHAMPION CHASE and RYANAIR CHASE

Long odds-on Champion Chase favourite Douvan arrives at Cheltenham looking to make it a perfect ten over fences. Last year's Arkle winner sauntered home in the Hilly Way Chase at Cork in December before adding the Paddy Power Cashcard Chase at Leopardstown over Christmas in similar fashion. He easily dealt with another

Races with the 'festival factor'

Stanjames.com International Hurdle

Cheltenham, December 10, 2016, 2m1f, soft

1 **The New One** 8 11-8 R Johnson 13-8f
2 **My Tent Or Yours** 9 11-0 B Geraghty 7-4
3 **Old Guard** 5 11-8 S Twiston-Davies 12-1
Trainer: Nigel Twiston-Davies
Distances: 3½l, 12l; 6 ran

Festival pointer Rooster Booster (2002-03) is the only winner of this race to land the Champion Hurdle since Comedy Of Errors (1974-75) and it has been a poor guide recently, with Katchit the only runner to have gone on to festival success in the past decade. In the past 20 years, two who were beaten here went on to take the Champion Hurdle crown and four of the last seven winners to line up in the Champion finished in the first three

🐎*One festival winner in the past ten years*

---

32 Red King George VI Chase

Kempton, December 26, 2016, 3m, good

1 **Thistlecrack** 8 11-10 T Scudamore 11-10f
2 **Cue Card** 10 11-10 P Brennan 5-4
3 **Silviniaco Conti** 10 11-10 N Fehily 20-1
Trainer: Colin Tizzard
Distances: 3¼l, shd; 5 ran

Festival pointer Eight of the last ten festivals have featured at least one winner who had run here and last year there were two (faller Don Cossack in the Gold Cup and runner-up Vautour in the Ryanair Chase). Desert Orchid (1988-89) was the last to complete the King George/Gold Cup double until 2002-2003, since when the double has been done by five of the 11 to try. Since Desert Orchid, 25 festival winners have come out of this race (in the Gold Cup, Champion Chase or Ryanair Chase)

🐎*11 festival winners in the past ten years)*

straightforward task in the Tied Cottage Chase at Punchestown in February, a race contested by the last two Irish-trained Champion Chase winners. Douvan can get in tight occasionally but generally jumps with aplomb and will take all the beating.

Frodon: winner of Cheltenham's Caspian Caviar Gold Cup

Races with the 'festival factor'

32Red.com Christmas Hurdle

Kempton, December 26, 2016, 2m, good

1 **Yanworth** 6 11-7 B Geraghty 5-4f

2 **The New One** 8 11-7
   S Twiston-Davies 13-8

3 **Ch'Tibello** 5 11-7 H Skelton 14-1

Trainer: Alan King

Distances: 3¼l, 2¼l; 5 ran

Festival pointer Faugheen in 2015-16 is the only one to have completed the Christmas/Champion Hurdle double since Kribensis (1989-90). Four beaten horses in the past 15 runnings have landed the Champion (the most recent was 2011 runner-up Rock On Ruby)

🐎*Four festival winners in the past ten years*

Lexus Chase

Leopardstown, December 28, 2016, 3m, yielding

1 **Outlander** 8 11-10 J Kennedy 11-1

2 **Don Poli** 7 11-10 David Mullins 12-1

3 **Djakadam** 7 11-10 R Walsh 5-4f

Trainer: Gordon Elliott

Distances: 2¼l, hd; 13 ran

Festival pointer Four of the past 11 runnings have featured that season's Gold Cup winner. Two were British raiders who won here (Denman and Synchronised) while the two Irish-trained Gold Cup winners to come out of this race were both beaten here (War Of Attrition was runner-up and Lord Windermere was seventh)

🐎*Three festival winners in the past ten years*

Vital statistics

Races with the 'festival factor'

Coral.ie Hurdle

Leopardstown, January 22, 2017, 2m, good

1 **Ice Cold Soul** 7 10-2 S Flanagan 20-1

2 **Tudor City** 5 10-0 R Colgan 16-1

3 **Golden Spear** 6 10-2 D O'Regan 5-1

4 **Derulo** 6 10-3 A Heskin 25-1

Trainer: Noel Meade

Distances: ½l, ½l, ¾l; 20 ran

Festival pointer Five of the eight Irish-trained County Hurdle winners in the past 14 years had run in this race (only Final Approach, in 2011, won both) – two of the other three ran in the Betfair Hurdle at Newbury. Xenophon followed up victory here by taking the Coral Cup in 2003

🐎*Four festival winners in the past ten years*

Galliardhomes.com Cleeve Hurdle

Cheltenham, January 28, 2017, 3m, soft

1 **Unowhatimeanharry** 9 11-8
   B Geraghty 10-11f

2 **Cole Harden** 8 11-0 G Sheehan 20-1

3 **West Approach** 7 11-2 R Walsh 14-1

Trainer: Harry Fry

Distances: 1¾l, 1½l; 15 ran

Festival pointer Principally a World Hurdle trial (four of the past nine winners did the double, most recently Thistlecrack last year) but has been used as a successful prep for a variety of races – the Champion Hurdle, National Hunt Chase and Ultima Handicap Chase (three times in the past seven years)

🐎*Nine festival winners in the past ten years*

Fox Norton finished behind Douvan at the Cheltenham and Aintree festivals last spring. Sold to Ann and Alan Potts and switched to Colin Tizzard, he won twice at Cheltenham before Christmas, accounting for Simply Ned and Special Tiara in the Shloer Chase on the second occasion. The Shloer, first run in 2009, has supplied the last three winners of the Champion Chase, as well as Uxizandre the season he won the Ryanair. After a midwinter

break, Fox Norton was put in his place by Altior in the Game Spirit Chase at Newbury. A brilliant novice, Altior would be a major contender were he added to the Champion Chase mix, but Nicky Henderson is sticking to the original plan of the Arkle.

A regular in the top two-mile events, Special Tiara later won Kempton's Desert Orchid Chase, an event won by three of the last five Champion Chase scorers, but he had only half

Vital statistics

Races with the 'festival factor'

BHP Insurance Irish Champion Hurdle

Leopardstown, January 29, 2017, 2m, good

1 **Petit Mouchoir**
6 11-10 David Mullins 9-10f

2 **Footpad** 5 11-8 D Jacob 12-1

3 **Ivanovich Gorbatov** 5 11-8
B Geraghty 13-2

Trainer: Henry de Bromhead

Distances: 1l, 37l; 4 ran

Festival pointer The most important hurdle race in Ireland before the festival, with eight of the 12 Irish-trained winners in the past 18 runnings of the Champion Hurdle having run here (six won)

Three festival winners in the past ten years

Betfair Hurdle

Newbury, February 11, 2017, 2m½f, soft

1 **Ballyandy** 6 11-1 S Twiston-Davies 3-1f

2 **Movewiththetimes** 6 11-2 B Geraghty 6-1

3 **Clyne** 7 11-9 A Wedge 6-1

4 **Song Light** 7 10-8 K Jones 14-1

Trainer: Nigel Twiston-Davies

Distances: ¾l, 6l, 2l; 16 ran

Festival pointer One abandonment means there have been only nine runnings of this valuable handicap hurdle in the past decade. The race is a good pointer, although Wicklow Brave (11th in 2015 before landing the County Hurdle at 25-1) is the only winner to emerge since 2010. However, also-rans from the last six editions have gone on to take five seconds and five thirds at the festival

Three festival winners in the past ten years

Vital statistics

Races with the 'festival factor'

Flogas Novice Chase

Leopardstown, February 12, 2017, 2m5½f, soft

1 **Disko** 6 11-10 S Flanagan 6-1

2 **Our Duke** 7 11-10 R Power 11-4

3 **Balko Des Flos** 6 11-10 David Mullins 20-1

Trainer: Noel Meade; Distances: 1¾l, 6l; 6 ran

Festival pointer This has emerged as an excellent guide in recent years, with four of the last eight RSA Chase winners having run here (two won, one was second and the other was third), as well as an Arkle winner who finished second here and then dropped in trip

Five festival winners in the past ten years

Deloitte Novice Hurdle

Leopardstown, February 12, 2017, 2m2f, soft

1 **Bacardys** 6 11-10 Mr P Mullins 12-1

2 **Bunk Off Early** 5 11-9 P Townend 11-2

3 **Brelade** 5 11-9 B Geraghty 8-1

Trainer: Willie Mullins

Distances: ¾l, 2¼l; 10 ran

Festival pointer This race produced a festival winner each year from 2002 to 2004 and after a long gap has enjoyed a resurgence with Champagne Fever, Vautour (both won here) and Windsor Park (second) scoring at the festivals of 2013, 2014 and 2015. Most winners since 2000 have dropped back in trip to land the Supreme but Windsor Park was the second runner-up to step up and win the Neptune over 2m5f (as did the top-class Istabraq and Danoli in the 1990s)

Three festival winners in the past ten years

---

a length to spare over Sir Valentino, who was giving him 6lb.

Un De Sceaux was found out by Sprinter Sacre in last year's Champion Chase, holding second by just a whisker from Special Tiara. On his return in December he responded willingly to beat former champ Sire De Grugy in the Tingle Creek before impressing in the Clarence House Chase, which had been rerouted to Cheltenham from Ascot. His

trainer Willie Mullins has intimated that Un De Sceaux is set to contest the Ryanair rather than cross swords with stablemate Douvan in the shorter event.

Uxizandre was Sir Anthony McCoy's final festival winner in the 2015 Ryanair Chase, but that was the last we saw of the gelding until he resumed at Cheltenham this January. That comeback run behind Un De Sceaux in the Clarence House was brimful of promise and the extra half-mile of the Ryanair is sure to suit. Trainer Alan King has the option of putting headgear back on him too.

Empire Of Dirt advertised his Ryanair claims in the Irish Gold Cup, travelling as smoothly as anything and only giving best on the run-in. That was his first run out of handicaps and next stop should be the Ryanair, which is sponsored by his owner. Gigginstown have another Ryanair horse in Sub Lieutenant, who beat Outlander in the Titanic Belfast Chase at Down Royal in November. He's run solid races in defeat since, behind Djakadam and Outlander at Punchestown and Sizing John at Thurles. On both occasions he was ahead of Black Hercules.

Josses Hill won the Peterborough Chase at Huntingdon in convincing style, jumping with an assurance he hasn't always shown. He was beaten only seven lengths when last of five in the King George afterwards and at least we know the Ryanair is his festival target.

Verdict It's hard to see past Douvan in the Champion Chase. Uxizandre makes plenty of appeal in the Ryanair *(Richard Lowther)*

STAYERS' HURDLE Unowhatimeanharry
has gone the same traditional route that Thistlecrack took prior to winning at last season's festival and he has passed with flying colours. First up was a smooth success over Nigel Twiston-Davies's tough Ballyoptic in the Grade 2 Long Distance Hurdle at Newbury's Hennessy meeting in November. That was followed by a more workmanlike win in the Grade 1 Long Walk at Ascot in December, when he emerged out of thick fog to defeat reliable Lil Rockerfeller, with Ballyoptic coming to grief when held at the last.

He then completed the hat-trick with another ready success back at Cheltenham in the Grade 2 Cleeve on Trials Day in January, idling after taking the measure of 2015 World Hurdle winner Cole Harden. In each of those three outings he recorded an RPR of 167. Winner of all four outings at Cheltenham, and adaptable regards going conditions, he has a huge chance of taking his form to an even higher level by landing the Stayers' Hurdle at the festival.

Cole Harden has been rejuvenated after looking in decline. A solid third in the Relkeel on bad ground on New Year's Day was backed up by a cracking effort to push Unowhatimeanharry in the Cleeve, again on going plenty soft enough. He was in receipt of 8lb and will renew rivalry on level weights, but he adores a sound surface and holds strong claims of going close again. It is worth remembering he is still only an eight-year-old.

This race is among a host of options for Vroum Vroum Mag. Having successfully taken over from Quevega in the Mares' Hurdle last year, Willie Mullins' versatile eight-year-old became a strong Stayers' contender when taking the Grade 1 Christmas Hurdle at Leopardstown. She was narrowly on top of stablemate Shaneshill prior to his final-flight fall and is well served by a decent test now. Despite a valuable mares' allowance of 7lb, her form falls short of Unowhatimeanharry's.

Shaneshill gained compensation when taking the Grade 2 Galmoy at Gowran Park in January, the same trial won by Alpha Des Obeaux prior to a fine second to Thistlecrack last season. He has been runner-up at the past three festivals and better ground in March would bring him into play.

However, the biggest challenge from Ireland comes in the shape of 2014 Champion Hurdle winner Jezki. Jessica Harrington's nine-year-old successfully returned from injury that forced him to miss last term in a conditions hurdle at Navan in January, although he was then beaten at Gowran. He has been aimed at this race and won a Grade 1 on his only previous start over 3m. He certainly has the class to have a big say.

Verdict JP McManus holds the key, with Unowhatimeanharry having taken the three top trials and ticking all the right boxes. McManus's Jezki is a big contender as well and remains unexposed as a stayer. The 2015 winner Cole Harden makes strong each-way appeal back on a sound surface *(Dave Orton)*

ROA

RACEHORSE OWNERS
ASSOCIATION

TOP-NOTCH BENEFITS FOR OWNERS

ROA membership is the equivalent of just 63p* a day but the benefits are immense

- **SIS sponsorship (worth an average of £4,000 against ownership costs alone – annually per horse)**

- **Free racecourse admission and priority car parking (worth over £200 a year)**

- **Automatic third-party insurance (worth £290 a year)**

- **BHA 20% fee discounts (worth £55 on average)**

- **Thoroughbred Owner & Breeder magazine (worth £55 for 12 issues)**

Plus much more

Join 7,700 owners today.
Call 020 7152 0200
or visit **roa.co.uk**

*£230/365 days - £0.63
Terms and conditions may apply to benefits

NOVICE CHASES Even before old rival Min defected, the Arkle was Altior's to lose. Last year's Supreme winner has been pretty flawless since his chasing debut at Kempton in November. He then took the Grade 1 Henry VIII at Sandown from the gutsy runner-up Charbel before comfortably completing a hat-trick in the Grade 2 Wayward Lad at Kempton's Christmas meeting. However, it was a foray out of novice company in the Grade 2 Game Spirit at Newbury in February, usually a strong pointer for the Champion Chase, that cemented him as the real deal. Nicky Henderson also used that as an Arkle prep for the brilliant Sprinter Sacre in 2012 and Altior could not have been more impressive on ground softer than ideal. He soared over the final five fences and easily saw off Champion Chase contender Fox Norton. The handicapper gave him an official rating of 170 afterwards, already putting him 1lb ahead of last year's winner Douvan at the end of his novice campaign and also 1lb better than Sprinter Sacre heading into his Arkle tilt.

Plausible alternatives are thin on the ground. Nine-year-old Some Plan *(below)* took the Irish Arkle at Leopardstown in January. That was a highly eventful race, though, and the form is miles below Altior's level.

Henderson also trains Top Notch, runner-up in the 2015 Triumph Hurdle, who has really come good this season over fences. He is the next best to the hot favourite on form, but it

GREAT
BRITISH
AGRICULTURE
ENTERTAINMENT
FOOD & DRINK

ENGLAND'S ROYAL 4 DAY SHOW
WWW.BATHANDWEST.COM
31 MAY - 3 JUNE 2017

2 CHILDREN GO FREE WITH EACH ADVANCE ADULT TICKET

would be a huge surprise if he ran in the Arkle rather than JLT over 2m4f on the Thursday. That looks one of the weakest Grade 1s at this year's festival and the six-year-old stamped himself as one of the leading players with a clear-cut success in the Grade 1 Scilly Isles at Sandown in February over 2m4f. He isn't too tall but coped fine with the daunting fences that day. With some give underfoot, he will be a threat to all.

The JLT revolves around last season's Neptune winner Yorkhill, who made it two out of two over fences in a Grade 3 at Leopardstown in January. Despite not looking a complete natural so far, he is surely capable of more and would be a firm favourite if confirmed for the JLT. After injuries to Willie Mullins' big guns, however, reverting to the smaller jumps for the Champion Hurdle is a live possibility.

Another serious Irish contender is Disko, who ran his rivals ragged in the Grade 1 Flogas Novice Chase at Leopardstown in February. That usually falls to a high-class novice and Noel Meade's grey proved right at home switched to front-running, reversing form with old rival Our Duke, who just got the better of him in a Grade 1 over 3m at the Leopardstown Christmas meeting.

The JLT has so far eluded champion trainer Paul Nicholls. Politologue is a live chance this year, though, with his best form not far off the market principals, and he arrives after a breeze at Kempton in February.

The staying division is muddling. Henderson trains RSA ante-post favourite Might Bite, who would have been a wide-margin winner of the Grade 1 Kauto Star at Kempton on Boxing Day but for a final-fence fall. The form of that race was boosted when the lucky winner Royal Vacation subsequently took apart a handicap at Cheltenham in January from a mark of 143. Might Bite got back on track in a soft affair at Doncaster and heads an ordinary bunch on form, although the last eight-year-old to win the RSA was Rule Supreme in 2004.

With Bellshill having plenty to prove after a flat run in the Flogas, Ireland's chief RSA hope looks to be Coney Island, who won the Grade 1 Drinmore at Fairyhouse in December, before splitting Our Duke and Disko at Leopardstown when upped to 3m later that month. He is open to plenty of improvement as a stayer, although a run in 2017 would be preferred.

The National Hunt Chase looks something of a mixed bag. Noel Meade is due to saddle A Genie In Abottle, who looked a dour stayer when just touched off by Anibale Fly, second in the Drinmore, in a key trial at Navan in January. The six-year-old can take his form to the requisite level over this marathon distance.

The British defence is headed by horses coming out of handicaps. Nicky Henderson has yet another festival hope here in Beware The Bear, who is two out of two over fences and has improved 18lb to a mark of 148. That puts him firmly in the mix.

Verdict Only the fences stand in the way of Altior winning the Arkle. With doubts surrounding Yorkhill, Nicky Henderson can also take the JLT with the tenacious Top Notch. However, his Might Bite is vulnerable to an improver in a cloudy RSA. A Genie In Abottle stands out in the National Hunt Chase *(Dave Orton)*

NOVICE HURDLES Willie Mullins'
much-hyped Melon delivered on his belated hurdling debut at Leopardstown in January. The French Flat winner powered away from a useful sort and appeared to have a lot of scope. That was only a maiden hurdle, but the form doesn't put him too far off the best novices and Mullins found it hard to hide his excitement. Inexperience is a worry, and he was guessy at times on his debut, but if Melon is slick in that department he can have a big say.

Mullins also has Bunk Off Early, runner-up in the key Grade 1 Deloitte at Leopardstown behind stablemate Bacardys in February. It was just his second start over hurdles, after taking his maiden there at the Christmas meeting, and the former Flat winner was unfortunate not to have followed up. He ran freely and found himself in front soon enough

BOURTON VALE
equine clinic

Wyck Road
Lower Slaughter
Cheltenham
Gloucestershire
GL54 2EX
Tel: 01451 820137
Email: office@bvec.co.uk

Practical, Cost Effective, Expert Treatment For All Equines

@TheEquineClinic   @BVEquineClinic
@BourtonValeEquineClinic
#BVEC   #BourtonValeEquineClinic   #EquineVets

after travelling easily to the last. Back at 2m in a strongly run race on a sound surface, he ought to peak.

Nicky Henderson broke Mullins' dominance last season when Altior gave him a first win since 1992. This time he looks set to rely on Charli Parcs, who made it two out of two as a hurdler on his British debut at Kempton in December. Henderson sent out Binocular at the same age to finish runner-up to Captain Cee Bee in 2008 and Charli Parcs will hold sound claims of being the first juvenile to succeed since Hors La Loi in 1999.

Moon Racer would be a danger to all if he goes for this race. Absent since landing a messy Grade 2 at the course in November, he had some decent types behind that day and his 2015 Champion Bumper win also came off a long break. However, the last eight-year-old to win the Supreme was Like-A-Butterfly in 2002.

Harry Fry has a Supreme contender if Neon Wolf takes his place, but it is more likely that the unbeaten six-year-old will head to the Neptune Novices' Hurdle instead. He has impressed for Fry, making deep ground look more like good to firm in the Grade 2 Rossington Main at Haydock in January. An Irish point winner, he is likely to improve for a step up in trip and it is worth noting his win between the flags came on a sound surface.

Finian's Oscar, ante-post favourite for the Neptune, took the 2m Grade 1 Tolworth on bad ground at Sandown in January, having scooted home over 2m5f at Hereford on his rules debut the previous month, and landed a hat-trick in a weak Listed race at Exeter in February. He is flattered by his five-length Tolworth win as runner-up Capitaine, who had taken the Grade 2 Kennel Gate at Ascot, hit the second-last when still going well. However, Colin Tizzard's unbeaten five-year-old is another who could have plenty more to offer back up in distance. There is also the option of the Supreme, should it be wet on the first day.

Ballyandy, last year's Champion Bumper winner, turned a corner when landing a gamble in the competitive Betfair Hurdle in February and would have sound claims if turning up. He loves a big field.

Bacardys' success in the Deloitte shot him to the front of Willie Mullins' Neptune pecking order. He is proven at the festival, having finished third in last year's Champion Bumper, and shapes as though he is crying out for a stiffer test.

The smart Death Duty made it four out of four over jumps in the Grade 1 Lawlor's Hotel Novice Hurdle at Navan in January. He was just on top prior to Augusta Kate falling at the last. Going over 3m in the Albert Bartlett promises further progress and he is a solid favourite.

West Approach, only 11th in the Albert Bartlett last year, finished third in the Grade 2 Cleeve on Trials Day in January and has to be considered a serious player back against novices. He is held by old rival Wholestone on earlier Cheltenham form, though, and Nigel Twiston-Davies's dual Grade 2 winner is the most solid of the home defence.

It looks like a decent Triumph Hurdle. JP McManus won it with Ivanovich Gorbatov last year and his main hope is Defi Du Seuil, a worthy favourite after five wins since going hurdling for Philip Hobbs. He is three out of three at Cheltenham and rates well up to an official mark of 150.

The Irish contingent have been beating themselves. The key trial is the Grade 1 Spring Juvenile Hurdle at Leopardstown in February when it was Mega Fortune's turn to come out on top, winning in first-time cheekpieces from Bapaume, who had him two places back when taking a Grade 2 there in December.

Verdict Charli Parcs rates a value alternative to Melon in the Supreme, as he has greater experience and the stronger form despite being a juvenile. Neon Wolf, who took a key trial and has yet to come out of second gear, makes definite appeal in the Neptune. Death Duty will take plenty of beating in the Albert Bartlett, while Defi Du Seuil rates a standout in the Triumph Hurdle *(Dave Orton)*

KimBaileyRacing.com

THE STABLES · THE TRAINER · THE DIFFERENCE

'What separates the winners from the losers is how a person reacts to each new twist of fate'. Donald Trump

Imagine how you would have felt if you had been jocked off one of the favourites at the Cheltenham Festival, to ride what looked like a complete outsider for the race?

It seemed like our stable jockey David Bass was dealt a cruel twist of fate when he was told he would not be riding the favourite Un Ace but long shot Darna instead in the Brown & Merriebelle Stable Plate Chase at the Cheltenham Festival.

However, if you had subscribed to Kim Bailey's Racing Insights you would have known that David was actually on a horse the stable also felt had a great chance in the race and he duly won at 33/1!

You can now get the low down on all our horses's prospects and our festival runners by subscribing to Kim Baileys Racing Insights.

Also, why not keep up to date with all the goings on at a top National Hunt yard by reading Kim's daily blog. The winner of the Racing Post's best Trainers Blog 5 years in a row!

Or enhance your racing experience by becoming an owner in one of our successful syndicates, which includes free access to Kim's racing insights. please visit kimbaileyracing.com and click on "horses for Sale" for the latest horses available or call Peter on 07901763643 for further information.

James Thomas of Racing Post Bloodstock looks for some clues

Melon: plenty in his favour on breeding

Switch of codes

The festival may be the premier fixture of the jumps calendar but that has not stopped the progeny of sires more commonly associated with the Flat scooping some notable prizes. Examples include Galileo striking with Celestial Halo and Dubawi providing Champion Chase hero Dodging Bullets.

An eyecatching Flat-bred with a big chance this year is Melon, a son of Medicean. The five-year-old caught the attention of pedigree buffs before his easy Leopardstown win, being a half-brother to Italian Oaks winner Night Of Magic and German Listed scorer Night Serenade.

Kayf the one to beat

The leading sire crown at last year's festival went to Kayf Tara, who supplied three winners in Thistlecrack, Blaklion and Ballyandy. The Overbury Stud resident is set to be represented by that same trio again and, with a supporting cast including Tea For Two, Identity Thief, Lifeboat Mona and Cantlow, he has every chance of retaining his no.1 position.

Bred for success

Oscar has had a glut of festival successes – including

Leading festival sires in past five years

Stallion	Sire	Stud	Winners
King's Theatre	Sadler's Wells	Dead	10
Robin Des Champs	Garde Royale	Glenview Stud	8
Oscar	Sadler's Wells	Grange Stud	6
Kayf Tara	Sadler's Wells	Overbury Stud	5
Milan	Sadler's Wells	Grange Stud	4
Presenting	Mtoto	Glenview Stud	4
Westerner	Danehill	Castle Hyde Stud	4

winners of the Gold Cup, Champion Hurdle and Champion Chase – and has a potential star in Colin Tizzard's Finian's Oscar. With his dam being a half-sister to Champion Chase winner Finian's Rainbow, Finian's Oscar has the pedigree to shine at Cheltenham.

New names in frame

It is worth noting the next wave of up-and-coming jumps sires, and two that boast particularly strong reputations are Blue Bresil and Getaway. Blue Bresil has already supplied his first festival winner, Ibis Du Rheu in last year's Martin Pipe Conditional Jockeys' Handicap Hurdle, and could be represented this year by that same horse as well as Mick Jazz and Le Prezien. Getaway is yet to have a festival runner but is sire of Getabird, early favourite for the Champion Bumper.

Inside the stables

Willie Mullins and Paul Nicholls discuss their
main hopes, plus a broader view of the Irish
challenge, trainer analysis and jockeys to watch

'Melon short of experience but has the ability'

Ireland's champion jumps trainer Willie Mullins talks about his leading contenders

Airlie Beach Mares' Novice Hurdle
She has an unblemished record, winning all of her seven races, six of them over hurdles. We never saw her as being a Grade 1-winning mare but she has been a revelation this season and achieved that Grade 1 success in the Royal Bond at Fairyhouse in December. She had a busy time of it and we decided to give her a good break and to train her for the festival. She's entered for a few races but it's most likely that her target will be the mares' novice hurdle.

Augusta Kate Mares' Novice Hurdle
She won three bumpers before making a successful debut over hurdles at Thurles in November. We ran her in a Grade 1 over 2m4f at Naas in January and, although it was a big step up for a mare with only one run over

hurdles behind her, she ran very well and had every chance when she fell at the final hurdle. She's very smart and, although she lacks the experience of Airlie Beach, we're thinking in terms of the mares' novice for her.

Bapaume Triumph
He has shown good form in his three races for us, winning a Grade 2 at Leopardstown's Christmas meeting before finishing second in a Grade 1 at the same track on Irish Gold Cup day. He was beaten fair and square by Mega Fortune but he deserves a shot at the Triumph. He jumps and stays well and better ground than he encountered last time will help his chance.

Bacardys Supreme/Neptune/Albert Bartlett
He fell when travelling well on his hurdling debut at Cork and then went on to win a maiden at Leopardstown's Christmas meeting. We had to give him a short break after that win and when he went back to Leopardstown for the Grade 1 Deloitte, we were hoping he would jump better and benefit from the experience. So the fact he won that race, coming from behind, was very encouraging. He was staying on well at the end of the two and a quarter miles, giving the impression that longer trips would suit. He's in the three novice hurdles at the festival and it will be a late call as to which of them he'll run in, although stamina is probably his forte.

Bellshill RSA Chase
He won a couple of Grade 1 novice hurdles last season, one of them over three miles at the Punchestown festival, and started off well over fences, winning his first two starts. He jumped well at Gowran Park and Limerick but for some reason he was very disappointing at Leopardstown on Irish Gold Cup day. He was well out of contention when he fell at the final fence. He was fine afterwards and it wasn't the first time he had run below expectations at Leopardstown. The RSA remains the plan once we're happy with him.

Bunk Off Early Supreme
He was impressive when winning well on his hurdling debut at Leopardstown's Christmas meeting, then went back to Leopardstown for the Grade 1 Deloitte and was a good second to Bacardys. He was a bit keen in both races but a strong pace at Cheltenham would suit him and he jumps very well. He has plenty of pace and the way he travels would suggest that dropping back to two miles in the Supreme rather than going up to 2m5f in the Neptune would be the logical thing to do.

Carter McKay Bumper
A point-to-point winner who has won both his bumpers and put up a good performance on his second start when easily accounting for his three rivals in a 2m3f race at Naas. We have a few other possibles for the race but Carter McKay deserves to take his chance. He stays well and should be capable of further improvement.

Clondaw Warrior Stayers' Hurdle
We've stepped him up to three miles this season and he put up his best performance when running Vroum Vroum Mag close in a Grade 1 over the trip at Leopardstown in December. On the back of that run, he started favourite for the Galmoy Hurdle at Gowran Park but could only finish third behind Shaneshill. Better ground at Cheltenham will suit him and he deserves to take his chance in the Stayers'.

Djakadam Gold Cup
He hasn't won in four visits to Cheltenham but he has run cracking races in the Gold Cup, finishing second to Coneygree and Don Cossack. A third tilt at the race has been the plan all season and we've given him a light campaign with that in mind. He won the John Durkan at Punchestown in December for the second year running and then finished a good third in the Lexus Chase. We decided against running him in the Irish Gold Cup to leave him fresh for Cheltenham. You'd like to think he might improve on his previous attempts.

Douvan Champion Chase
We've thought the world of him ever since we first worked him and his performances, over hurdles and fences, have emphasised his huge level of ability. He's unbeaten in nine starts over fences and has won his three races this season by wide margins. He's answered every question put to him and, while you can never take anything for granted, we're hoping he can justify his position as hot favourite for the Champion Chase.

Footpad Champion Hurdle
He stayed on well for second in the Irish Champion Hurdle, getting to within one length of Petit Mouchoir, who had beaten him by more than 14 lengths in December. He jumps and stays well and his owners are keen to let him take his chance in the Champion Hurdle.

Isleofhopendreams Pertemps Final
He's a ten-year-old with very little racing done due to past problems. After he won well over fences at Cork in November, we decided to switch back to hurdles and he was very unlucky in the Pertemps qualifier at Leopardstown's Christmas meeting when he finished well to be beaten only a head. He went on to win the Punchestown qualifier in good style and we hope there will be more improvement to come.

Let's Dance Mares' Hurdle/novice hurdles
Although she failed to win last season, she

gained plenty of experience running in high-grade races and being placed a couple of times in Grade 1s. That experience has stood her in good stead and she is four from four this season. We have plenty of options for her and I'd imagine she'll go for one of the staying races. Stamina appears to be her forte.

Melon Supreme

He won on the Flat in France and showed us plenty at home when we started working him. We had to give him time to come right and we started him off in a maiden hurdle at Leopardstown in January when he won by ten lengths. He jumped very well apart from the final hurdle and, as first runs over hurdles go, it was an impressive performance. We would have liked to get another race into him but there was nothing suitable. He lacks experience but has a lot of ability.

Nichols Canyon Champion/Stayers' Hurdle

He's been twice placed at the festival, finishing third in the Champion Hurdle last year and third in the Neptune in 2015. He won the Morgiana Hurdle in November for the second year running but failed to run to his best when beaten seven lengths in the Ryanair Hurdle at Leopardstown in December and he looked held in second place when he fell at the last in the Irish Champion Hurdle. He finished third in a Grade 1 in the US in May on his only attempt over three miles. Which race he goes for hasn't been decided but it will probably be the Champion.

Penhill Albert Bartlett

He's won five of his seven starts over hurdles and has proved himself quite adaptable in terms of going. He got three miles well when winning a Grade 2 by seven lengths at Limerick's Christmas meeting and the Albert Bartlett is his target.

Shaneshill Stayers' Hurdle

He has finished second on each of his three visits to the festival and is a versatile performer who has been running over hurdles

since he ran in the RSA Chase last year. He won the Galmoy over three miles at Gowran Park in January and we decided against running him again before Cheltenham. The Stayers' Hurdle is his target and he should represent us well.

Un De Sceaux Ryanair Chase

He has delivered two excellent performances this season, winning the Tingle Creek at Sandown and the Clarence House at Cheltenham. He's shown he's much more than an out-and-out front-runner and has found plenty in the closing stages of his two races. He's in the Champion Chase but with Ruby [Walsh] keen on riding both him and Douvan at the festival, it's much more likely that he will run in the Ryanair. He has won over the distance over hurdles, so the trip shouldn't be a problem.

Vroum Vroum Mag Mares'/Stayers' Hurdle

She is entered for six races at the festival – three over hurdles and three over fences – and it's most likely that she'll run in one of the hurdle races as she hasn't run over fences for a long time. She won the Grade 1 mares' race at the meeting 12 months ago and, while we'll be keeping our options open until late in the day, she could bid for a repeat. She wasn't at her best when winning at Doncaster on her most recent start and we gave her a break before preparing her for the festival.

Yorkhill JLT

His win in the Neptune, in which he beat Yanworth, was one of three Grade 1 novice hurdle wins for him last season. We thought long and hard about what route to take this season – stay hurdling or go novice chasing. We eventually came down in favour of a chasing campaign and, while he is two from two over fences, his jumping has been a bit iffy with his tendency to jump to the left at most of his fences. He has a great engine and a lot of ability and hopefully he'll be able to brush up his jumping. He's also in the Arkle but the JLT is his more likely target.

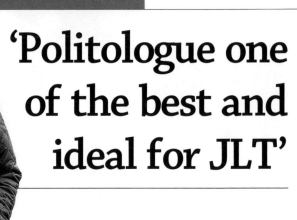

'Politologue one of the best and ideal for JLT'

Britain's champion jumps trainer with the lowdown on his main hopes

Arpege D'Alene National Hunt Chase
He's a good staying chaser and won his novice chase this season at Aintree. He was just beaten in the Pertemps Final at Cheltenham last year and has been running well over fences including at Cheltenham in January when he had plenty of weight in a handicap. He'll go for the National Hunt Chase and four miles will suit him really well. He's by Dom Alco and there's no question of him not staying; he's been crying out for a trip. He doesn't want the ground bottomless and this has been the target from the start. Will Biddick will ride.

Capitaine Supreme
He won at Ascot before Christmas and it's turned out a good race. I don't know why we didn't make the running at Sandown in the

Tolworth, probably because we were a bit nervous about the ground, but he ran okay and made a mistake when he didn't need to. He'll be a great chaser next season.

Cliffs Of Dover Triumph
I schooled him just before he was going to go to Musselburgh and he knocked himself. It might be a race against time to get him there. If we can't quite get him right this season for whatever reason he'll be better next season when he'll be a really good hurdler. He wants looking after and we could do with a few more like him.

Diego Du Charmil County Hurdle
He'll have an entry for the County, but it might pay to wait for the Scottish Champion Hurdle or something like that. He likes to be fresh.

Dodging Bullets Grand Annual
He's not the horse he was. The season he won the Champion Chase, he got to a level he hadn't managed before or since. He looks great and I suspect he'll end up running in the Grand Annual.

El Bandit Pertemps Final
He won well at Musselburgh and surprised us a bit. He'll go for the Pertemps Final and there are races to be won with him.

Frodon JLT
I haven't made a plan and there are some good races you can win either side of the

festival. He's tough and likes Cheltenham, but handicaps are out now as he's rated 153 and it'll have to be a novice chase.

Modus Coral Cup

He's rated 155 after winning the Lanzarote, so the handicapper hasn't missed him.

Movewiththetimes Supreme/Neptune/ Coral Cup/County Hurdle

We thought he'd win his bumper and he duly obliged. He started off over hurdles at Fontwell in October and won well and was then beaten three and three-quarter lengths by Moon Racer at Cheltenham, but he couldn't have got in any more trouble if we'd tried. It was one of those races where they all got into a muddle and it was a bit of a funny race. He got an awful run and the race never worked out. He then won again at Wincanton and I thought it was an awesome display to run Ballyandy so close in the Betfair Hurdle. He's still learning about racing and will enjoy better ground. One thing for sure is he'll make a really smart chaser in time and we like him a lot.

Politologue JLT

It was a good run from him at Haydock, giving 3lb to the winner, and he was rated 152 off the back of that, which is not far off

what Denman was at the end of his novice season. I was nervous about running him so soon after having a hard race but he was nice and relaxed in the hood at Kempton last time and that was job done. He's one of the best novices around and I think he'll go well at Cheltenham, and some of ours are definitely better on better ground. He's the ideal horse to run in the JLT.

Saphir Du Rheu Gold Cup/Ultima Handicap Chase

He ran well at Cheltenham in January and was entitled to win at Kelso last time. He's got his jumping together and I know the owners are keen to run in the Gold Cup. We really fancied him for the Hennessy but he didn't jump well enough. However, that might have woken him up a bit.

Zubayr County Hurdle/Coral Cup

He surprised us last year by winning the Adonis at Kempton. He was dropped right out last and they went quick and he stayed on strongly. He was disappointing in the Betfair Hurdle on his first run since he had a little wind op. We haven't quite found the key to him. I just think he'll be better in the spring. He probably does want two and a half miles, but there's more to come from him.

Saphir Du Rheu:
could have a crack
at the Gold Cup

Mullins v Elliott an intriguing subplot in Cheltenham drama

By Alan Sweetman

THE bar has been set high for Ireland's Cheltenham raiding party in 2017 after last year's record-equalling tally of 14 wins. That later became a record-breaking 15 when the Enda Bolger-trained Josies Orders was awarded the Glenfarclas Chase following the disqualification of Any Currency, who tested positive for a prohibited substance.

Last year Annie Power was promoted from the bench by Willie Mullins to became the fourth consecutive Irish-trained winner of the Champion Hurdle and the Gordon Elliott-trained Don Cossack spearheaded a clean sweep of the first four placings in the

Cheltenham Gold Cup, but the big-race picture looks less promising this year.

A high rate of attrition among leading jumpers in Britain and Ireland this season has taken an unforgiving toll on Irish hopes. Annie Power, her stablemate Faugheen, winner of the 2015 Champion Hurdle, and Don Cossack are three of the major names missing.

Against the background of a domestic campaign largely defined by Elliott's increasingly potent threat to the Mullins dominance, the pair's rivalry will provide an intriguing subplot to the Irish challenge. Another layer of drama involves Gigginstown-owned horses previously trained by Mullins, now in other hands. One of them, Petit Mouchoir, has prospered since his transfer to Henry de Bromhead and holds a claim as Ireland's leading Champion Hurdle hope

following two Grade 1 wins at Leopardstown. Those races simultaneously dented the championship aspirations of the Mullins-trained Nichols Canyon, third to Annie Power last year.

The other side of the coin for De Bromhead is the loss of horses owned by Alan and Ann Potts, notably Sizing John, who was stepped up from the two-mile division by Jessica Harrington to beat two former Cheltenham Festival winners, Empire Of Dirt and Don Poli, in the Stan James Irish Gold Cup.

A handicap winner at last year's fixture for the now retired Colm Murphy, Empire Of Dirt has maintained his rate of progression since joining Elliott. Don Poli, third in the race for Mullins last year, and another ex-Mullins horse Outlander, who gave a stout performance to beat Don Poli and

Cruise control: progressive chaser Empire Of Dirt, a festival winner last year, comes home in good style to win the Troytown

Djakadam in the Lexus at Leopardstown, help to give Elliott a fighting chance of a second Gold Cup. Djakadam, second last year and also-runner-up to Coneygree in 2015, will represent Mullins again.

Douvan, whose 13-race unbeaten record for Mullins has included the 2015 Supreme Novices' Hurdle and the 2016 Arkle Chase, towers above his rivals in the Queen Mother Champion Chase. Stablemate Un De Sceaux, second to a rejuvenated Sprinter Sacre in that contest a year ago, is poised to step up in trip to lead the Irish challenge for the Ryanair Chase following victories in the Tingle Creek and the Clarence House Chase.

In 2016 Mullins won the OLBG Mares' Hurdle for the eighth consecutive year and also sent out Limini to win the inaugural mares' novice hurdle. Despite a plethora of candidates – including the multiply entered Vroum Vroum Mag, Limini, the highly progressive Let's Dance and Airlie Beach – the stable's supremacy in the Grade 1 mares' race is threatened by Apple's Jade, second in the Triumph for Mullins last season and back in form for Elliott when narrowly beating Vroum Vroum Mag in the Hatton's Grace at Fairyhouse in December.

Let's Dance, who has won all four races since chasing home Apple's Jade at Punchestown last spring, and Airlie Beach, who stretched her unbeaten sequence to seven when winning the Royal Bond at Fairyhouse in December, are eligible for the novice races. Mullins could target the mares' novice race with one of the pair, leaving the other to broaden his options for the three Grade 1 novice events in which he already holds a strong hand with the geldings.

The range of choice open to Mullins with his novice hurdlers makes these races a minefield for ante-post punters. Elliott may also delay some crucial decisions, although Death Duty, arguably the leading Irish staying novice, seems to be heading for the Albert Bartlett rather than the Neptune in which a high standard is set by the ex-Irish pointer Finian's Oscar, a winner in this season's autumn campaign before joining Colin Tizzard.

Bacardys, winner of the Deloitte Novice Hurdle at Leopardstown, may represent the best hope for Mullins in one of the longer races. Melon and Deloitte runner-up Bunk Off Early will probably be among those on duty in the Supreme.

Mullins will also ponder the options for his novice chasers. Yorkhill, the pick of his team in this division, will presumably bypass Altior in the Arkle to contest the JLT. Eddie Harty's Drinmore Chase winner Coney Island is perhaps the most interesting of the Irish contingent for the RSA Chase.

In broad terms, the Irish novice chasers may make a less significant impact than the hurdlers, who also include a group of credible Triumph Hurdle contenders, comprising such as Mega Fortune (Elliott), Bapaume (Mullins) and Landofhopeandglory, whose trainer Joseph O'Brien was the 'de facto' handler of last year's winner Ivanovich Gorbatov.

Last year's eventual 15-winner haul was achieved despite a failure to win one of the races most readily associated with the Irish challenge, the Weatherbys Champion Bumper, Mullins, who has won the race on eight occasions, is set to bring a typically strong team, headed by Carter McKay, a winner at Leopardstown and Naas, and Ballyward, who won by a huge margin at the Leopardstown Christmas meeting.

Enda Bolger, for whom the promoted Josies Orders was a fifth winner of the cross-country event since its inauguration in 2005, supplies a leading candidate again in Cantlow. The County Limerick maestro will aim to create a slice of Cheltenham Festival history when On The Fringe lines up for the St James's Place Foxhunter Chase, bidding to go one better than the other seven horses who have won the race twice in the post-war era. The 12-year-old warmed up with a highly satisfactory second at Leopardstown and will not have to contend with the high-class winner Foxrock, who is ineligible.

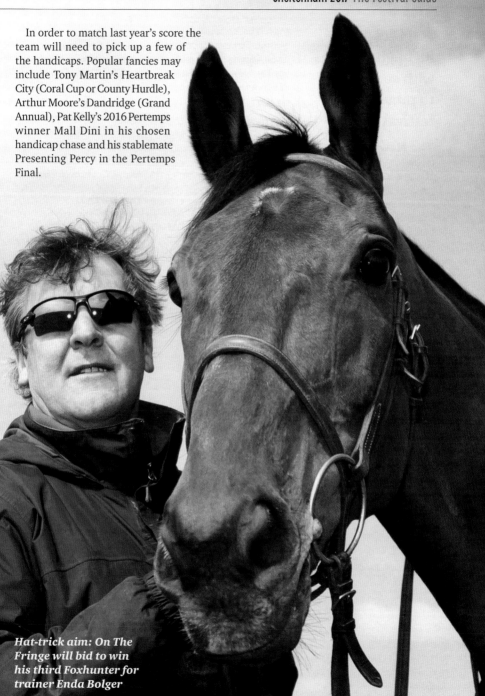

In order to match last year's score the team will need to pick up a few of the handicaps. Popular fancies may include Tony Martin's Heartbreak City (Coral Cup or County Hurdle), Arthur Moore's Dandridge (Grand Annual), Pat Kelly's 2016 Pertemps winner Mall Dini in his chosen handicap chase and his stablemate Presenting Percy in the Pertemps Final.

Hat-trick aim: On The Fringe will bid to win his third Foxhunter for trainer Enda Bolger

Jon Lees highlights horses with something to prove at the festival

The New One
(below left)
The fatal fall of Our Conor in the 2014 Champion Hurdle robbed The New One, who was badly hampered, of his best chance of victory. He finished third behind Jezki but in two return visits he hasn't got as close, finishing around nine lengths behind both Faugheen and Annie Power. Having clinched a record-equalling third win in the International Hurdle this season, The New One clearly acts on the course and it is understandable Nigel Twiston-Davies has not given up on winning the big prize, but The New One's best does not look quite good enough.

Djakadam
Willie Mullins has saddled 48 festival winners but the one race that continually eludes him is the Cheltenham Gold Cup. He has saddled the runner-up four years running and Djakadam has finished second in the last two. They are the only times he has got round the course as he has fallen on his two other visits.

Un De Sceaux
He had looked so good last season that he was sent off 4-6 favourite for the Champion Chase in a field containing a rejuvenated Sprinter Sacre and when he eased into the lead after the fourth-last punters looked set to collect. The appearance proved deceptive as he was unable to muster a challenge once Sprinter Sacre took him on. He has won both starts this season but has never run over a trip as far as the Ryanair Chase over fences.

Yanworth
He was predicted to be one of the stars of last year's festival after a hugely impressive win on Festival Trials Day but in March he was outgunned by the superior Yorkhill. He looked a certain candidate for the Stayers' Hurdle but has been switched to the Champion Hurdle and his preparation hasn't been totally smooth.

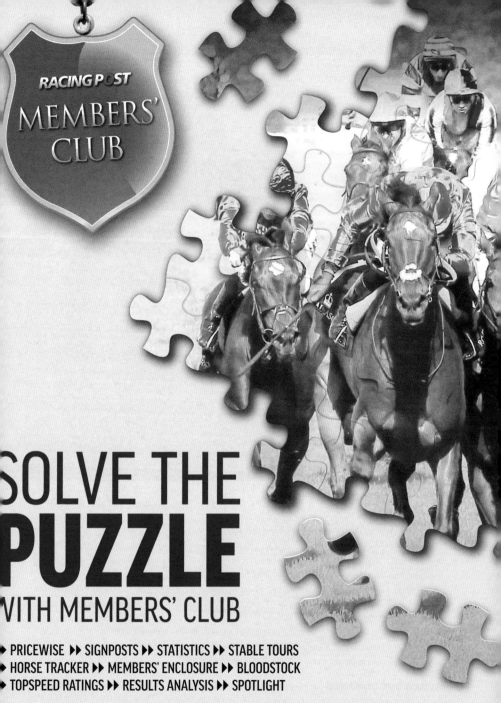

All change at the top

The main four feature races are set to have new champions again this year, with the 2016 winners either retired, injured or otherwise engaged.

Don Cossack never raced again after his Cheltenham Gold Cup triumph and was retired in January with a tendon injury, Sprinter Sacre has also been retired after crowning his career with a second Queen Mother Champion Chase success, Annie Power was ruled out of her Champion Hurdle defence in January with a leg injury and Thistlecrack has moved from World Hurdle winner to Gold Cup favourite in his first season over fences.

That means all four races will have a different winner to last year, a scenario that has now occurred for five consecutive years. Before that, going back to 2003 to take account of the foot-and-mouth abandonment, the trend had been for at least one repeat winner (that happened eight times out of ten).

When this year's new champions are crowned, many will fast-forward 12 months and wonder if they can do it again. Recent festivals prove how difficult a repeat victory is to achieve.

Beaten but unbowed

Merely getting to be favourite in a Grade 1 race at the festival is evidence of strong form, clear ability and/or a big home reputation, and the evidence from last year's results is that beaten favourites should not be dismissed as having been over-hyped and exposed as not good enough.

In the 14 Grade 1 races in 2015, there was an even split of seven favourites who won and seven who were beaten. Yet those beaten favourites were well worth sticking with last year.

Six of the seven beaten market leaders from the 2015 Grade 1 races returned for another crack at the festival and, guess what, four of them won. Not only that, three of them (Don Cossack, Annie Power and Sprinter Sacre) took championship feature races. The other who made a successful return was Black Hercules (sixth as 5-2 favourite in the 2015 Albert Bartlett but the 4-1 winner of the JLT Novices' Chase last year).

Following those six returning beaten favourites last year would have yielded

Un De Sceaux finished second in last year's Champion Chase at the festival, where Limini (below) landed the mares' novice hurdle

Big day for Ireland

Only Thistlecrack in the World Hurdle could hold back the Irish tide on the Thursday of last year's festival when six of the seven races went to the raiders in a rare show of strength on what is traditionally a day dominated by the home team.

The JLT Novices' Chase, the opening race on the card, has become an Irish benefit with five of the six winners since it was introduced, but the other established Thursday races have been difficult for the Irish to win.

Mall Dini's Pertemps Final win last year was the first for Ireland since 2006; Vautour took the Ryanair Chase from Britain for the first time since it was introduced in 2005; the Plate went to Empire Of Dirt, the first Irish winner since 1982; and Cause Of Causes' Kim Muir victory was only Ireland's second since 1983.

The Trull House Stud Mares' Novices' Hurdle, won in its inaugural year by Limini, may become another benefit for Ireland (more specifically Willie Mullins) along with the JLT, but whether Ireland can keep up last year's winning run in the other Thursday races is still open to question.

a profit of +11.75pt to a level stake.

Once again, six beaten favourites from last year's Grade 1 races are set to return for another go. The six are Yanworth, More Of That, Un De Sceaux, Augusta Kate, Bristol De Mai and Shantou Village, which doesn't look a bad shortlist in its own right.

Ireland's champion aiming to lead for fifth straight year

WILLIE MULLINS

Favourites have a high strike-rate, particularly in Grade 1s

County and Martin Pipe handicap hurdles have proved profitable

Ten of his 11 chase winners were in novice races

The Irish colossus has been leading trainer at the festival for the past four years and, while last year's seven-winner haul was just short of his record eight in 2015, Nicky Henderson (seven in 2012) is the only other trainer to have had more than five at a single meeting.

Mullins now has 48 winners going back to Tourist Attraction's Supreme Novices' Hurdle success in 1995 and has moved to seven behind Henderson, the festival's winningmost trainer on 55 (amassed over a decade longer than Mullins).

One big difference for Mullins this season is that he has lost the patronage of Gigginstown House Stud but, while that compromises his chance of an 11th Irish title, it may not affect him too badly at the festival. Only two of the 24 winners that made him leading trainer for the past four years were in Gigginstown colours (the same horse, Don Poli, both times – in the 2014 Martin Pipe Conditional Jockeys' Handicap Hurdle and the 2015 RSA Chase).

Mullins relies on a big opening day to get him off and running. Seven of his 15 winners in the past two years came on the Tuesday, all in Grade 1 company and with six of the seven returned as favourite at no bigger than 5-2.

The market tells its story. At the past four festivals, Mullins has had a total of 34 favourites and 17 (50%) have won, perhaps surprisingly producing a profit in three of the years (+9.09pt overall). Only seven of his 24 winners in that period did not start favourite (and four of those were second favourite).

Traditionally the stable's main strength in Grade 1 races has been over hurdles, particularly over 2m, but Mullins has won six Grade 1 chases in the past two years (having not done so since 2009).

He drew a blank in handicap hurdles last year but has had six winners since 2010 (four at double-figure odds). Excluding the Fred Winter Juvenile Handicap Hurdle, which he has never won, his strike-rate in that period is 6-49 (+35.5pt) and the key targets have been the County Hurdle (3-19, +39pt) and Martin Pipe Conditional Jockeys' Hurdle (3-12, +14.5pt).

Of his eight Champion Bumper winners, six were five-year-olds who had won their sole outing prior to arriving at Cheltenham.

Strong opening hand with Altior and Buveur D'Air

NICKY HENDERSON

Last seven favourites in Grade 1 novice races have finished 1112111

Never one to discount in handicaps at rewarding odds

The master of Seven Barrows is the most successful trainer at the festival with 55 winners and his totals in the past eight years read 3/3/2/7/4/1/2/2, preceded by rare blanks in 2007 and 2008. In that period, however, Willie Mullins has outscored him 36-24 and is now up to 48 overall, putting pressure on Henderson's top spot.

Henderson has assembled a strong team this year, however, and perhaps he could have a festival to rank with his 'magnificent seven' of 2012. With Altior set to lead the charge in the Arkle Chase, swiftly followed by Buveur D'Air and Brain Power in the Champion Hurdle, the opening day could develop into a major battleground with Mullins, traditionally strongest on the Tuesday. How they fare that day should be a good pointer to their chances through the week.

Altior's victory in the Supreme Novices' Hurdle was one of Henderson's brace last year, along with Sprinter Sacre's emotionally charged triumph in the Queen Mother Champion Chase. Already being compared to Sprinter Sacre, Altior is unbeaten in nine starts over jumps and became the fourth-highest-rated chaser of the season with his Newbury success in February.

Henderson has strong claims of taking the Champion Hurdle for a record sixth time with Buveur D'Air, diverted from a chasing campaign once the race started to cut up, or progressive handicapper Brain Power.

Opening-day support could come in particular from Charli Parcs in the Supreme Novices' Hurdle (although the Triumph is an alternative on the Friday), along with Beware The Bear (National Hunt Chase) and Kotkikova (Mares' Hurdle).

The rest of the week looks highly promising for Henderson too. Might Bite (probably in the RSA Chase) and Top Notch (JLT) are another pair of highly rated novice chasers, with good back-up from Whisper and O O Seven, and the rest of the novice hurdling team includes Consul De Thaix, Lough Derg Spirit and Constantine Bay.

Josses Hill (Ryanair Chase) is another decent chance and then there are the handicaps, where Henderson has a knack of turning up a good-priced winner or two. Second-season hurdlers are always worth noting, along with the booking of claiming jockeys – four of Henderson's seven handicap winners since 2009 have had the benefit of a weight allowance.

Handicap hurdles now offer best route to success

PAUL NICHOLLS

Thirteen of his last 15 festival winners have been over hurdles

Seven of his last eight successes were achieved in handicaps

Does well with young, unexposed horses in handicaps

No longer the force he was in Grade 1 chases

The ten-time champion trainer has held on to his no.1 spot in Britain despite being unable to unearth a superstar to rank with the likes of Kauto Star, Denman, Master Minded and Big Buck's, but he is no longer top dog at the Cheltenham Festival. He was leading trainer five times in six years between 2004 and 2009 but has not had that accolade since then.

The change in status is reflected in his type of winners. Whereas he used to dominate the Grade 1 races, seven of his eight winners in the past four years have been in handicaps. Last year's three winners all came in that sphere – Diego Du Charmil (Fred Winter Juvenile Handicap Hurdle), Ibis Du Rheu (Martin Pipe Conditional Jockeys' Handicap Hurdle) and Solar Impulse (Grand Annual Handicap Chase). That was his second consecutive three-winner haul and, with three seconds as well last year (also all in handicaps), he seems to be back as a festival force.

The key to finding a Nicholls handicap winner at the festival, especially over hurdles, is to identify a young, lightly raced type yet to be exposed to the handicapper. Eight of his ten handicap hurdle winners were aged four or five, and nine of his 14 handicap winners overall have carried between 10st 10lb and 11st 1lb (the only two above that weight were in the Martin Pipe).

Once again the Nicholls team is hardly brimming with big chances in the Grade 1 contests, but Politologue has live claims in the JLT Novices' Chase. The grey is one of the main hopes for a return to the halcyon days of top-level chasers, which saw Nicholls claim 14 of his first 25 festival winners in Grade 1 chases up to Kauto Star's second Gold Cup in 2009. Since then, only Dodging Bullets in the 2015 Queen Mother Champion Chase has won a festival Grade 1 over fences for the yard.

Among the handicappers, Diego Du Charmil could bid for a second festival success, this time in the County Hurdle, Brio Conti and Lac Fontana (also a previous festival winner, in the 2014 County) are possibles for the Martin Pipe and the progressive El Bandit is set to go for the Pertemps Final.

It is worth noting that Nicholls has won the County on four occasions and the Grand Annual Chase three times – both are over 2m, and that is another factor to take into account when looking for his best handicap chances.

Staying chases the strong suit
Jonjo O'Neill

O'Neill is a consistent trainer of winners at the festival, with only two blanks since the turn of the century. His total now stands at 26, which puts him in a clear fourth place among current trainers behind Nicky Henderson, Willie Mullins and Paul Nicholls.

Last year his sole winner was Minella Rocco in the National Hunt Chase, his sixth success in that race. His first five came in 12 runnings from 1995 to 2007 but the recent changes in the race conditions (which have made it a higher-class contest) appeared to have taken away his edge until Minella Rocco's victory.

There is enough quality (and stamina) in O'Neill's string for him to continue to do well in the NH Chase and the Kim Muir, the other big chase for amateur riders, and it is worth taking note when he has a fancied runner. Minella Rocco, his first NH Chase runner for five years, was 8-1 and since 2010 his five participants in the NH Chase and Kim Muir priced under 10-1 have finished 41419.

Staying races are clearly where O'Neill does best, with 21 of his 26 festival victories coming in races over 3m or further, and he also has a good record in the Pertemps Final (four wins) and the Ultima Handicap Chase (three wins). Handicap chasers to note this year are Holywell, Beg To Differ and Another Hero.

Excellent record in races over 3m-plus

Twelve of his 15 winners in the past decade came over fences

Big chance of Defi Triumph
Philip Hobbs

The Somerset trainer has drawn a blank at the past two festivals but has a big hope this year in long-time Triumph Hurdle favourite Defi Du Seuil. Hobbs has not had a Triumph runner for five years but has a good record in the Grade 1 contest, having won with Made In Japan in 2004 and Detroit City in 2006. The stable regularly delivers with fancied runners – four of the last five winners were sent off no bigger than 6-1.

Hobbs's 18 winners have come in 14 different races but four of the last six have been gained over fences. Several of his early festival winners came in handicap hurdles (two wins in both the County and the Coral Cup) but he has had only one in that sphere since 2004.

His runners in big handicaps always merit respect, however, and last year he had the third in the Pertemps Final and the third and fourth in the County Hurdle. He won the Pertemps in 2014 with Fingal Bay and could have decent chances this year with Big Easy and For Good Measure. Wait For Me, fourth when favourite for the County last year and third in the 2015 Champion Bumper, could have another crack at the County, while No Comment could go for the Martin Pipe Conditional Jockeys' Handicap Hurdle.

Over fences there is no standout but Garde La Victoire, who has won four of his seven chase starts, has outside place claims in the Champion Chase.

Watch the market closely

Each-way prospects in big handicap hurdles

Yanworth bids to go one better
Alan King

King had a golden period with 11 festival winners from 2004 to 2009 but has scored only in singles since then (in 2011, 2013, 2014 and 2015) to take his score to 15. He remains a competitive force, with ten runners finishing in the first four at the past three festivals in addition to his two winners.

Yanworth was seen as one of the British bankers last year but had to settle for second behind Yorkhill in the Neptune Novices' Hurdle. He will be back again for the Champion Hurdle, having been diverted from the planned route to the Stayers' Hurdle as owner JP McManus has Unowhatimeanharry for the longer race.

Another Grade 1 hope is Uxizandre, who was King's most recent festival winner in the 2015 Ryanair Chase. He had been absent since that race until his January return at Cheltenham and is now set to make a repeat bid.

King has a good record with juveniles and won the Triumph Hurdle with Penzance (2005) and Katchit (2007). In the past ten years eight of his 32 runners (25%) in the Triumph and Fred Winter made the first three and his record is particularly good with fancied runners under 10-1 (01223F30).

Defi Du Seuil looks tough to beat in the Triumph, but Cosmeapolitan, Coeur De Lion and Fidux are King juveniles to bear in mind, especially if they turn up in the Fred Winter.

Most of King's chase wins at the festival have been with novices, including in handicaps.

Strong squad of juvenile hurdlers

Watch out for his novice chasers in handicaps

Best hopes with novice hurdlers
Nigel Twiston-Davies

Twiston-Davies lacks the strength in depth of the other top stables and consequently his festival record has fits and starts. He had two winners in 2009, three in 2010 (including the Gold Cup with Imperial Commander), two in 2013 and two again last year, but he drew a blank in the other four years in that period.

Last year's two winners both came in Grade 1 races – the RSA Chase with Blaklion and the Champion Bumper with Ballyandy – and his overall total now stands at 17. It was notable last year that his fancied runners all did well. Five were priced at under 10-1 and they finished 41122. Again, in 2013, he had a winner and a second from two runners priced at under 10-1.

His best hopes on the ante-post prices are Ballyandy – once the Betfair Hurdle winner's target is decided – and Wholestone, his other high-class novice hurdler who is set to go for the Albert Bartlett.

Twiston-Davies traditionally does well with novice chasers. He has landed the RSA twice and the National Hunt Chase, and also taken the Grand Annual and Kim Muir with first-season chasers. Foxtail Hill is one to note.

Novice chasers are a traditional strength

The New One is the yard's only festival winner over hurdles since 2008

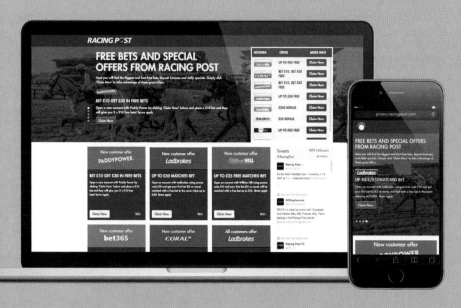

Focus on handicap chase fancies
David Pipe

Pipe has a long way to go to match father Martin's 34 festival winners but he is now up to 14 and has failed to register at only two festivals since landing the 2007 Fred Winter Juvenile Handicap Hurdle with Gaspara in his first season.

Last year's sole winner came on familiar territory as Un Temps Pour Tout took the Ultima Handicap Chase. Ten of Pipe's 14 wins have been in chases and handicaps are the main route – he has won the Ultima twice and both the Kim Muir and the Stable Plate on three occasions.

Watch the market closely. From 23 runners priced at 12-1 or below in those three handicap chases, he has had six winners (26%, +29.83pt), two seconds and a third.

His battalion of chasers could be led this year by Champers On Ice in the RSA or National Hunt Chase. Others to note include Un Temps Pour Tout (again), Vieux Lion Rouge, Doctor Harper, What A Moment and Starchitect.

Two of Pipe's four wins over hurdles have been in the Pertemps Final, although both came early in his training career with course specialist Buena Vista.

He has yet to win a Grade 1 over hurdles at the festival but has high hopes in the Supreme Novices' Hurdle with Moon Racer, the 2015 Champion Bumper winner.

Ten of his 14 festival victories have come over fences

Note his fancied runners in staying handicap chases

Gold top with exciting line-up
Colin Tizzard

These are exciting times for Tizzard's expanding training operation in Dorset and, if everything went perfectly to plan, he could get close to doubling his festival tally of five winners. He has a strong team in the Gold Cup, headed by Thistlecrack, and leading fancies in a couple of the Grade 1 novice hurdles, as well as several handicap possibilities.

In previous years Tizzard has sent no more than a dozen runners to the festival and now, with a stronger team of fancied runners, much more is expected. It is worth noting that he has had only seven runners priced under 10-1 at the past five festivals and they finished 201521F (the faller was Cue Card three out in last year's Gold Cup when going well).

If all his leading hopes make it to Cheltenham, Tizzard could well have three runners under 10-1 in the Gold Cup alone, with Thistlecrack set to be joined by Native River and Cue Card (although there is the option of sending the latter back to the Ryanair he won in 2013).

Away from the main event, Tolworth Novices' Hurdle winner Finian's Oscar holds strong claims in the Neptune (or Supreme) and likewise West Approach in the Albert Bartlett after his Cleeve Hurdle third. Fox Norton has good place claims in a Champion Chase featuring the formidable Douvan (with the Ryanair a possibility) and Festival Trials Day winner Royal Vacation holds a solid chance in the RSA or National Hunt Chase.

Fancied runners usually perform well

But don't rule out a surprise. Three of his five festival winners were returned at huge prices (40-1 twice and 28-1)

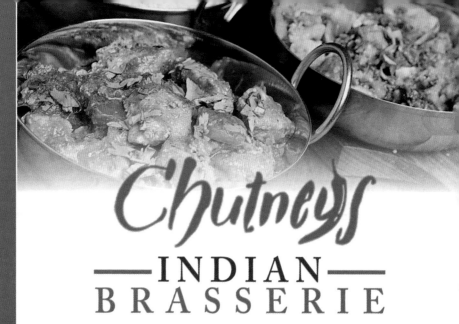

Chutneys

—INDIAN—
B R A S S E R I E

36 St. Michael's Street. Oxford. OX1 2EB

Close finish? Make it a perfect one and stop by for something to end the day perfectly at the oldest Indian restaurant in Oxford

QUOTE "CHELTENHAM10"
for a 10% discount!
Call 01865 724 241

Authentic Indian Cuisine

www.chutneysoxford.co.uk
facebook.com/chutneysoxford

Twiston-Davies profits from Nicholls success

Sam Twiston-Davies

Ruby Walsh has been top jockey at ten of the past 13 festivals since his first success in 2004 but he may come under more pressure this year with the Willie Mullins team depleted by injury to some of its stars, and Twiston-Davies could be worth a shot at 12-1 in the leading rider market.

Now well settled into Walsh's old job as stable jockey to Paul Nicholls, Twiston-Davies recorded his fastest century this season despite missing seven weeks through injury and he appears to have a book of rides that will help him build on last year's successful festival.

His victories aboard Diego Du Charmil in the Fred Winter Juvenile Handicap Hurdle and Solar Impulse in the Grand Annual Handicap Chase were his third and fourth for Nicholls at the festival from 31 rides (13%, +21pt) and he had another winner on his father Nigel's Ballyandy in the Champion Bumper.

With both stables heading to the festival in great form, Twiston-Davies will have plenty of ammunition this year. Politologue looks one of his most exciting mounts in the JLT Novices' Chase but it is worth noting that three of his four festival winners for Nicholls have been in handicaps.

The trainer has had more success at targeting handicaps in the past couple of years and, as well as his two winners with Twiston-Davies in 2016, they also went close when 14-1 shot Bouvreuil was beaten half a length in the novice handicap chase.

Of course Walsh will be difficult to unseat from his Cheltenham throne, and certainly so if he repeats last year's seven winners, but five of his ten leading rider titles have been gained with a total of just three and Twiston-Davies looks up to reaching that figure again.

Claimers for Willie Mullins

While it may have become near impossible to profit from the Ruby Walsh-Willie Mullins partnership, it is worth noting the trainer's use of riders with a weight claim. Since 2008 he has done this on just nine occasions but three of those runners won (33%, +30.25pt).

Amateurs to note

There is rich talent among the amateur jockeys and two of the best are Ireland's top point-to-point riders **Derek O'Connor** and **Jamie Codd**, who each landed a winner at last year's festival.

O'Connor scored on the Jonjo O'Neill-trained 8-1 shot Minella Rocco in the National Hunt Chase and that took his record to three winners, five seconds, two thirds and two fourths from 28 mounts (+21pt). He seems to be O'Neill's preferred amateur these days and their link-ups are worth noting.

Codd's festival record is 5-29 (17%, +16.83pt). Notably he is 2-4 (+10.33pt) when riding for David Pipe, with two Kim Muir wins aboard the gambled-on pair Junior (2012) and The Package (2015), but last year's success came for Gordon Elliott on 9-2 shot Cause Of Causes in the Kim Muir and that is a combination to watch.

Paddy Brennan

Brennan's headline act is Cue Card *(right)*, who will make another bid for the Cheltenham Gold Cup following last year's unfortunate fall three out, but the talented freelance will be much in demand across the four days.

One trainer who has used him regularly this season is the up-and-coming Fergal O'Brien and they have had a great deal of success together – 38 winners by early February at a strike-rate of 26 per cent. Backing the combination blind this season would have returned a level-stake profit of +68.43pt. O'Brien runners could include Colin's Sister (Mares' Hurdle/ novice hurdle), Barney Dwan (Pertemps Final). Bells 'N' Banjos (National Hunt Chase) and Imperial Eloquence (Champion Bumper).

Adrian Heskin

The Irishman was an immediate hit when he became Tom George's stable jockey this season and their partnership could be worth watching at this year's festival.

Heskin has ridden two festival winners (A New Story in the Cross Country Chase in 2010 and Martello Tower in the 2015 Albert Bartlett Novices' Hurdle), while George has to go back to 2002 for his sole success with Galileo in what is now the Neptune Novices' Hurdle.

Their biggest victory this season came with Sir Valentino in the Grade 2 Haldon Gold Cup at Exeter but they have churned out a steady stream of winners (by mid-February they had a 23 per cent strike-rate and a healthy profit of +46.6pt).

TOP JOCKEYS

Festival award winners

2016	Ruby Walsh	7
2015	Ruby Walsh	4
2014	Ruby Walsh	3
2013	Ruby Walsh	4
2012	Barry Geraghty	5
2011	Ruby Walsh	5
2010	Ruby Walsh	3
2009	Ruby Walsh	7
2008	Ruby Walsh	3
2007	Robert Thornton	4

Total festival winners

Ruby Walsh	52
Barry Geraghty	34
Richard Johnson	20
Davy Russell	17
Tom Scudamore	9
Timmy Murphy	8
Sam Twiston-Davies	7
Paddy Brennan	6
Nina Carberry	6
Bryan Cooper	6

TOP TRAINERS

Festival award winners

2016	Willie Mullins	7
2015	Willie Mullins	8
2014	Willie Mullins	4
2013	Willie Mullins	5
2012	Nicky Henderson	7
2011	Willie Mullins	4
2010	Nicky Henderson	3
2009	Paul Nicholls	5
2008	Paul Nicholls	3
2007	Paul Nicholls	4

Total festival winners

Nicky Henderson	55
Willie Mullins	48
Paul Nicholls	40
Jonjo O'Neill	26
Philip Hobbs	18
Edward O'Grady	18
Nigel Twiston-Davies	17
Alan King	15
David Pipe	14

Nick Pulford on some of the jockeys and trainers looking for a first success at the festival

Jack Kennedy

Still only 17, the richly talented jockey has to be top of the list as the 'one most likely to' be the next new name on the festival roll of honour. Kennedy had a second place on his festival debut 12 months ago, beaten four lengths on the Venetia Williams-trained 33-1 shot Tango De Juilley in the Stable Plate, but the committed backing of leading Irish trainer Gordon Elliott will give him any number of good rides. He has proved he can be trusted with top talent, having landed Grade 1 wins this season on the Elliott-trained Neptune Novices' Hurdle fancy Death Duty and Outlander in the Lexus Chase.

Sean Flanagan

Flanagan, 28, has yet to ride a winner in Britain, let alone at Cheltenham, but he is armed with much better ammunition having become stable jockey to Noel Meade this season. He is having the best campaign of his career in Ireland, where his high-profile winners have included Disko in the Grade 1 Flogas Novice Chase and Ice Cold

Soul in the Coral.ie Hurdle. He may have to give up some top rides to Gigginstown's retained jockey Bryan Cooper but is set to have one or two decent chances.

The Mullins boys

The Mullins name resonates through Cheltenham's history and jockeys Danny and David Mullins may soon be added to the family roll of honour. Both are grandsons of Dawn Run's trainer Paddy Mullins and sons of festival-winning trainers,

as well as nephews of Willie Mullins. Danny – the 24-year-old son of trainers Tony and Mags Mullins (who won the 2015 Albert Bartlett with Martello Tower) – is having his best season, highlighted by Royal Bond Novice Hurdle victory on Airlie Beach for uncle Willie, and should pick up some good rides. David, whose father Tom Mullins won twice at the festival with Alderwood, hit the heights last year with his Grand National victory

Names to note: Jack Kennedy (main) and (clockwise from top left) Sean Flanagan, Charlie Longsdon, Danny Mullins, David Mullins and Ben Pauling

Albert Bartlett Novices' Hurdle second favourite Barters Hill was beaten into fourth by Unowhatimeanharry. He may not have a leading contender of that ilk this time but a solid team includes Grade 2 winner Willoughby Court (Neptune Novices' Hurdle) and High Bridge (Supreme Novices' Hurdle).

Four more to watch

Gavin Cromwell, a farrier by trade who shoed last year's Gold Cup winner Don Cossack, trains a small string in County Meath that includes Jer's Girl, a dual winner of Grade 1 novice hurdles last season and now set to go for the Mares' Hurdle.

Debra Hamer, who trains in Carmarthenshire, has guided Tobefair to a remarkable seven-timer in handicap hurdles and could bid to make it eight in the Pertemps Final.

Lucy Wadham, a mainly jumps trainer in Newmarket, is aiming for the Kim Muir with her highest-rated horse, Potters Legend.

Jack Barber, British champion point-to-point trainer for the past two seasons, has a leading chance in the Foxhunter with Ask The Weatherman.

on Rule The World at the age of 19 and this season has won the Irish Champion Hurdle on Petit Mouchoir, the Thyestes Handicap Chase with Champagne West and a Grade 3 handicap hurdle at Ascot on Brain Power, the Nicky Henderson-trained Champion Hurdle contender.

Charlie Longsdon

The highest-ranked British trainer still without a festival winner on his CV was a little unlucky last year with Our Kaempfer, beaten around three lengths into fifth when well fancied for the Pertemps Final, and the same horse could be back for one of the chases – possibly the JT McNamara National Hunt Chase for amateur riders. Hope also lies with Forth Bridge, likely to go for the Fred Winter Juvenile Handicap Hurdle.

Ben Pauling

Hopes of breaking his duck were dashed last year when

Get Champers On Ice for National Hunt Chase

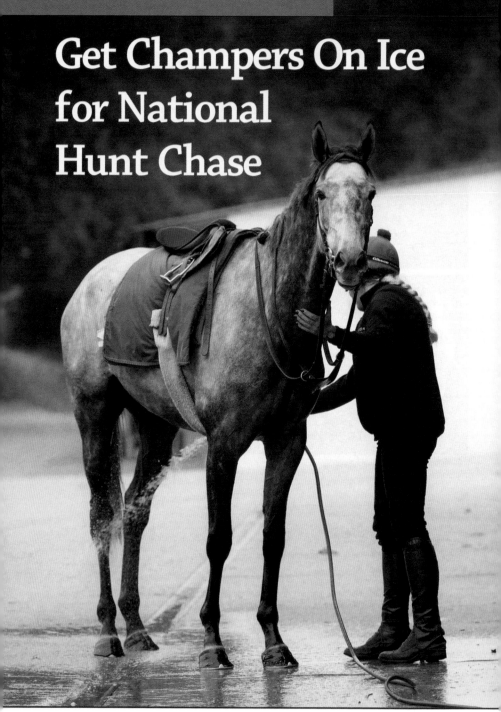

The Racing Post's regional correspondents pick their fancies

Lambourn James Burn

No trainer has won more Champion Hurdles than Nicky Henderson and he can take the outright record with a sixth success courtesy of **Buveur D'Air**.

Third in the Supreme last term, JP McManus's six-year-old went novice chasing this term and won twice, but connections switched him back over hurdles and it looks an inspired move.

He bolted up in the Contenders Hurdle at Sandown and, with no Annie Power or Faugheen around, he should be hard to stop.

Henderson looks set for a great opening day as **Charli Parcs** seems sure to be a player in the Supreme. He is entered in the Triumph Hurdle as well but appears to be more likely to run in the Supreme and do not be surprised if he is a Champion Hurdle contender in 12 months' time.

Those two are held in the highest regard, as is Warren Greatrex's **La Bague Au Roi**, who is in the mix for the mares' novice hurdle.

Successful in six of her seven starts, she has been aimed at the race all season and should be raring to go after a mid-season break.

West Country Andrew King

Colin Tizzard appears to hold the key to the Timico Cheltenham Gold Cup if the betting is any guide and the highly progressive **Native River** might take a lot of catching if allowed to dominate as his jumping is so accurate.

The Harry Fry-trained **Neon Wolf** is a smart performer in the making who has impressed with his attitude in three outings this season. There is no reason he cannot carry on the good work in the Neptune Investment Management Novices' Hurdle.

Fry also looks to have the answer to the Sun Bets Stayers' Hurdle with **Unowhatimeanharry**, who can follow up last year's victory at the festival. If anything he has improved at the age of nine and with his proven stamina he looks a banker.

Champers On Ice (left) might appear to have been disappointing at Cheltenham on Trials Day in January, but things did not pan out for him over a trip far too short. He will have things in his favour in the 4m National Hunt Chase.

Ireland Kevin Walsh

Death Duty's unbeaten run has been one of the stories of the Irish season and Gordon Elliott's durable six-year-old can cap a terrific season with Albert Bartlett victory. The form of his four consecutive victories looks like a bit of a mixed bag but Monalee has developed into a reliable benchmark recently and the step up to three miles could see Death Duty at his most effective.

At around 25-1, **Marinero** could emerge as a real each-way threat if he takes up the National Hunt Chase option. In finishing less than four lengths behind Thistlecrack at Cheltenham in November, he looked to be crying out for a step up in trip and seems to have gone under the radar. The favourite A Genie In Abottle is also owned by Gigginstown, but Marinero's previous course visit could prove invaluable in this energy-sapping contest.

The North Colin Russell

Nietzsche from the Brian Ellison yard looks one of the north's best chances of the week in the Fred Winter Juvenile Handicap Hurdle.

He was progressive on the Flat and has won three of his six races over hurdles. He looks an ideal type as he should get into the race but is considered better than his current mark of 130.

Ellison also has an interesting candidate in **Forest Bihan** in the Racing Post Arkle Chase but, with Altior in the field, he may be one to back in the 'without the favourite' market.

Cloudy Dream, beaten by Forest Bihan at Doncaster last time, is another Arkle possible but would be of more interest stepped up in trip in the JLT Novices' Chase.

TUESDAY, MARCH 14 (OLD COURSE)

PAUL KEALY
ON THE KEY
CONTENDERS

1.30 Sky Bet Supreme Novices' Hurdle   ITV/RUK

2m½f   Grade 1   £125,000

Willie Mullins and Ruby Walsh have turned up at the Cheltenham Festival with a Supreme banker for the past four years, delivering with the first three (Champagne Fever, Vautour and Douvan) before Min was beaten into second by Altior last year. They head the market again with Melon but his prominence owes more to his trainer's recent record in the race and a tall reputation than the substance of his ten-length maiden win at Leopardstown. There are plenty with stronger form, including Betfair Hurdle winner Ballyandy, Grade 2 Cheltenham scorer Moon Racer (like Ballyandy a former winner of the Champion Bumper) and Deloitte one-two Bacardys and Bunk Off Early (both stablemates of Melon). Charli Parcs, a twice-raced juvenile with the Triumph as an alternative target, is another highly regarded contender for Nicky Henderson, last year's winning trainer.

Melon

5 ch g; Trainer Willie Mullins
Hurdles form 1 (left-handed)
Best RPR 138

It took a while for the obligatory Willie Mullins-trained Supreme Novices' Hurdle favourite to emerge, but Melon assumed that role with an impressive ten-length success on his hurdles debut at Leopardstown in January. Quite what he achieved in doing so is hard to gauge as the runner-up, who had been 100-1 second to Anibale Fly on his hurdles debut in December 2015, had since run in six bumpers, winning only the last of them, and then got chinned at odds of 4-11 next time, but Melon's jumping was good and he's clearly got a lot of talent. There are obvious downsides, though, as he clearly hasn't shown anywhere near the sort of form usually associated with a Supreme winner (last year Altior had run an RPR nearly 20lb higher and went off a bigger price than Melon is now) and the last scorer to have run just once over hurdles was Flown back in 1992. Melon's sire, Medicean, is not known for producing high-class jumpers either, with Sempre Medici much his best. On the upside, this looks a surprisingly weak year.

Going preference Unknown. Not raced on soft
Star rating ✪✪

Charli Parcs

4 b g; Trainer Nicky Henderson
Hurdles form 11 (left-handed)
Best RPR 139

Won sole start in France and snapped up for €250,000 by JP McManus. Charli Parcs certainly looked the part on his British debut at Kempton, where he settled well, jumped fluently, took it up a long way out and strode away for an eight-length win from Master Blueyes, to whom he was conceding 5lb and who subsequently won at Ludlow. Put in at odds-on against ownermate and Triumph Hurdle favourite Defi Du Seuil (rated 155) at Cheltenham on Trials Day in January, with Barry Geraghty set to ride, but he didn't run – although Nicky Henderson was still keen to find one more outing for him. Could go for the Triumph, but owner has a stack of juvenile hurdlers and this one looks very speedy, so maybe this easier course will suit better. Only 13 four-year-olds have run in the Supreme since Hors La Loi won at that age in 1999 and most of those would not have won a Cheltenham Festival race at any age, but McManus's Binocular finished second in 2008 and the 8lb weight-for-age allowance will be tempting.

Going preference Won on good and soft
Star rating ✪✪✪✪

Moon Racer

8 b g; Trainer David Pipe
Hurdles form 11
Left-handed 1, best RPR 140
Right-handed 1, best RPR 130
Cheltenham form 111 (bumpers and hurdles), best RPR 140
At the festival 11 Mar 2015 Slowly into stride and had to be held up in rear, good progress on inner from 3f out, ridden 2f out, closed to lead just over 1f out, ran on well, won Champion Bumper by one and a half lengths from Modus

Champion Bumper winner two seasons ago when had the likes of Yanworth (fourth) and Bellshill (tenth) behind, but injury problems meant he was not seen again for another 13 months until running second in a Grade 1 bumper at Punchestown. Had two starts over hurdles in the autumn, each time accounting for last season's Champion Bumper winner Ballyandy, but hard to rate the form highly given slow pace in small fields, especially with Mirsaale (beaten out of sight next three starts) finishing runner-up in the second of them. Yet another who hasn't achieved the usually required level of form to win this race, but that is also true of the only two other horses quoted in single figures at the beginning of February and he's already a festival winner who is unbeaten on the course. The worry is another absence since November for a horse who is obviously fragile, but trainer David Pipe reported all well with him in early February. You have to go back to 2002 and Like-A-Butterfly to find the last winner aged eight (she may have been second had Adamant Approach not fallen at the last but he was also eight), but only five have tried since.

Going preference Has won on good and soft
Star rating ✪✪✪

Bunk Off Early

5 ro g; Trainer Willie Mullins
Hurdles form (all left-handed) 12, best RPR 145

Had peak official rating of 82 on the Flat in Ireland. Moved from Andrew Oliver to Willie Mullins for a jumps campaign and began very well, scoring by an easy five and a half lengths on debut at Leopardstown over Christmas from a much superior Flat rival (Outspoken, trained by Joseph O'Brien) who has since won easily. Took big step up in the class in February's Grade 1 Deloitte Novice Hurdle and again performed with plenty of credit, finishing a three-quarter-length second to strong-staying stablemate Bacardys. Indeed, he raced keenly for a lot of the way in that 2m2f soft-ground contest and left no doubt he'll be suited by the shorter trip of the Supreme. Obviously has better form than the stable's favourite for this race and is one to take very seriously.

Going preference Clearly handles soft but hard to believe better surface won't suit just as well
Star rating ✪✪✪

Finian's Oscar

5 b g; Trainer Colin Tizzard
Hurdles form (all right-handed) 111, best RPR 147

Point winner who was well talked up as Colin Tizzard's best novice hurdler and duly dotted up on Hereford debut over 2m5½f in December. Dropped in trip for the 2m Grade 1 Tolworth Hurdle at Sandown next time and, having been put in at 8-1 in the ante-post market by one firm when the entries came out, was backed as if defeat was out of the question and went off at just 11-10 before

---

TRAINER'S VIEW

David Pipe on Moon Racer "He found plenty when asked for his effort [at Cheltenham in November] and was well on top on the run-in. I've always held the opinion that he's a top-notch two-mile hurdler and this did nothing to dissuade me" *Had subsequent Betfair Hurdle one-two Ballyandy and Movewiththetimes behind in third and fifth in Cheltenham Grade 2*

winning by five lengths from previous Grade 2 scorer Capitaine. Cruised up to lead at the second-last and looked like winning easily, but made a mistake at the final flight and ultimately it was hard work on sticky ground. Full of promise and favourite for Neptune, but prepped over 2m at Exeter (wasn't impressive at odds of 1-16) and connections still undecided.

Going preference Won point on good/yielding; any faster an unknown
Star rating ✪✪✪

Defi Du Seuil

4 b g; Trainer Philip Hobbs
Hurdles form 11111 (all left-handed), best RPR 150
Cheltenham form 111, best RPR 136

Has the most experience and an RPR of 150 gives him much the best form when you figure in an 8lb weight-for-age allowance, but favourite for the Triumph and most likely goes there.

Going preference Won on anything from good to soft, but said to prefer it easy
Star rating ✪✪✪✪

Ballyandy

6 b g; Trainer Nigel Twiston-Davies
Hurdles form 2321, best RPR 151
Left-handed 31, best RPR 151
Right-handed 22, best RPR 135
Cheltenham form (all) 113, best RPR 136
At the festival 16 Mar 2016 Close up behind leaders, trapped behind weakening rival 4f out and dropped to midfield 3f out, ridden and rallied 2f out, chased leader 1f out, led near finish, just held on, won Champion Bumper by a nose from Battleford

Last year's Champion Bumper winner made a bit of a slow start over hurdles, coming off second or third best on his first three outings, but there wasn't much disgrace in losing to 2015 Champion Bumper winner Moon Racer twice or subsequent Challow Hurdle winner Messire Des Obeaux. Those races were all run with small fields off a slow gallop and Ballyandy had already shown how well suited he was to the hurly-burly of a big-field contest

by storming up the hill at Cheltenham last March, having been hampered around half a mile out. It was therefore not too surprising that Nigel Twiston-Davies put him away once handicapped and targeted him at the Betfair Hurdle at Newbury, a plan brought off when Ballyandy won by three-quarters of a length from fellow novice Movewiththetimes. He doesn't boast the Grade 1 form of some of those shorter in the betting, but you would be hard pushed to suggest the Newbury form doesn't put him right up there with them as the front two pulled six lengths clear of the 5lb well-in Clyne, who had won four in a row before pushing Twiston-Davies's The New One to a length at Haydock. Two recent novice winners of the Betfair Hurdle, My Tent Or Yours and Get Me Out Of Here, went on to run close seconds in the Supreme and Ballyandy has to have a big shout. Sam Twiston-Davies thinks he's more of a stayer, so the Neptune is a serious option, but connections will wait and see what the ground looks like and a soft surface is likely to see him line up here.

Going preference Seems to handle anything
Star rating ✪✪✪✪

Bacardys

6 b g; Trainer Willie Mullins
Hurdles form F11, best RPR 147
Left-handed 11, best RPR 147
Right-handed F, best RPR 129
Cheltenham form (bumper) 3
At the festival 16 Mar 2016 Held up in midfield, progress over 4f out to track leaders 3f out, ridden and no impression 2f out, stayed on final furlong to take 3rd last 100yds, finished third, beaten two lengths by Ballyandy in Champion Bumper

Third in last year's Champion Bumper and beat Bunk Off Early in the Grade 1 Deloitte, so has to feared wherever he goes, but did all his best work late at Leopardstown, so probably more likely to run in the Neptune.

Going preference Handles soft well but third on good ground at last year's festival
Star rating ✪✪

High Bridge

6 b g; Trainer Ben Pauling
Hurdles form (left-handed) 111, best RPR 136
Cheltenham form (bumper) 6, best RPR 129
At the festival 16 Mar 2016 Prominent, tracked leader over 3f out, ridden to challenge well over 1f out, faded final furlong, finished sixth, beaten four and a half lengths by Ballyandy in Champion Bumper

Had a big reputation when with John Ferguson and sent off at 12-1 for the Champion Bumper last year, in which he performed with credit in sixth. Briefly went back to Godolphin and Charlie Appleby when Ferguson packed in training, but chinned at odds-on in a Thirsk maiden and swiftly shipped back out again, this time to Ben Pauling although still in Bloomfields' ownership. Has won all three starts over hurdles, but all in relatively low-class novice races, so needs a lot more to be competitive. Connections have faith and he's got a turn of foot, so he's worth his place.

Going preference Doesn't seem dependent
Star rating ✪✪

Neon Wolf

6 b g; Trainer Harry Fry
Hurdles form 11, best RPR 149
Left-handed 1, best RPR 149
Right-handed 1, best RPR 131

Considered more likely to run in the Neptune, so dealt with in more detail in Wednesday's section. However, boasts form that puts him right up there with the best and, while he might indeed want further in time, the winners of five Gold Cups have finished second in the Supreme this century and it would be madness not to take him very seriously if he runs here.

Going preference Won point on good/yielding; any faster an unknown
Star rating ✪✪✪

Movewiththetimes

6 ch g; Trainer Paul Nicholls
Hurdles form 1512, best RPR 151
Left-handed 152, best RPR 151
Right-handed 1, best RPR 126
Cheltenham form 5, best RPR 139

Comes out the same horse as Ballyandy on Betfair Hurdle form (gave 1lb, beaten three-quarters of a length) and has much less experience, so every reason to think he can improve again. While some were not impressed that he appeared to hang in behind Ballyandy on the run-in, that can easily be put down to inexperience. He boasts some of the best 2m form on offer but his pedigree suggests he'll get further with no problem. The main concern is that Nicholls has said he will handle very deep ground well and those conditions are unlikely.

Going preference Soft ground best
Star rating ✪✪✪

OTHERS TO CONSIDER

The Willie Mullins mares **Airlie Beach** and **Let's Dance** have the figures to be competitive, but you'd be surprised if they weren't kept to their own sex. Nicky Henderson's **Consul De Thaix** was being prepped for the Betfair Hurdle and was among the favourites until inflammation in a hind leg caused his withdrawal the day before. His form with Champion Hurdle candidate Brain Power is solid, but with a mark of 140 he'll have handicap options, most likely the County. Henderson's **Beyond Conceit** was talented on the Flat and showed courage to make it 2-2 over hurdles at Ascot in February, while **Mick Jazz** is also reported by Gordon Elliott to be heading to the County.

VERDICT

This looks the most open Supreme in years and while the Mullins faithful will happily lump on Melon at any price he can't represent value. I'd be more interested in Mullins' Bunk Off Early at the prices, but I've backed both BALLYANDY and MOVEWITHTHETIMES for this race and the Neptune on non-runner no bet as their Betfair Hurdle form is right up there with the best and both have more to come. If you listen to the gossip Charli Parcs is the best four-year-old Henderson has ever had and if that's the case everyone is in trouble.

SUPREME NOVICES' HURDLE RESULTS AND TRENDS

	FORM	WINNER	AGE & WGT	Adj RPR	SP	TRAINER	BEST RPR LAST 12 MONTHS (RUNS SINCE)
16	61111	**Altior** CD	6 11-7	163[T]	4-1	N Henderson	won Kempton class 2 nov hdl (2m) **(0)**
15	2111	**Douvan** D	5 11-7	160[-3]	2-1f	W Mullins (IRE)	won Punchestown Gd2 nov hdl (2m) **(0)**
14	2-111	**Vautour** D	5 11-7	157[T]	7-2j	W Mullins (IRE)	won Gd1 Deloitte Hurdle (2m2f) **(0)**
13	-1231	**Champagne Fever** C, D	6 11-7	157[-13]	5-1	W Mullins (IRE)	won Gd1 Deloitte Hurdle (2m2f) **(0)**
12	-2111	**Cinders And Ashes** D	5 11-7	152[-6]	10-1	D McCain	won Aintree class 4 mdn hdl (2m1f) **(2)**
11	-F311	**Al Ferof** D	6 11-7	146[-17]	10-1	P Nicholls	won Newbury class 3 nov hdl (2m½f) **(0)**
10	11212	**Menorah** D, BF	5 11-7	160[-3]	12-1	P Hobbs	won Kempton class 2 nov hdl (2m) **(1)**
09	12121	**Go Native** D	6 11-7	153[-8]	12-1	N Meade (IRE)	won Punchestown Listed nov hdl (2m) **(2)**
08	1/711	**Captain Cee Bee** D	7 11-7	151[-2]	17-2	E Harty (IRE)	won Punchestown hdl (2m) **(0)**
07	21	**Ebaziyan** D	6 11-7	121[-43]	40-1	W Mullins (IRE)	2nd Cork mdn hdl (2m) **(1)**

WINS-RUNS: 4yo 0-4, 5yo 4-81, 6yo 5-64, 7yo 1-18, 8yo 0-4, 9yo 0-1 **FAVOURITES:** -£4.75

TRAINERS IN THIS RACE (w-pl-r): Willie Mullins 4-2-22, Nicky Henderson 1-9-19, Paul Nicholls 1-1-9, Philip Hobbs 1-1-7, Alan King 0-1-4, Dermot Weld 0-0-3, David Pipe 0-0-6, Harry Fry 0-0-1, Gordon Elliott 0-0-2, Henry de Bromhead 0-1-2, Nigel Twiston-Davies 0-0-4, Mouse Morris 0-0-2, Colin Tizzard 0-0-1

FATE OF FAVOURITES: 3253402112 **POSITION OF WINNER IN MARKET:** 0464362112

Key trends

🐎 Won at least 50 per cent of hurdle starts, 10/10

🐎 Ran within the last 59 days, 9/10

🐎 Won last time out, 9/10

🐎 Adjusted RPR of at least 151, 8/10

🐎 Previously contested a Graded race, 7/10 (six won)

🐎 Rated within 8lb of RPR top-rated, 7/10 (only two were top-rated)

Other factors

🐎 Ireland has won this 14 times in the past 26 years

🐎 Only one winner had come via the Flat. Seven of the other nine started their careers in bumpers, where they had earned an RPR of at least 110. The other two started over hurdles in France

🐎 Three winners had previously run in the Champion Bumper (Al Ferof second in 2010, Cinders And Ashes fifth in 2011 and Champagne Fever won in 2012)

🐎 For many years, the shortest-priced Irish runner was often beaten by a compatriot. However, of the last nine to win, seven were the most fancied

Notes

Altior has been favourite for this race ever since he ran away with last year's Supreme Novices' Hurdle by seven lengths and has become a bigger banker with each run over fences, most impressively when slamming seasoned rivals Fox Norton and Dodging Bullets (the 2015 Champion Chase winner) in the Grade 2 Game Spirit. That took his aggregate winning distance to 100 lengths in four chase starts and earned an exceptional Racing Post Rating of 175 (4lb higher than erstwhile stablemate Sprinter Sacre after he took the Game Spirit en route to winning the Arkle in 2012). He has taken so well to fences that Nicky Henderson felt compelled to give him an entry in the Champion Chase, but the trainer is likely to hold fire on a clash with Douvan. Opposition may be thin on the ground come the opening day but among the possibles are Yorkhill, Identity Thief, Charbel and Cloudy Dream – all decent but far from Altior's class.

Altior *(right)*

7 b g; Trainer Nicky Henderson
Chase form (all right-handed) 1111, best RPR 175
Cheltenham form (hurdles) 11, best RPR 163
At the festival 15 Mar 2016 Travelled and jumped well, mid-division, headway after 5th, challenged after 2 out, ridden to lead before last, quickened clear, impressive, won Supreme Novices' Hurdle by seven lengths from Min

Superb winner of last season's Supreme Novices' Hurdle and would undoubtedly be a short price for the Champion Hurdle if he'd been kept over the smaller obstacles given that the eight-and-a-half-length third Buveur D'Air is now vying for market favouritism in that. Nicky Henderson always had him down as a chaser, though, and it's hard to argue with that assessment after four wins this season by an aggregate of 100 lengths. It's true more than half that distance came in a two-runner affair at Kempton on his debut, but Altior fairly toyed with the classy Charbel (six lengths)

in the Grade 1 Henry VIII Novices' Chase at Sandown in December and did the same to the decent Marracudja (18 lengths) in a Grade 2 at Kempton over Christmas. However, he saved his best for his Cheltenham prep as he drew comparisons with the stable's brilliant Sprinter Sacre by slamming three high-class established two-milers in the Game Spirit at Newbury in February. He was getting 5lb from runner-up Fox Norton, but that one was rated 167 and was second favourite for the Champion Chase yet was beaten hollow by the winner, who strolled 13 lengths clear without coming out of a canter. A Racing Post Rating of 175 puts him within 3lb of odds-on Champion Chase favourite Douvan's best and is 4lb higher than Sprinter Sacre achieved at the same stage of his career – and he doesn't appear to have anything of the quality Sprinter Sacre had to beat in the Arkle. Something has to go badly wrong for him not to win.

TRAINER'S VIEW

Nicky Henderson on Altior "His times have been extraordinary – he just cruises at such a rate. He's hugely talented, even if he's got a long, long way to go to fill Sprinter Sacre's boots" *Has followed a similar route to the Arkle as Sprinter Sacre in 2011-12, winning the Wayward Lad with an RPR of 167 (Sprinter Sacre recorded 162) and the Game Spirit with 175 (Sprinter Sacre 171)*

Going preference Trainer says he doesn't want it too soft, which is scary given his best run has come on such a surface
Star rating ✪✪✪✪

Yorkhill

7 ch g; Trainer Willie Mullins
Chase form 11, best RPR 150
Left-handed 1, best RPR 150
Right-handed 1, best RPR 145
Cheltenham form 1 (hurdles), best RPR 158
At the festival 16 Mar 2016 Took keen hold, held up in rear, not fluent 4th and 7th, not much room bend before 3 out, progressed to track leaders 2 out, squeezed through on inner to lead on bend before last, 3 lengths up and fine jump last, edged right and ridden out, won Neptune Investment Management Novices' Hurdle by a length and three-quarters from Yanworth

Over the top when beaten at odds-on on final start last season, but otherwise enjoyed a superb hurdles campaign, winning at Cheltenham from hotpot Yanworth in the Neptune and following up at Aintree. Clearly a high-class performer but had a tendency to both hang and jump left at his hurdles and that has been magnified over fences. Has still won both races very easily, but length-and-a-quarter runner-up at Leopardstown had only a 132 rating over hurdles, so it's fair to say he hasn't been tested in a proper race (RPR some 25lb below that achieved by Altior). Undoubtedly has the pace for 2m, though, and left-leaning tendencies won't be severely punished with a rail on his left throughout at Cheltenham. At the time of writing, though, he was favourite for the JLT and among the market leaders for the Champion Hurdle, for which he was not even entered. With stablemates Faugheen and Annie Power both absent this year, though, anyone who has backed him for either of the chases has serious cause for concern.

Going preference Handles any, but well suited by good ground
Star rating ✪✪✪✪

Identity Thief

7 b g; Trainer Henry de Bromhead
Chase form 11PU, best RPR 146
Left-handed PU
Right-handed 11, best RPR 146
Cheltenham form (hurdles) 6, best RPR 154
At the festival 15 Mar 2016 Tracked leaders, hit 4th, ridden before 2 out, weakened before last, finished sixth, beaten 18 and a half lengths by Annie Power in Champion Hurdle

Won last season's Fighting Fifth Hurdle and had peak official rating of 159 in that sphere and, while not coming up to scratch in the Champion Hurdle, he was still a high-class performer. Made respectable start over fences, winning easily on debut at Punchestown and following up at the same track in more workmanlike fashion, but then the wheels fell off. He was pulled up lame when second favourite behind Min in the Grade 1 Racing Post Novice Chase at Leopardstown over Christmas and his return a month later in the Irish Arkle wasn't what the doctor ordered as he unseated at the first. Raw talent to be a player if he gets it right, but missed final prep with a setback and major questions to answer.

Going preference Has won on yielding and soft, not proven on any quicker
Star rating ✪✪

Charbel

6 b g; Trainer Kim Bailey
Chase form 12, best RPR 153
Left-handed 1 , best RPR 150
Right-handed 2, best RPR 153
Cheltenham form (hurdles) 5, best RPR 150
At the festival 15 Mar 2016 Led, ridden and headed after 2 out, 4th and held when hit last, lost 4th final strides, finished fifth, beaten 12 and a half lengths by Altior in Supreme Novices' Hurdle

Good novice over hurdles, with the pick of his runs being an 11-length thumping of Brain Power at Musselburgh and his fifth in a strong Supreme at the festival. Promising to be at least as good over fences, too, as he started with victory over Le Prezien at Uttoxeter before finding Altior too fast for him in the Grade 1 Henry VIII at Sandown in December. Trainer of the opinion he wants further, so appears

likely to run in the JLT, but would have a big shout of picking up the pieces here if for some reason Altior didn't fire.

Going preference Seems to handle anything
Star rating ✪✪

Cloudy Dream

7 gr g; Trainer Malcolm Jefferson
Chase form 1122, best RPR 150
Left-handed 112, best RPR 150
Right-handed 1, best RPR 139

Yet to finish out of the first three in 11 starts under rules and signed off hurdling career with an excellent second to Ch'Tibello (now a stone higher) in the Scottish Champion Hurdle at Ayr, where he was arguably unlucky when hampered having to switch round an omitted hurdle. Chasing has gone well, too, winning his first two at odds-on and then running second to Buveur D'Air and Forest Bihan at Haydock and Doncaster respectively. Those defeats might hint at limitations, but they were hardly disgraces as the uber-talented Buveur D'Air has switched back to hurdles and into favouritism for the Champion Hurdle and Forest Bihan has so far lost only to Waiting Patiently, himself unbeaten in three. Also has a JLT entry, but trainer on record as saying he doesn't think Cloudy Dream needs to go further – and something has to take on Altior!

Going preference Handles good and soft, said to prefer it quicker
Star rating ✪✪

Some Plan

9 b g; Trainer Henry de Bromhead
Chase form 1F11
Left-handed F11 ,best RPR 153
Right-handed 1, best RPR 142
Cheltenham form (all) 200F, best RPR 142
At the festival 10 Mar 2015 Led, ridden and headed after 3 out, losing place when hampered before next, soon weakened, finished tenth, beaten 34¾ lengths by Douvan in Supreme Novices' Hurdle
18 Mar 2016 Mid-division, ridden after last (usual 2 out), never threatened, weakened before omitted last, finished 16th, beaten 19½ lengths by Superb Story in County Hurdle

Usually the winner of the Irish Arkle at Leopardstown would warrant serious respect (both Un De Sceaux and Douvan won it) but Some Plan's success came in a four-runner race in which two of his rivals unseated within three fences, while the other one, 5-1 outsider Royal Caviar, looked to be going best when coming down at the last. That's not to say he doesn't have talent, because he does, as he has won two of his other three chase starts and was yet to be asked a question when falling two out against Le Prezien at Cheltenham in November. That added to his chequered record at Prestbury Park, though, as he beat only two home in Douvan's Supreme when trained by Tom George and didn't fare much better for Paul Nicholls in last season's County Hurdle. Can better those efforts for Henry de Bromhead, but as a nine-year-old is surely an unlikely winner.

Going preference Seems to act on any
Star rating ✪✪

Forest Bihan
6 ch g; Trainer Brian Ellison
Chase form 1211, best RPR 150
Left-handed 211, best RPR 150
Right-handed 1, best RPR 135

Fair hurdler when joining Brian Ellison from France last season, but failed to win in that sphere in Britain. Looks an altogether different kettle of fish over fences, though, having won three of his four starts and gone down only to the unbeaten Waiting Patiently. Earned a generous-looking mark of 140 for 19-length drubbing of Chidswell at Newcastle in January, which led many to put him near the top of their lists for the novice handicap at the festival (with a ceiling rating of 140), a race nominated by the trainer. However, he spoiled that by winning the Grade 2 Lightning Novices' Chase at Doncaster three weeks later by just under two lengths from Cloudy Dream. Arguably better than he showed there, too, as he gave the third-last a right belt and was three lengths down at the time, so it was a good effort to reel in a promising rival even in receipt of 3lb. Has form over further, but only entry is in Arkle.

Going preference Seems equally at home on good or soft
Star rating ✪✪✪

Royal Caviar
9 b g; Trainer Willie Mullins
Chase form 1F, best RPR 151
Left-handed F, best RPR 151
Right-handed 1, best RPR 142

Another going chasing late in life, but he probably would have made it 2-2 had he not fallen at the last in the Irish Arkle at Leopardstown in January. Hard to gauge what that form is worth given two of his four rivals were out of the race after less than half a mile, but other than Yorkhill, who has two arguably more likely options, he is Willie Mullins' shortest-priced contender for this, so you'd imagine he'll run, assuming problems that have restricted him to 11 starts in four years do not resurface.

Going preference Seems versatile
Star rating ✪✪

OTHERS TO CONSIDER

Trying to find any more dangers to Altior is difficult, largely because there is a JLT to go for and the likes of Top Notch, Politologue and Le Prezien and plenty of others will head that way to avoid him as long as they have the requisite stamina. The one you'd like to see in there is the unbeaten **Waiting Patiently**, whose form ties in with plenty of decent British novices, but he's said to want soft ground and trainer Malcolm Jefferson does not seem keen on sending him to Cheltenham this year.

VERDICT

It is probably no coincidence that since the JLT was created in 2011 four of the six Arkle winners have gone off at odds-on. ALTIOR is set to make it five out of seven as his form is head and shoulders above those likely to turn up. At some point bookmakers will offer betting without the favourite and Forest Bihan, who impressed with his attitude after a mistake three out at Doncaster, would be the pick at likely fair odds.

FORM	WINNER	AGE & WGT	Adj RPR	SP	TRAINER	BEST RPR LAST 12 MONTHS (RUNS SINCE)
16	-1111 **Douvan** C, D	6 11-4	180^T	1-4f	W Mullins (IRE)	won Leopardstown Gd1 nov ch (2m1f) **(1)**
15	1-F11 **Un De Sceaux** D	7 11-4	181^T	4-6f	W Mullins (IRE)	won Leopardstown Gd1 nov ch (2m1f) **(0)**
14	1-261 **Western Warhorse**	6 11-4	148^{-23}	33-1	D Pipe	won Doncaster class 3 nov ch (2m3f) **(0)**
13	11-11 **Simonsig** C, D	7 11-7	174^T	8-15f	N Henderson	won Kempton Gd2 nov ch (2m) **(0)**
12	3-111 **Sprinter Sacre** D	6 11-7	179^T	8-11f	N Henderson	won Newbury Gd2 ch (2m1f) **(0)**
11	22221 **Captain Chris** C, D	7 11-7	163^{-4}	6-1	P Hobbs	2nd Sandown Gd1 nov ch (2m4½f) **(1)**
10	41111 **Sizing Europe** C, D	8 11-7	170^T	6-1	H de Bromhead (IRE)	won Leopardstown Gd1 nov ch (2m1f) **(0)**
09	-1222 **Forpadydeplasterer** D	7 11-7	160^{-6}	8-1	T Cooper (IRE)	2nd Gd1 Dr PJ Moriarty Nov Ch (2m5f) **(0)**
08	-1112 **Tidal Bay** C, BF	7 11-7	160^T	6-1	H Johnson	won Carlisle class 3 nov ch (2m4f) **(2)**
07	21211 **My Way De Solzen** C, D	7 11-7	161^{-1}	7-2	A King	won Haydock Gd2 nov ch (2m4f) **(0)**

WINS-RUNS: 5yo 0-10, 6yo 3-30, 7yo 6-46, 8yo 1-15, 9yo 0-3, 10yo 0-1, 12yo 0-1 **FAVOURITES:** -£3.82

TRAINERS IN THIS RACE (w-pl-r): Nicky Henderson 2-3-9, Willie Mullins 2-1-9, David Pipe 1-0-5, Henry de Bromhead 1-1-3, Alan King 1-0-3, Colin Tizzard 0-1-1, Gordon Elliott 0-0-2, Nigel Twiston-Davies 0-0-1, Paul Nicholls 0-1-11, Venetia Williams 0-0-2

FATE OF FAVOURITES: 23F0411211 **POSITION OF WINNER IN MARKET:** 2233411811

Key trends

🏇Finished in the first two on all completed chase starts, 10/10

🏇RPR hurdle rating of at least 153, 9/10

🏇SP no bigger than 8-1, 9/10

🏇Aged five to seven, 9/10

🏇Rated within 6lb of RPR top-rated, 9/10

🏇Adjusted RPR of at least 160, 9/10

🏇Achieved hurdles RPR of at least 143, 9/10

🏇Three to five chase runs, 8/10 (both exceptions had fewer)

Other factors

🏇Six winners had previously won a 2m-2m1f Graded chase (no race has proved a reliable guide)

🏇Seven winners had previously run at the festival, showing mixed form in a variety of hurdle races

🏇A French-bred has finished in the first three on eight occasions (four won)

Notes

2.50 Ultima Handicap Chase · ITV/RUK

🏇 3m1f · 🏇 Grade 3 · 🏇 £105,000

The most prestigious handicap chase of the meeting has been won by just two favourites since 1977 (Antonin at 4-1 in 1994 and Wichita Lineman at 5-1 in 2009) but 12 of the past 18 winners were sent off 10-1 or lower.

Last year's winner Un Temps Pour Tout was the first horse since Dixton House in 1989 to land the prize having not won a race over fences before, although he did continue the recent trend of inexperienced chasers taking this competitive handicap. In the last nine years only two horses, Golden Chieftain (2013) and The Druids Nephew (2015), had run more than ten times over fences before landing the prize.

Eight-year-olds have won the race seven times in the last 16 years, along with five seven-year-olds. Together they account for 75 per cent of winners (12-16) in that period.

An official rating of 131 was required to get into last year's race and in the last ten seasons no horse rated under 129 has qualified. However, no winner has had a mark above 150 since 1983. Holywell won with 11st 6lb in 2014 (off a mark of 145), the highest weight carried successfully since Unguided Missile's 11st 10lb in 1998 (off 149).

While second-season chasers have traditionally done well, Un Temps Pour Tout's success in 2016 meant that a raw novice has landed the race five times in the last 13 runnings.

Jonjo O'Neill has the best recent record in the race, winning three times in the last eight runnings. Holywell gave him his most recent success in 2014, following on from Wichita Lineman (2009) and Alfie Sherrin (2012).

The only winner in the past 12 years without any previous course form was the Irish-trained Dun Doire, who completed a six-timer over fences in this race for Tony Martin in 2006. While Irish-bred horses account for nine of the last ten winners, those trained across the Irish Sea have not done so well, having been successful only twice since 1966 with Youlneverwalkalone (2003) and Dun Doire.

There have been only two dual winners of the contest, Sentina (1957-1958) and Scot Lane (1982-1983) but the O'Neill-trained Holywell could make it three. While only three horses have managed to carry 11st-plus to victory since 2000, his trainer clearly targets the race and the 2015 Gold Cup fourth could run another big race at a track he loves.

Black Hercules (nearest) is towards the head of the market for Willie Mullins

	FORM WINNER	AGE & WGT	OR	SP	TRAINER	BEST RPR LAST 12 MONTHS (RUNS SINCE)
16	-1224 **Un Temps Pour Tout** D, BF	7 11-7	148-15	11-1	D Pipe	2nd Newbury Gd2 nov ch (2m7½f) **(1)**
15	-1275 **The Druids Nephew**	8 11-3	146T	8-1	N Mulholland	2nd Cheltenham Gd3 hcap ch (3m3½f) **(1)**
14	32U11 **Holywell** C, D	7 11-6	145-9	10-1	J O'Neill	won Doncaster class 4 nov ch (3m) **(0)**
13	P3633 **Golden Chieftain** D	8 10-2	132-1	28-1	C Tizzard	won Worcester class 3 hcap ch (2m4f) **(5)**
12	-PF75 **Alfie Sherrin** (1oh) D	9 10-0	129-5	14-1	J O'Neill	7th Kempton class 3 hcap ch (2m4½f) **(0)**
11	F2-52 **Bensalem** C, BF	8 11-2	143T	5-1	A King	fell Festival Handicap Chase (3m½f) **(3)**
10	-3701 **Chief Dan George** D	10 10-10	142-6	33-1	J Moffatt	won Doncaster class 2 hcap ch (3m) **(0)**
09	9-121 **Wichita Lineman** C, D	8 10-9	142T	5-1f	J O'Neill	won Chepstow class 3 nov ch (3m) **(0)**
08	3-P61 **An Accordion** D	7 10-12	143-6	7-1	D Pipe	won Doncaster Listed hcap ch (3m) **(0)**
07	76-78 **Joes Edge**	10 10-6	130-8	50-1	F Murphy	13th Cheltenham Gold Cup (3m2½f) **(4)**

WINS-RUNS: 6yo 0-14, 7yo 3-43, 8yo 4-50, 9yo 1-50, 10yo 2-30, 11yo 0-22, 12yo 0-4, 13yo 0-1 **FAVOURITES:** -£4.00

FATE OF FAVOURITES: 2312F02000 **POSITION OF WINNER IN MARKET:** 0310270325

OR 121-133 3-2-35, **134-148** 7-24-152, **149-161** 0-4-31

Key trends

🐎Aged seven to ten, 10/10

🐎Officially rated 129-146, 9/10

🐎Ran no more than five times that season, 9/10

🐎Carried no more than 11st 3lb, 8/10

🐎Won over at least 3m, 8/10

🐎No more than 11 runs over fences, 8/10

🐎Top-three finish on either or both of last two starts, 7/10

Other factors

🐎Eight winners had run at a previous festival, three recording at least one top-four finish

🐎Five winners had run well in a handicap at Cheltenham earlier in the season (three placed, one fourth and one sixth). Bensalem, the 2011 winner, had run well in a Grade 2 hurdle at the course

🐎This was once seemingly an impossible task for novices but four of the past ten winners have been first-season chasers

Notes

3.30 Stan James Champion Hurdle ITV/RUK

2m½f ⚡Grade 1 ⚡£400,000

The complexion of this race changed completely in the space of a fortnight in late January/early February when both Annie Power and Faugheen – the last two winners – were ruled out through injury by Willie Mullins. That led to a quick rethink of plans in various quarters and not least from Nicky Henderson, who rerouted Buveur D'Air from fledgling novice chaser back to hurdling and quickly into Champion Hurdle favouritism having taken the Contenders Hurdle at Sandown. Henderson also has rising handicapper Brain Power as he bids for a record sixth triumph, while Buveur D'Air's owner JP McManus has another challenger in the Alan King-trained Christmas Hurdle winner Yanworth and possibly a third if 2014 winner Jezki runs here rather than in the Stayers' Hurdle. Irish Champion Hurdle winner Petit Mouchoir is the shortest-priced of the confirmed Irish raiders, although Mullins could cause another shake-up if he diverts Yorkhill (who would need to be supplemented) or Vroum Vroum Mag to this contest.

Buveur D'Air

6 b g; Trainer Nicky Henderson
Hurdles form 11311, best RPR 156
Left-handed 131, best RPR 156
Right-handed 11, best RPR 155
Cheltenham form 3, best RPR 154
At the festival 15 Mar 2016 Held up in rear, headway from 3 out, not fluent 2 out, soon ridden, went 3rd at the last, kept on but not pace to get on terms, finished third, beaten eight and a half lengths by Altior in Supreme Novices' Hurdle

High-class novice who possibly wasn't quite the finished article in relation to stablemate Altior and it showed when he was beaten eight and a half lengths into third by that one in the Supreme, a slight mistake at the second-last not losing him enough ground to suggest he'd have fared any better without it. Won the Top Novices' Hurdle at Aintree on next start, a battling neck victory over 40-1 chance Petit Mouchoir looking a lot better now than it did then, but even so was not considered a serious Champion Hurdle contender at the time. Got the job done easily enough in two novice chase starts – particularly the first when cruising past Cloudy Dream – but jumped very low at his fences and once Annie Power and then Faugheen were ruled out of Champion Hurdle contention connections decided on a change of tack. Promoted to favouritism after cantering past Rayvin Black in four-runner Contenders Hurdle at Sandown in February, but with only realistic danger Irving not running to form it's hard to work out what he achieved as he was getting 4lb from a horse rated 10lb inferior. Plenty have struggled to win impressively on that sort of ground, though, and the handicapper was impressed enough to raise him 4lb to 155. From a ratings point of view, though, it's still a surprise he is favourite as while horses rated under 160 can win, the last four to do so went off at 10-1, 10-1, 16-1 and 33-1. Easy enough to argue that it won't take a huge performance to win this year's renewal, though, and there's little doubt he has plenty more in the locker, but he does need to prove he has the raw pace for 2m on decent ground.

Going preference Acts on good to soft, seems well suited by easier.
Star rating ✪✪✪✪

Petit Mouchoir

6 gr g; Trainer Henry de Bromhead
Hurdles form 1348223F11, best RPR 166
Left-handed 3482F11, best RPR 166
Right-handed 123, best RPR 155

Cheltenham form 8, best RPR 147
At the festival 15 Mar 2016 Tracked leaders, hit 2 out, soon ridden, faded before last, finished eighth, beaten 15 lengths by Altior in Supreme Novices' Hurdle

Only win last season came in maiden hurdle on debut and well beaten in the Supreme, though raced keenly tracking the leaders in a hood. Had much more use made of him at Aintree and nearly caused a 40-1 shock when running Buveur D'Air to a neck and that progress has continued bar a tame reappearance run at Down Royal in November. Had just taken it up and looked to be travelling best when coming down three out in the Fighting Fifth at Newcastle after that and since then he has been given his head and taken his form to a new level, thrashing Nichols Canyon by seven lengths in the Ryanair Hurdle at Leopardstown in December and confirming that in the Irish Champion back

there a month later. Only won by a length from Footpad there (Nichols Canyon beaten when falling at the last) but looked to have gone hard up front and runner-up is surely flattered by proximity. Looks likely to be the one they'll all be aiming at from the off and probably doesn't have enough in hand if his jockey doesn't get the fractions right, but position in market has been earned on merit.

Going preference Seems to act on any
Star rating ✪✪✪✪

TRAINER'S VIEW

Henry de Bromhead on Petit Mouchoir
"It's hard to do what he has now done twice – go a strong pace from the front and keep going. He's not a fast horse at home but he is a great galloper" *Recorded RPRs of 166 and 165 in his two Grade 1 wins, up from his previous best of 156*

Yanworth *(below, left)*

7 ch g; Trainer Alan King
Hurdles form 11112111, best RPR 165
Left-handed 112, best RPR 160
Right-handed 11111, best RPR 165
Cheltenham form (all) 412, best RPR 160
At the festival 11 Mar 2015 Held up towards rear, progress over 3f out, not clear run over 2f out and lost place, driven and ran on from over 1f out, nearest finish, finished fourth, beaten three and a quarter lengths by Moon Racer in Champion Bumper
16 Mar 2016 Held up in rear, progress on wide outside after 7th, close up when mistake 3 out, challenged after 2 out, chased winner before last, stayed on but not pace to challenge, finished second, beaten one and three-quarter lengths by Yorkhill in Neptune Investment Management Novices' Hurdle

Fourth in 2015 Champion Bumper and rapidly developed into top-class novice hurdler last season, his on-the-bridle seven-length win at Cheltenham on Trials Day making him hot favourite for the Neptune. Alan King's horses were not quite at their best at the festival when Yanworth was beaten by Yorkhill, but it was no disgrace to be beaten by a very talented rival with the front two seven lengths clear. There was talk of running in the Stayers' Hurdle and he looked in need of all of Ascot's 2m3½f to overhaul Lil Rockerfeller on his return in the Ascot Hurdle in November, and he displayed more speed when dismissing The New One in the 2m Christmas Hurdle at Kempton, taking time to get on top, but ultimately winning with a fair bit to spare. However, he then made hard work of beating a 149-rated rival in the Kingwell at Wincanton on bad ground that he handles so well and there has to be a big doubt whether he has the speed against top-notch two-milers. Will certainly be better suited to a stiffer test at Cheltenham, though, and plenty of strong stayers have won the Champion Hurdle over the years.

Going preference Acts on any, looked a superstar on heavy in January 2016
Star rating ✪✪✪✪

Brain Power

6 b g; Trainer Nicky Henderson
Hurdles form 1213811, best RPR 162
Left-handed 8, best RPR 134
Right-handed 121311, best RPR 162
Cheltenham form 8, best RPR 162

Fair novice last season when owner Michael Buckley accused him of not living up to

his name – "He is really stupid and doesn't concentrate" – but he is really starting to look the part now. Beat stablemate Consul De Thaix by three-quarters of a length in a Listed handicap off a mark of 142 in December and then confirmed that form when strolling home by five lengths from the same rival in what used to be the Ladbroke at Ascot two weeks later. Undeniably impressive there, but it was only off a mark of 149 against inferior rivals and taking on 160-plus-rated rivals off levels is a different task altogether. Also of mild concern is the fact he didn't show much promise on his return at Cheltenham when beaten 20 lengths in the Greatwood Hurdle in November. It might have been rustiness, but other than a debut bumper win for another trainer in February 2015, his two runs left-handed have resulted in heavy defeats.

Going preference Acts on good and good to soft, well beaten sole start on soft
Star rating ✪✪

Yorkhill

7 ch g; Trainer Willie Mullins
Hurdles form 11114, best RPR 158
Left-handed 11, best RPR 158
Right-handed 114, best RPR 150
Cheltenham form 1, best RPR 158
At the festival 16 Mar 2016 Took keen hold, held up in rear, not fluent 4th and 7th, not much room bend before 3 out, progressed to track leaders 2 out, squeezed through on inner to lead on bend before last, 3 lengths up and fine jump last, edged right and ridden out, won Neptune Investment Management Novices' Hurdle by a length and three-quarters from Yanworth

Would be following in the footsteps of Istabraq and Hardy Eustace if winning the Champion Hurdle after taking the 2m5f Neptune the year before, but there's one big stumbling block to that – he's not even entered. However, with Willie Mullins losing Annie Power and Faugheen to season-ending injuries there has been plenty of speculation that he will be supplemented, and while trainer said it wasn't in his plans, neither was Vautour's Ryanair run at this point last year. Such is his reputation that all firms going non-runner no

bet make him favourite or joint-favourite, but his on-track achievements do not quite merit such a position, if only because he has yet to race outside novice company. His defeat of Yanworth in the Neptune earned him a peak Racing Post Rating of 158 and there was a suspicion the runner-up wasn't in his best form (had run a bigger figure on the bridle before) and he ran to only 149 when beating Le Prezien at Aintree before flopping at Punchestown. Two chase runs this season have both resulted in wins, but his tendency to edge to his left over hurdles has been magnified over the bigger obstacles, which is half the reason people expect the switch. Still, he is a very short price for the JLT, so a dangerous betting vehicle for this without the NRNB concession.

Going preference Acts on any
Star rating ✪✪

Vroum Vroum Mag *(left)*

8 b m; Trainer Willie Mullins
Hurdles form 121111211, best RPR 157
Left-handed 12111, best RPR 155
Right-handed 1112, best RPR 157
Cheltenham form 1, best RPR 146
At the festival 15 Mar 2016 Towards rear of midfield, smooth headway from 4 out, tracked leaders 2 out, led before last, ran on well, ridden out, won OLBG Mares' Hurdle by two and three-quarter lengths from Rock On The Moor

Has won 12 of 13 starts over hurdles and fences since joining Willie Mullins from France and impressive strike-rate has earned her something of a cult following among punters, some of whom seem to think she could win any of the big races at the festival. Connections have done their best to play along with the wind-up by entering her for the Champion Hurdle, Champion Chase, Ryanair, Stayers' Hurdle and Gold Cup, but in truth she has to be considered an odds-on shot to defend her Mares' Hurdle title, which will not be a shoo-in this season. The reality is she has run 19 times in her life, has an official rating of 154 and has never posted a Racing Post Rating higher than 157 despite having never been sent off at odds-against in Britain or Ireland.

If she was a gelding a rating like that would entitle her to be considered no more than a good Grade 2 performer, but the 7lb sex allowance gives her a shot in the top races and she has won a couple of Grade 1s outside of mares' company, albeit coming off second best at the weights in substandard affairs to Identity Thief (rated 157) over 2m and Clondaw Warrior (155) over 3m. She does have commendable versatility to be able to win at a range of trips, but doesn't appear to have as much up her sleeve as it seems when let down – which is why Apple's Jade fought back to beat her at Fairyhouse in December – and she would need a career best by some margin to win anything other than the Mares' Hurdle. The form of her scrambling head victory over Midnight Jazz on her Doncaster prep probably wouldn't be good enough to win the Mares' Hurdle and would give her no chance in any of the other races.

Going preference Seems to act on any
Star rating ✪

The New One

9 b g; Trainer Nigel Twiston-Davies
Hurdles form 11121211231111151214F121, best RPR 171
Left-handed 111212131111514F11, best RPR 171
Right-handed 12122, best RPR 171
Cheltenham form (hurdles) 121131541, best RPR 171
At the festival 14 Mar 2012: tracked leaders, ridden and outpaced 2f out, hung left over 1f out, rallied final 100yds, no impression on front three, finished sixth, beaten six lengths by Champagne Fever in Champion Bumper
13 Mar 2013: tracked leaders, not fluent 2 out, driven to lead approaching last, ran on strongly run-in, won Neptune Investment Management Novices' Hurdle by four lengths from Rule The World
13 Mar 2013 Tracked leaders, not fluent 2 out, driven to lead approaching last, ran on strongly run-in, won Neptune Investment Management Novices' Hurdle by four lengths from Rule The World
11 Mar 2014 Tracking leaders when badly hampered and dropped to 7th 3rd, effort to close after 3 out, ridden approaching 2 out and

one pace, rallied under pressure approaching last, stayed on well for 3rd final 50yds, closing on leading duo but always held, finished third, beaten two and three-quarter lengths by Jezki in Champion Hurdle
10 Mar 2015 Raced keenly, jumped right a few times, not fluent 2nd, chased winner until 3 out but still upsides, ridden and outpaced approaching last, hung left after and one pace, finished fifth, beaten eight and three-quarter lengths by Faugheen in Champion Hurdle
15 Mar 2016 Led to 1st, remained prominent, shaken up when every chance 2 out, ridden and outpaced before last, edged left under pressure run-in, kept on but not pace of leaders, finished fourth, beaten eight and three-quarter lengths by Annie Power in Champion Hurdle

Wonderfully consistent campaigner who hasn't always got the love he's deserved from some, largely because he always seems to come up a bit short on the big days. Arguably unlucky on first crack at this race in 2014 as he was badly hampered by the ill-fated Our Conor, but no real excuses when well beaten fifth and fourth on next two tries and plenty of evidence to suggest he is better suited to the New Course, on which he landed his third International Hurdle in December. That showed he's not a mile off his best even at the age of nine and, while he proved no match for Yanworth in the Christmas Hurdle at Kempton, that track really doesn't suit and nor does Haydock, where he scrambled home against Clyne. There are plenty who would like to see him stepped up in trip for the Stayers' Hurdle, but no doubt he is worthy of another crack at this and he'll run his usual gallant race and will probably beat a few who are ahead of him in the market.

Going preference Doesn't really want it too soft but arguably needs it to be to make the race a test
Star rating ✪✪

Jezki

9 b g; Trainer Jessica Harrington
Hurdles form 11113111241122341112, best RPR 171
Left-handed 1113241234111, best RPR 171
Right-handed 11111212, best RPR 168

Cheltenham form 314, best RPR 171
At the festival 12 Mar 2013 Midfield, headway to track leaders 3 out, effort and switched left when mistake last, stayed on same pace final 75yds, finished third, beaten two and three-quarter lengths in Supreme Novices' Hurdle
11 Mar 2014 Took keen hold, tracked leaders, not fluent 4 out, slight lead 2 out, edged left and ridden approaching last, stayed on well under pressure run-in, all out, won Champion Hurdle by a neck from My Tent Or Yours
10 Mar 2015 Raced keenly, upsides and in 2nd place from 3 out, ridden and not quicken approaching last where mistake and lost 2nd, stayed on same pace run-in, finished fourth, beaten eight and a quarter lengths by Faugheen in Champion Hurdle

Terrific performer over the years who finished third in a very good Supreme in 2013 before turning the form around with runner-up My Tent Or Yours and winning the Champion Hurdle by a neck the following season. Appeared to be losing a bit of his speed the following campaign, but won 2m4f Aintree Hurdle and then beat Hurricane Fly in 3m World Series Hurdle, but sidelined by injury and missed all of last season and didn't return until winning a six-runner 2m hurdle at Navan in January. Hard to know what he achieved that day as he was getting 6lb from a 149-rated rival, but he was expected to need it and won pretty much as he liked. Ran on heavy ground in the Red Mills Trial Hurdle at Gowran after that but beaten by Navan third Tombstone and took big walk in market for this and Stayers' Hurdle. Trainer Jessica Harrington wasn't unduly concerned, though, reasoning that he'd been beaten on heavy ground several times before. Decision over festival target is still apparently some way off, but no doubt he'll enjoy better ground wherever he goes.

Going preference Acts on any but always considered best on decent going
Star rating ✪✪✪

Superb Story

6 b g; Trainer Dan Skelton
Hurdles form 1544121P1, best RPR 150
Left-handed 4121, best RPR 148
Right-handed 144P1, best RPR 150

Cheltenham form 21, best RPR 148
At the festival 18 Mar 2016 Mid-division, headway after 2 out (usual 3 out), going well in 3rd after next, led before omitted last, ran on strongly, won County Hurdle by two and a half lengths from Fethard Player

Won last season's County Hurdle in fine style off a mark of 138 and after flopping in the Galway Hurdle (said not to have travelled well) was back on the upgrade in the Scottish County Hurdle at Musselburgh. Was pretty much all out to land that prize off a mark of 145, though, and an RPR of 150 puts him at least a stone off the required standard even in what seems a substandard year. Plenty to prove and will be given an entry in the County again.

Going preference Decent ground suits best
Star rating ✪

OTHERS TO CONSIDER

Apple's Jade almost certainly heads to the Mares' Hurdle, but if the ground turned very soft and she was given her chance she'd be one of the more interesting outsiders on that one piece of form at Aintree last season (RPR 162). **Nichols Canyon** was third last year and that form is up there with the best on offer, but he hasn't run to it on his last two starts after winning so well at Punchestown and he has a heavy fall to recover from. **Footpad** was almost certainly flattered to have got so close to Petit Mouchoir at Leopardstown. While **Sutton Place** was introduced by a couple of firms after his strong-staying 2m5f win at Navan in February, he is not entered and looks a stayer on that evidence anyway.

VERDICT

It's hard to argue BUVEUR D'AIR should be favourite on form but he does give the impression he could be a bit special and he'd be a strong fancy if the ground turned soft. Petit Mouchoir is tough, but an open year normally means a big field and that will make it harder to make all. The New One has had his share of goes, but always runs his race and this will be the weakest Champion Hurdle he's run in. Don't be surprised if he manages to nick a place at tidy odds.

	FORM WINNER	AGE & WGT	Adj RPR	SP	TRAINER	BEST RPR LAST 12 MONTHS (RUNS SINCE)
16	1F-11 **Annie Power** C, D	8 11-3	173^T	5-2f	W Mullins (IRE)	Won Gd1 Punc Mares Hurdle (2m2f) **(1)**
15	1-111 **Faugheen** C, D	7 11-10	173^{-4}	4-5f	W Mullins (IRE)	Won Gd1 Christmas Hurdle (2m) **(0)**
14	-1124 **Jezki** D	6 11-10	169^{-8}	9-1	J Harrington (IRE)	2nd Gd1 Ryanair Hurdle (2m) **(1)**
13	1-111 **Hurricane Fly** CD	9 11-10	177^T	13-8f	W Mullins (IRE)	won Gd1 Irish Champion Hurdle (2m) **(0)**
12	23-12 **Rock On Ruby** C, D	7 11-10	170^{-7}	11-1	P Nicholls	2nd Gd1 Christmas Hurdle (2m) **(0)**
11	1-111 **Hurricane Fly** D	7 11-10	172^{-2}	11-4f	W Mullins (IRE)	won Gd1 Irish Champion Hurdle (2m) **(0)**
10	3-531 **Binocular** D	6 11-10	171^{-2}	9-1	N Henderson	won Sandown Listed hdl (2m½f) **(0)**
09	1-1F3 **Punjabi** D, BF	6 11-10	168^{-8}	22-1	N Henderson	won Gd1 Punchestwn Champ Hdl (2m) **(3)**
08	-1321 **Katchit** CD	5 11-10	166^{-8}	10-1	A King	won Gd2 Kingwell Hurdle (2m) **(0)**
07	444-1 **Sublimity** D	7 11-10	146^{-31}	16-1	J Carr (IRE)	4th Gd1 Supreme Nov Hdl (2m½f) **(2)**

WINS-RUNS: 5yo 1-29, 6yo 3-33, 7yo 4-23, 8yo 1-15, 9yo 1-7, 10yo 0-4, 11yo 0-4, 12yo 0-2, 13yo 0-1 **FAVOURITES:** £1.68

TRAINERS IN THIS RACE (w-pl-r): Willie Mullins 4-4-14, Nicky Henderson 2-7-21, Alan King 1-0-6, Paul Nicholls 1-1-8, Nigel Twiston-Davies 0-2-5, David Pipe 0-1-3, Henry de Bromhead 0-0-2, Dan Skelton 0-0-1

FATE OF FAVOURITES: 6030131411 **POSITION OF WINNER IN MARKET:** 6597141511

Key trends

🐎 Adjusted RPR of at least 166, 9/10

🐎 Rated within 8lb of RPR top-rated, 9/10

🐎 No more than 12 hurdle runs, 9/10

🐎 Aged between six and eight, 8/10

🐎 Ran within the past 51 days, 8/10

🐎 Won a Grade 1 hurdle, 8/10

🐎 Won last time out, 7/10

🐎 Topspeed of at least 151, 7/10

Other factors

🐎 Katchit (2008) broke a long-standing trend when he became the first five-year-old to win since See You Then in 1985. In the intervening years 73 failed while 25 have come up short since

🐎 Only two winners had not run since the turn of the year (Rock On Ruby and Faugheen).

Notes

4.10 OLBG Mares' Hurdle

2m4f Grade 1 £110,000

ITV/RUK

Quevega famously won this race six years in a row and Willie Mullins' domination has continued since her retirement, with the victories of Glens Melody (who benefited from the final-flight fall of stablemate and odds-on favourite Annie Power) and Vroum Vroum Mag making it eight in a row for the Irish champion trainer. His strength in depth in this division was underlined last year when Limini took the inaugural running of the Trull House Stud Mares' Novices' Hurdle and she could line up here for Mullins. Whether Vroum Vroum Mag bids for back-to-back wins is open to question as she has a range of other entries but Mullins looks likely to face a stronger challenger than usual in the shape of Apple's Jade, who used to be one of his own. Now with Gordon Elliott following the Gigginstown House Stud split from Mullins, Apple's Jade beat Vroum Vroum Mag by a short head in the Grade 1 Hatton's Grace Hurdle over 2m4f at Fairyhouse in December. Vroum Vroum Mag has the edge on Racing Post Ratings with a mark of 157, against 153 for Apple's Jade and 148 for Limini. A little further behind them on RPRs is the Gavin Cromwell-trained Jer's Girl (a dual Grade 1 novice hurdle winner last spring).

OLBG MARES' HURDLE RESULTS AND TRENDS

	FORM WINNER	AGE & WGT	Adj RPR	SP	TRAINER	BEST RPR LAST 12 MONTHS (RUNS SINCE)
16	1-111 **Vroum Vroum Mag** D	7 11-5	160[T]	4-6f	W Mullins (IRE)	won Ascot Gd2 hdl (2m7½f) (0)
15	7521 **Glens Melody** D	7 11-5	162[-11]	6-1	W Mullins (IRE)	won Warwick Listed hdl (2m5f) (0)
14	1/11- **Quevega** CD	10 11-5	171[T]	8-11f	W Mullins (IRE)	won Gd1 Punchestown World Hdl (3m) (0)
13	/111- **Quevega** CD	9 11-5	168[T]	8-11f	W Mullins (IRE)	won Gd1 Punchestown World Hdl (3m) (0)
12	1/1-1 **Quevega** CD	8 11-5	168[T]	4-7f	W Mullins (IRE)	won Gd1 Punchestown World Hdl (3m) (0)
11	3911- **Quevega** CD	7 11-5	166[T]	5-6f	W Mullins (IRE)	won Gd2 Mares' Hurdle (2m4f) (1)
10	11-39 **Quevega** CD	6 11-5	168[T]	6-4f	W Mullins (IRE)	3rd Gd1 Punchestown Champ Hdl (2m) (1)
09	19-31 **Quevega** D	5 11-3	156[-4]	2-1f	W Mullins (IRE)	won Punchestown hdl (2m4f) (0)
08	23121 **Whiteoak**	5 11-0	139[-23]	20-1	D McCain	won Ascot class 3 nov hdl (2m) (0)

WINS-RUNS: 4yo 0-3, 5yo 2-24, 6yo 1-45, 7yo 3-40, 8yo 1-28, 9yo 1-10, 10yo 1-3 **FAVOURITES:** £5.03

TRAINERS IN THIS RACE (w-pl-r): Willie Mullins 8-1-12, Alan King 0-1-5, Ben Case 0-0-1, David Pipe 0-0-4, Dan Skelton 0-0-2, Gordon Elliott 0-0-1, Harry Fry 0-1-4, Fergal O'Brien 0-0-1, Colin Tizzard 0-0-1, Jessica Harrington 0-1-6, Neil Mulholland 0-0-3, Nicky Henderson 0-3-10, Paul Nicholls 0-0-2, Oliver Sherwood 0-0-2, Tim Vaughan 0-0-3, Peter Bowen 0-0-1

FATE OF FAVOURITES: 3111111F1 **POSITION OF WINNER IN MARKET:** 711111121

Key trends

- Top-three finish in a Grade 1 or 2 hurdle, 9/9
- At least nine career starts, 9/9
- Won last time out, 8/9
- Trained by Willie Mullins, 8/9
- Adjusted RPR of at least 156, 8/9

Other factors

- Nicky Henderson has yet to win this but has had three places from ten runners (two seconds, one third)
- A runner priced 16-1 or bigger has finished in the first three in all nine renewals
- Quevega used to come here fresh when defending her crown but the other three winners had between three and five outings that season

This is the longest and oldest race at the festival. The structure of the race has changed and it has gradually lost its reputation for producing shocks. Before 2002, horses who had won over hurdles were excluded and since 2010 chase winners have not had to carry penalties. It was awarded Listed status in 2014 and is now more of a four-mile RSA Chase in quality, with this year's renewal the first to have Grade 2 status.

This means the big yards have a greater chance of producing the winner. In the last six years, three favourites have obliged and the other three winners were sent off at 8-1. It is notable that three of those past six winners had the highest official rating, while Shotgun Paddy (top-rated in 2014) was beaten only a neck.

NATIONAL HUNT CHASE RESULTS AND TRENDS

FORM	WINNER	AGE & WGT	Adj RPR	SP	TRAINER	BEST RPR LAST 12 MONTHS (RUNS SINCE)
16 -3P62	**Minella Rocco**	6 11-6	159-7	8-1	J O'Neill	2nd Ascot Gd2 nov ch (3m) **(0)**
15 20-75	**Cause Of Causes**	7 11-6	159-2	8-1	G Elliott (IRE)	2nd Kim Muir hcap ch (3m1½f) **(3)**
14 61U21	**Midnight Prayer**	9 11-6	154-12	8-1	A King	won Warwick class 3 nov ch (3m2f) **(0)**
13 /2111	**Back In Focus**	8 11-6	161T	9-4f	W Mullins (IRE)	won Leopardstown Gd1 nov ch (3m) **(0)**
12 321P1	**Teaforthree**	8 11-6	161T	5-1f	R Curtis	won Chepstow class 3 nov ch (3m) **(2)**
11 11F25	**Chicago Grey** C	8 11-6	163T	5-1f	G Elliott (IRE)	2nd Cheltenham class 2 nov ch (3m1½f) **(1)**
10 -2951	**Poker De Sivola**	7 11-6	145-8	14-1	F Murphy	2nd Kelso class 3 hcap ch (3m1f) **(3)**
09 42212	**Tricky Trickster**	6 11-11	140-18	11-1	N Twiston-Davies	2nd Chelt class 2 nov hcap ch (2m5f) **(0)**
08 27322	**Old Benny**	7 11-7	135-18	9-1	A King	2nd Newbury class 2 nov ch (3m) **(0)**
07 11430	**Butler's Cabin** C	7 12-0	131-20	33-1	J O'Neill	won Aintree class 3 hcap ch (2m4f) **(4)**

WINS-RUNS: 6yo 2-26, 7yo 4-71, 8yo 3-51, 9yo 1-22, 10yo 0-7, 12yo 0-2 **FAVOURITES:** £5.25

TRAINERS IN THIS RACE (w-pl-r): Alan King 2-1-9, Gordon Elliott 2-0-4, Nigel Twiston-Davies 1-0-7, Rebecca Curtis 1-0-4, Willie Mullins 1-2-10, Colin Tizzard 0-1-2, David Pipe 0-2-7, Nicky Henderson 0-1-3, Mouse Morris 0-1-3, Charlie Longsdon 0-0-3, Noel Meade 0-0-3, Paul Nicholls 0-1-7, Warren Greatrex 0-0-2, Fergal O'Brien 0-0-1, Henry de Bromhead 0-0-1, Mark Bradstock 0-0-1, Margaret Mullins 0-0-1, Neil Mulholland 0-0-1, Philip Hobbs 0-0-2, Sue Smith 0-0-2, Tim Vaughan 0-1-4, Tom George 0-0-2, Victor Dartnall 0-0-1

FATE OF FAVOURITES: F545111004 **POSITION OF WINNER IN MARKET:** 0457111435

Key trends

- ☙Ran at least three times over fences, 10/10
- ☙Achieved hurdles RPR of at least 118, 10/10
- ☙Finished first or second in a chase over at least 3m, 9/10
- ☙Top five-finish last time out, 9/10 (exception unplaced in Class 1 chase)
- ☙Top-three finish on either or both of last two starts, 9/10
- ☙Aged seven or eight, 7/10
- ☙Had won over at least 3m (hurdles or chases), 7/10

Other factors

- ☙The four winners from 2007 to 2010 had adjusted RPRs of 131-145. The last six were 154-163
- ☙The three winners in 2011, 2012 and 2013 were outright favourites (Chicago Grey, Teaforthree and Back In Focus) – the last to oblige before them was Keep Talking in 1992
- ☙Jonjo O'Neill landed this contest five times between 1995 and 2007 and last year won for the first time since
- ☙Paul Nicholls has never won this race despite strong representation

5.30 Close Brothers Novices' Handicap Chase RUK
2m4½f Listed £70,000

In its first six years this race was run on the New course over 2m5f but it was then moved to the Old course over half a furlong less and there has been a growing emphasis on quality. The last six winners carried the biggest weights so far successful. Five of the six had an official rating of 137 or more, while only one of the first seven winners was rated above 135.

The ceiling rating is now 140 and in last year's 20-runner contest a rating of 136 was required to get in, with only 4lb covering the handicap. It is therefore hardly surprising that strong recent form is important. Nine of the 12 winners secured a top-two finish last time out, six of them winning.

Last year's 12-1 scorer Ballyalton (aged nine) was the oldest winner in the race's 12-year history, breaking a run of three consecutive six-year-old winners. Seven-year-olds enjoy the best record in the race, having won six times.

Winners have been prominent in the betting, with ten sent off at odds between 9-2 and 12-1. The biggest-priced winner was 20-1 scorer L'Antartique in 2007.

One to watch this year is Forest Bihan, a progressive chaser open to improvement. The step up in trip should suit and this smooth traveller could go well if connections opt for this race instead of taking on Altior in the Racing Post Arkle.

CLOSE BROTHERS NOVICES' HANDICAP CHASE RESULTS AND TRENDS

	FORM WINNER	AGE & WGT	OR	SP	TRAINER	BEST RPR LAST 12 MONTHS (RUNS SINCE)
16	/U62F **Ballyalton** C	9 11-10	140-6	12-1	I Williams	2nd Market Rasen class 2 ch (2m5½f) **(1)**
15	7-323 **Irish Cavalier**	6 11-7	137-4	11-1	R Curtis	3rd Chelt class 2 nov hcap ch (2m5f) **(0)**
14	32121 **Present View** D	6 11-7	137-1	8-1	J Snowden	won Kempton class 3 hcap ch (2m4½f) **(0)**
13	-2F17 **Rajdhani Express** D	6 11-7	140T	16-1	N Henderson	won Kempton class 3 hcap ch (2m4½f) **(1)**
12	12111 **Hunt Ball** D	7 12-0	142-4	13-2f	K Burke	won Kempton class 3 hcap ch (2m4½f) **(0)**
11	31591 **Divers** D	7 11-4	132-6	10-1	F Murphy	won Musselburgh class 3 nov ch (2m4f) **(0)**
10	-1321 **Copper Bleu** D	8 11-1	139-3	12-1	P Hobbs	won Exeter class 4 ch (2m1½f) **(0)**
09	9-F21 **Chapoturgeon**	5 10-11	135-2	8-1	P Nicholls	won Doncaster class 2 nov ch (2m½f) **(0)**
08	-3F22 **Finger Onthe Pulse** D	7 10-12	135-7	9-1	T Taaffe (IRE)	2nd Leopardstown Gd2 nov ch (2m5f) **(0)**
07	221F2 **L'Antartique** D	7 10-11	133-16	20-1	F Murphy	won Bangor class 4 nov ch (2m4½f) **(2)**

WINS-RUNS: 5yo 1-17, 6yo 3-42, 7yo 4-75, 8yo 1-43, 9yo 1-18, 10yo 0-3 **FAVOURITES:** £-2.50

FATE OF FAVOURITES: 0F00515026 **POSITION OF WINNER IN MARKET:** 0325418365

OR 123-130 0-2-8, **131-140** 9-26-177, **141-148** 1-2-13

Key trends

- Officially rated 132-142, 10/10
- Top-three finish on last completed start, 9/10
- Won over at least 2m2f, 8/10
- Carried no more than 11st 7lb, 8/10
- Aged six or seven, 7/10
- Finished in the first four all completed starts over fences, 7/10

Other factors

- Five winners had fallen at least once over fences
- Three winners had contested novice hurdles at a previous festival
- Three winners had hurdle RPRs of at least 144, three in the 130s and three in the 120s
- Only two winners bigger than 12-1

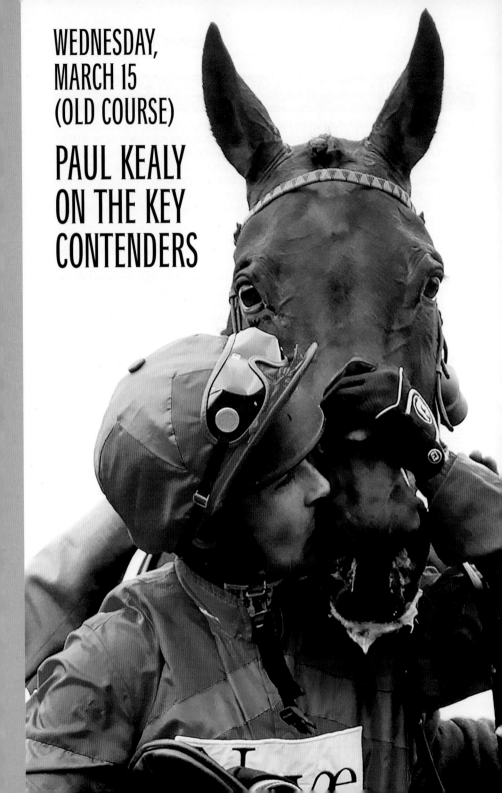

WEDNESDAY,
MARCH 15
(OLD COURSE)

PAUL KEALY
ON THE KEY
CONTENDERS

1.30 Neptune Investment Novices' Hurdle ITV/RUK
2m5f Grade 1 £125,000

Ireland has won the last three renewals but this year's ante-post market has a British feel with Finian's Oscar and Neon Wolf in the top two spots and Messire Des Obeaux and Ballyandy also prominent. Finian's Oscar, a £250,000 purchase for Ann and Alan Potts and described by Colin Tizzard as the best young horse in his yard, rocketed to the head of the betting with a dominant display in the Grade 1 Tolworth (also the proving ground for last year's winner Yorkhill). Harry Fry made his festival breakthrough last year with novice hurdler Unowhatimeanharry and Neon Wolf is another exciting prospect. The Alan King-trained Messire Des Obeaux is another Grade 1 scorer, having taken the Challow, while this is one of the options for Betfair Hurdle winner Ballyandy. The shortest-priced Irish challenger after all the main trials was Willie Mullins' Grade 1 Deloitte winner Bacardys.

Finian's Oscar
5 b g; Trainer Colin Tizzard
Hurdles form (all right-handed) 111, best RPR 147

Potentially top-notch novice who has choice of this or the 2m Supreme depending on which way connections want to go. Certainly won't have a problem with this 2m5f trip as has already won over it and a 3m point, but won 2m Tolworth – as did last year's winner Yorkhill – at Sandown, so clearly not short of speed either. Does travel powerfully through his races, but looked like winning Tolworth a lot more easily between the last two than he eventually did and, while he prepped over 2m at Exeter he didn't impress at odds of 1-16 (suspicion some of Colin Tizzard's horses not quite at their best at the time), so maybe the extra trip is what is needed. Reputation preceeded him before he hit the track and easy enough to argue that's what's keeping him at the top of the market.

Going preference All hurdles wins on soft, but won point on good-yielding
Star rating ●●●

Neon Wolf
6 b g; Trainer Harry Fry
Hurdles form 11, best RPR 149
Left-handed 1, best RPR 149
Right-handed 1, best RPR 131

Unbeaten in a point, a bumper and two hurdles, the first of them in January when he beat a modest field comfortably over 2m2½f at Exeter. Backed as if defeat was out of the question when dropped three furlongs in trip for the Supreme Trial at Haydock and had clockwatchers purring with his effort up the straight, where he poured it on, jumping fluently and pulling nine lengths clear of the 145-rated Elgin. Is going to need 3m in time according to jockey Noel Fehily (pedigree backs that up) and considered more likely to run here than in the Supreme, for which he

TRAINER'S VIEW

Harry Fry on Neon Wolf "He's an absolute monster in the making. To put up a performance like that [Grade 2 win at Haydock] over a sharp two miles, for a horse who's going to be a three-mile chaser, is something he just shouldn't be doing. We're looking at his chasing campaign next season really as he's a big tank of a horse and that's why we wouldn't want to go to Cheltenham this year if the ground wasn't on the slow side." *All three runs for Fry have been with 'soft' in the going description*

is also well up there in the betting, but final decision has yet to be made.

Going preference Won point on good/ yielding; any faster an unknown
Star rating ✪✪✪✪

Bacardys
6 b g; Trainer Willie Mullins
Hurdles form F11, best RPR 147
Left-handed 11, best RPR 147
Right-handed F, best RPR 129
Cheltenham form (bumper) 3
At the festival 16 Mar 2016 Held up in midfield, progress over 4f out to track leaders 3f out, ridden and no impression 2f out, stayed on final furlong to take 3rd last 100yds, finished third, beaten two lengths by Ballyandy in Champion Bumper

Third in last year's Champion Bumper and after blotting his copybook with a fall at odds of 1-3 on Cork debut in November he has really got his act together. Duly claimed his maiden at Leopardstown over Christmas and went back there for the Grade 1 Deloitte in February, causing something of a surprise by winning at 12-1. Short-priced stablemate Saturnas was bitterly disappointing in last, but there's no reason to think the form is any the weaker for it and Bacardys, who was only eighth jumping two out, really powered home to win. The way he finished there, and when third at the festival last March, suggests he's going to be even more at home of the Neptune trip, or even the Albert Bartlett (like so many Mullins horses he has all the options).

Going preference Handles soft well, but third on good ground at last year's festival
Star rating ✪✪

Messire Des Obeaux
5 b g; Trainer Alan King
Hurdles form 56371112, best RPR 146
Left-handed 563711, best RPR 146
Right-handed 12, best RPR 146
Cheltenham form 7, best RPR 128
At the festival 16 Mar 2016 Mid-division, headway after 5th, ridden to chase leaders after 2 out, kept on same pace approaching last, finished seventh, beaten nine and three-quarter lengths by Diego Du Charmil in Fred Winter Juvenile Handicap Hurdle

Second-season novice who has really come of age this season, bolting up by ten lengths in a handicap at Bangor on his return and then giving 7lb and a half-length beating to Champion Bumper winner and subsequent

Betfair Hurdle hero Ballyandy in the Grade 2 Winter Novices' Hurdle at Sandown in December. Better still when a commanding winner of the Challow Hurdle at Newbury, a race won by plenty of festival winners over the years but, strangely, never one of the Neptune. Lost unbeaten record for season when a neck second to Keeper Hill in the Sidney Banks Memorial, but no disgrace in trying to give 8lb to a clearly talented rival. That said, it does hint at limitations, especially as the winner's jumping left a lot to be desired at times.

Going preference Handles easy ground, trainer says he's not dependent on it
Star rating ✪✪✪

Death Duty *(below, left)*
6 b g; Trainer Gordon Elliott
Hurdles form 1111, best RPR 150
Left-handed 111, best RPR 150
Right-handed 1, best RPR 140

Red-hot favourite for the Albert Bartlett and dealt with in more detail in Friday's section, although has yet to run over 3m.

Going preference Obviously handles plenty of dig; fast ground an unknown
Star rating ✪✪✪✪

Ballyandy
6 b g; Trainer Nigel Twiston-Davies
Hurdles form 2321, best RPR 151
Left-handed 31, best RPR 151
Right-handed 22, best RPR 135
Cheltenham form (all) 113, best RPR 136
At the festival 16 Mar 2016 Close up behind leaders, trapped behind weakening rival 4f out and dropped to midfield 3f out, ridden and rallied 2f out, chased leader 1f out, led near finish, just held on, won Champion Bumper by a nose from Battleford

Dealt with in more detail in the Supreme section on Tuesday, but just as likely to go here if the ground is reasonably dry and Betfair Hurdle form among the best on offer. Obviously handles track and won't be as big as he is currently on a non-runner-no-bet basis wherever he ends up.

Going preference Seems to handle anything
Star rating ✪✪✪✪

Invitation Only
6 b g; Trainer Willie Mullins
Hurdles form 13, best RPR 141
Left-handed 3, best RPR 141
Right-handed 1, best RPR 132

Unbeaten in one point and two bumpers, showing useful form in latter sphere, before making hurdles debut with a fluent win at Gowran Park in November. Subsequently put in his place by Death Duty in Grade 2 Navan Novice Hurdle in December (was even-money favourite) and while no reason was given he had not raced by mid February, so there may have been a setback. Too early to write off, but may need 3m and has an Albert Bartlett entry.

Going preference Won on a range of going
Star rating ✪✪

Let's Dance
5 b m; Trainer Willie Mullins
Hurdles form 223421111, best RPR 146
Left-handed 223411, best RPR 146
Right-handed 211, best RPR 141

Second season novice who finished fourth in last season's Triumph Hurdle as a maiden and is really beginning to look the part now. Unbeaten in four starts since May, and has been very impressive in her most recent two wins when stepped up to 2m4f. The second of those was in a Grade 2 against the boys and she slammed some high 130s-rated rivals very easily. As usual she has a bunch of entries, which makes it hard to gauge where she is going to run, but trainer also has favourite Airlie Beach and Augusta Kate for the mares' novice hurdle and there has to be a chance at least one of them will go somewhere else. Let's Dance clearly stays very well, so that 2m1f contest might not be for her. She'd be a big player in this, or even the Albert Bartlett.

Going preference Latest best form on decent ground, but it's probably not an issue.
Star rating ✪✪✪

Willoughby Court
6 br g; Trainer Ben Pauling
Hurdles form 211, best RPR 147

Left-handed 11 ,best RPR 147
Right-handed 2, best RPR 121

Two-time bumper winner who excelled himself when fifth in the Aintree bumper at the Grand National meeting, but shaped like a stayer then and no surprise he started his hurdling career at 2m4f. Surprisingly beaten first time out at Market Rasen, but left that form well behind on next two starts, both at Warwick, where he also won a bumper. Maiden win was secured in battling fashion, but Grade 2 Leamington success was all the more impressive as, well backed, he made all and ground his rivals into submission, winning by eight lengths. That form arguably as good as any in the line-up, but came on deep ground and yet to prove himself on faster.

Going preference Very well suited by soft
Star rating ✪✪

Keeper Hill
6 b g; Trainer Warren Greatrex
Hurdles form 2111, best RPR 139
Left-handed 21, best RPR 125
Right-handed 11, best RPR 139

Steady improver who won two fairly run of the mill novice hurdles at Bangor and Hereford before stepping up in class in the Sidney Banks Memorial Novices' Hurdle at Huntingdon. Made much of the running before doing well to battle back and edge out Messire Des Obeaux by a neck. Was getting 8lb from the runner-up, though, so has a bit to make up formwise, but made his share of mistakes and jumped left at times, so potentially better than that. Doesn't look quite the finished article yet, but one to look forward to with another summer on his back.

Going preference Seems versatile enough
Star rating ✪✪

Movewiththetimes *(right)*
6 ch g; Trainer Paul Nicholls
Hurdles form 1512, best RPR 151
Left-handed 152, best RPR 151
Right-handed 1, best RPR 126
Cheltenham form 5, best RPR 139

Comes out the same horse as Ballyandy on Betfair Hurdle form (gave 1lb, beaten three-quarters of a length) and has much less experience, so every reason to think he can improve again. Indeed, the Betfair was the first occasion he was really asked to race and while some were not impressed that he appeared to hang in behind Ballyandy on the run-in that can easily be put down to inexperience. He is clearly not short of pace and boasts some of the best 2m form on offer, but his pedigree suggests he'll get further with no problem. The main concern is that Nicholls has said he will handle very deep ground well and those conditions are unlikely.

Going preference Soft ground best
Star rating ✪✪✪

OTHERS TO CONSIDER

It really is a nightmare trying to work out which Willie Mullins entries to put in and which ones to leave out. At the time of writing he had 29 entries, several of whom could be given a fair chance were they to get the go ahead. More obvious ones are **Melon** (Supreme favourite, surely goes there) and the mares **Augusta Kate** and **Airlie Beach**, although at least one will run in the mares' novice. Augusta Kate was giving the well-touted Death Duty a run for his money before coming down at the last at Naas and she has already won at 2m7f, so could go here or for the Albert Bartlett. Given Mullins does not train the favourite, there's every chance he'll be mob-handed, too and others that were shortest in the betting of his included **Bon Papa** and **Chateau Conti**.

VERDICT

This is probably even more open than quotes of 4-1 the field suggest. BALLYANDY, fresh from his Betfair Hurdle win, strikes me as very fair value at double-figure odds if he runs here, while I've also backed MOVEWITHTHETIMES for the same reasons, both on a non-runner no-bet basis. I'm also intending to back LET'S DANCE in whatever race she finally gets the go-ahead for as I think she has a bit of star quality about her.

NEPTUNE NOVICES' HURDLE RESULTS AND TRENDS

	FORM	WINNER	AGE & WGT	Adj RPR	SP	TRAINER	BEST RPR LAST 12 MONTHS (RUNS SINCE)
16	1-111	**Yorkhill**	6 11-7	159-8	3-1	W Mullins (IRE)	won Sandown Gd1 nov hdl (2m) (0)
15	-1142	**Windsor Park**	6 11-7	154-3	9-2	D Weld (IRE)	2nd Leopardstown Gd1 nov hdl (2m2f) (0)
14	1111	**Faugheen**	6 11-7	156T	6-4f	W Mullins (IRE)	won Limerick Gd3 nov hdl (3m) (0)
13	-1112	**The New One** CD, BF	5 11-7	162-1	7-2	N Twiston-Davies	2nd Cheltenham Gd2 nov hdl (2m4½f) (0)
12	1121	**Simonsig**	6 11-7	160T	2-1f	N Henderson	2nd Sandown Gd2 nov hdl (2m4f) (1)
11	-4131	**First Lieutenant**	6 11-7	152-8	7-1	M Morris (IRE)	won Leopardstown Gd1 nov hdl (2m) (0)
10	111	**Peddlers Cross**	5 11-7	155-1	7-1	D McCain	won Haydock Gd2 nov hdl (2m½f) (0)
09	21111	**Mikael D'Haguenet**	5 11-7	160-4	5-2f	W Mullins (IRE)	won Punchestown Gd2 nov hdl (2m) (0)
08	153-1	**Fiveforthree**	6 11-7	141-9	7-1	W Mullins (IRE)	won Fairyhouse mdn hdl (2m) (0)
07	21U53	**Massini's Maguire** CD	6 11-7	145-8	20-1	P Hobbs	won Cheltenham class 2 nov hdl (2m5f) (3)

WINS-RUNS: 4yo 0-3, 5yo 3-49, 6yo 7-63, 7yo 0-22, **FAVOURITES:** -£1.00

TRAINERS IN THIS RACE (w-pl-r): Willie Mullins 4-5-17, Dermot Weld 1-1-4, Mouse Morris 1-2-6, Nicky Henderson 1-0-12, Nigel Twiston-Davies 1-0-5, Philip Hobbs 1-0-1, Noel Meade 0-1-5, Alan King 0-2-9, Colin Tizzard 0-0-2, David Pipe 0-0-5, Jonjo O'Neill 0-0-1, Nick Williams 0-2-2, Paul Nicholls 0-1-5, Henry de Bromhead 0-0-1, Jessica Harrington 0-0-3

FATE OF FAVOURITES: 5013313132 **POSITION OF WINNER IN MARKET:** 8414412132

Key trends

- Aged five or six, 10/10
- Rated within 10lb of RPR top-rated, 10/10
- Started career in Irish points or bumpers, 9/10
- Adjusted RPR of at least 152, 8/10 (the last eight)
- Scored over at least 2m4f, 8/10
- Won at least 50 per cent of hurdle runs, 8/10
- At least three runs over hurdles, 7/10
- Finished first or second on all completed starts over hurdles, 7/10
- Won a Graded hurdle, 7/10

Other factors

- Three of the last ten favourites have obliged (Mikael D'Haguenet 2009, Simonsig 2012, Faugheen 2014) and in that period only one winner has started bigger than 7-1 (Massini's Maguire 20-1 in 2007)

2.10 RSA Chase

🏇 3m½f 🏇 Grade 1 🏇 £175,000

Nicky Henderson has a strong team of novice chasers and the likelihood is that his main representative in this race will be Might Bite, who crashed out at the last in the Grade 1 Kauto Star Novices' Chase at Kempton's Christmas meeting but still earned a Racing Post Rating of 165. He did not return until early February, where he had an easy spin round in a low-level race at Doncaster, but by then the form had been boosted considerably with the Cheltenham victory of Royal Vacation, the lucky Kempton winner who could well reoppose here. Possible Irish challengers include the Eddie Harty-trained Coney Island, last year's World Hurdle runner-up Alpha Des Obeaux, Grade 1 Flogas winner Disko and Bellshill (a Flogas faller). Henderson could have a second-string with Whisper, while Harry Fry has a decent shot with the front-running American.

Might Bite

8 b g; Trainer Nicky Henderson
Chase form 521F1, best RPR 165
Left-handed 5211, best RPR 155
Right-handed F, best RPR 165
Cheltenham form 157, bst RPR 148

Chasing career was put on hold after just one run after Might Bite made a few serious mistakes on his debut at Cheltenham in November 2015. Much more the finished article this season, though, and after getting chinned at odds of 1-2 on his return at Ffos Las, he bolted up at Doncaster and was in the process of running a stunning race in the Feltham at Kempton when coming down at the last. He was 18 lengths clear of subsequent trials day winner Royal Vacation when coming down and an RPR of 165 gives him a clear form edge over this field. Warmed up with straightforward wide-margin win over much inferior rivals at Doncaster, but did show tendency to be a little too brave at times. Has won at Cheltenham, but in five-runner novice hurdle against weak opposition and well beaten other two starts. Wide-margin wins at Newbury, Doncaster and Kempton over hurdles and fences confirm that flat tracks suit very well, so does have questions to answer regarding track.

Going preference Goes very well on decent ground
Star rating ✪✪✪

Might Bite (centre): perhaps best suited by a flat track

Coney Island

6 b g; Trainer Edward Harty
Chase form 212, best RPR 156
Left-handed 2, best RPR 156
Right-handed 21, best RPR 150

Smart novice hurdler and very closely matched with Bellshill in that sphere, having run that one to half a length in 3m Grade 1 at Punchestown in April. Quickly developed into at least as good a chaser in three starts, running second on debut, but then impressing when winning the Grade 1 Drinmore at Fairyhouse. Stepped back up to 3m for the Grade 1 Neville Hotels Novice Chase, but only gave way late on after a sustained battle with Our Duke to finish second, so hard to say he didn't stay. Well beaten fifth A Toi Phil won big handicap at Leopardstown off mark of 143, so form has solid look.

Going preference Seems to handle any ground
Star rating ✪✪✪

Alpha Des Obeaux

7 b g; Trainer Mouse Morris
Chase form 5113P, best RPR 146
Left-handed 5P, best RPR 125
Right-handed 113, best RPR 146
Cheltenham form (hurdles) 2, best RPR 170
At the festival 17 Mar 2016 Held up in touch, tracked leaders 3 out, went 2nd 2 out, ridden and briefly tried to challenge on bend between last 2, outpaced by impressive winner last, kept on and clear of others but no chance, finished second, beaten seven lengths by Thistlecrack in World Hurdle

High-class hurdler who finished second in the World Hurdle to Thistlecrack, posting an RPR of 170. Bit of a chequered start over fences, though, as was last of five when odds-on for debut before winning next two and then running third to Coney Island in the Drinmore. Was expected by many to leave previous form behind once stepped up to 3m over fences, but unfortunately suffered a reportedly quite bad bleed and was pulled up in the Neville

Hotels Novice Chase. Obviously has questions to answer after that, but largely jumps well and hurdles form at this track suggests he warrants serious respect should his trainer get him back fit and healthy.

Going preference Acts on any, best form on good

Star rating ✪✪✪

American

7 b g; Trainer Harry Fry
Chase form 11, best RPR 155
Left-handed 1, best RPR 155
Right-handed 1, best RPR 145

Has been brought along very quietly by trainer Harry Fry with just three runs over hurdles last term, but that largely because he is considered fragile and needs time between his races. Trainer clearly holds him in high regard, though, and novice chase win from Label Des Obeaux at Exeter in November was followed by impressive success in Listed contest at Warwick in January. Jockey Noel Fehily says he's a Welsh National horse in the making and that surely says a lot about his ground requirements and must be a doubt whether he would be risked on fast ground.

Going preference Goes very well on soft

Star rating ✪✪

Bellshill

7 b g; Trainer Willie Mullins
Chase form 11, best RPR 155
Left-handed F
Right-handed 11, best RPR 155
Cheltenham form (all) 00, best RPR 132
At the festival 11 Mar 2015 Settled towards rear, effort into midfield well over 2f out, ridden and no headway soon after, finished tenth, beaten 16 and a half lengths by Moon Racer in Champion Bumper
15 Mar 2016 Tracked leaders, not fluent 4th, pushed along after next, ridden after 3 out, soon outpaced, weakened after next, finished 13th, beaten 32 lengths by Altior in Supreme Novices' Hurdle

Had been as short as 3-1 favourite for this following two comfortable wins at Gowran Park and Limerick, but fluffed his lines when

sent off at just 6-5 for the Grade 1 2m4f Flogas Novice Chase at Leopardstown and has questions to answer now. Was ridden a fair way out of his ground at Leopardstown, but Ruby Walsh seemed happy enough even jumping three out. However, he failed to pick up and wasn't making serious inroads on the front three when coming down at the last. Perhaps he does need 3m at the top level (beat Coney Island in a Grade 1 3m hurdle at Punchestown) now, but he is following a remarkably similar path to the last two seasons. In 2015 he prepped with defeat at odds of 7-4 before running down the field in the Champion Bumper and last year he was defeated at 4-6 before finishing 13th of 14 in the Supreme. Each time he bounced back to run second at Aintree and then win at Punchestown, so maybe February is not his time of year and Cheltenham is not his track. Plenty to prove now whatever the case.

Going preference Has won on good to yielding, very well suited by soft/heavy

Star rating ✪✪

Disko

6 gr g; Trainer Noel Meade
Chase form 1331, best RPR 157
Left-handed 31, best RPR 157
Right-handed 13, best RPR 149

Hard to say he doesn' stay 3m as was close second to the imposing Our Duke at Leopardstown over Christmas, but best form dropped to 2m5½f when winning the Flogas Novice Chase in February. Surely more likely to run in the JLT and dealt with in more detail in Thursday's section.

Going preference Acts on soft and yielding, much faster would be an unknown

Star rating ✪✪

Whisper

9 b g; Trainer Nicky Henderson
Chase form 211, best RPR 160
Left-handed 11, best RPR 160
Right-handed 2, best RPR 137
Cheltenham form (all) 41315P811, best RPR 160
At the festival 12 Mar 2014 Always in leading

group, ridden to lead before last, hard pressed flat, just held on, won Coral Cup by a short head from Get Me Out Of Here
12 Mar 2015 Mid-division, headway when not fluent 2 out, ridden to briefly dispute 2nd before last, soon no extra, finished fifth, beaten ten and a half lengths by Cole Harden in World Hurdle
17 Mar 2016 Held up, mistake 8th, soon pushed along, weakened after 2 out, eased when well beaten before last, finished eighth, beaten 46 lengths by Thistlecrack in World Hurdle

Another who does stays 3m, but kept at shorter so far and dealt with in more detail for the JLT in Thursday's section.

Going preference Has won on all types of going
Star rating ✪✪✪

Royal Vacation
7 b g; Trainer Colin Tizzard
Chase form 221311, best RPR 155
Left-handed 211, best RPR 155
Right-handed 31, best RPR 149
Cheltenham form (all) 961, best RPR 155
At the festival 12 Mar 2014 Well in rear, ridden and still towards rear over 3f out, kept on final 2f, no danger, finished ninth, beaten 13 and a quarter lengths by Silver Concorde in Champion Bumper

Has more racecourse experience than most having run in the 2014 Champion Bumper and spent two seasons as a novice hurdler and didn't really give the impression he'd be starring in Grade 1 company any time soon. However, has got better with every run and while he was obviously no match for Might Bite, who gifted him the Feltham at Kempton by falling at the last, he improved again when romping home off a mark of 143 in the 2m5f novice handicap chase on trials day at Cheltenham. Had given the impression he was a strong stayer prior to that (had certainly looked outpaced by Politologue over the same trip at Ascot), so the way he travelled was a revelation. Doesn't have the sexy profile of some, but probably unwise to dismiss lightly.

Going preference Seems well suited by soft/heavy but has run well on good.
Star rating ✪✪✪

0 0 Seven
7 b g; Trainer Nicky Henderson
Chase form 131, best RPR 154
Left-handed 13, best RPR 153
Right-handed 1, best RPR 154
Cheltenham form (all) 081, best RPR 153
At the festival 11 Mar 2015 Prominent until weakened over 2f out, finished 16th, beaten 32 lengths by Moon Racer in Champion Bumper
16 Mar 2016 Took keen hold, pressed leaders, jostling match with rival after 6th, still challenging 2 out, weakened quickly well before last, finished eighth, beaten 23 lengths by Yorkhill in Neptune Investment Management Novices' Hurdle

Made no show in two previous festivals, but on the evidence of three chase starts this season he is going to be much better in this discipline. It was hard to know what he really achieved when a ten-length winner on his debut at Cheltenham in November as hot favourite Barters Hill unfortunately pulled up early on, but he jumped well and was impressive. However, next time he was beaten at odds-on by the 139-rated Present Man and Potters Legend at Doncaster on his first try at 3m over fences. Was better on final start, winning back down to 2m4f at Huntingdon, but he definitely does stay 3m (outbattled subsequent Albert Bartlett runner-up Fagan at that trip over hurdles) and this is his only entry so far. Nicky Henderson said he'd be put in one of the handicaps, but assessor awarded him with a mark of 152 and if he's up to that in handicap company he won't be far off up to this either.

Going preference Seems versatile
Star rating ✪✪

Singlefarmpayment
7 b g; Trainer Tom George
Chase form 321B, best RPR 150
Left-handed 31B, best RPR 150
Right-handed 2, best RPR 145
Cheltenham form (all) 11B, best RPR 150

Fair handicap hurdler, who would nevertheless have been some way below the best of these in that sphere. However, has always looked a chaser and is steadily progressing. Off the mark on his third start this season at Cheltenham in December, he was always travelling well, so connections decided to drop him to 2m5f on trials day and he was cantering when brought down in the race won by Royal Vacation. That was six out, so it was far too early to say what would have happened, but it also represented his first loss in three starts at the track, so it's clear he handles it well. Handicap mark of 142 looks tasty, but connections may think bigger.

Going preference Seems versatile
Star rating ✪✪

OTHERS TO CONSIDER

Shantou Village is a potential forgotten horse having started so well before a heavy fall at Wincanton, although you would like to see some evidence that he's fit and well first. **Martello Tower** is worthy of some respect as a previous Albert Bartlett winner but he doesn't look so good over fences, while **Bigbadjohn** and **Acapella Bourgeois** both won Graded races in February and could play a part, but it's likely neither wants the ground too fast.

VERDICT

There is little doubt Might Bite has the best form, and by some way, but he also has the profile of a horse well suited to flat tracks and he didn't jump well at Cheltenham on his chase debut last season. I wouldn't mind betting the one to turn him over could be ROYAL VACATION, who was the chief beneficiary when Might Bite fell in the Feltham. He has a good 20 lengths to make up on that run, but he has improved his RPR with every start over fences and was impressive in the 2m5f novice handicap chase at the trials meeting. If Singlefarmpayment runs he wouldn't be without a chance at a price.

TRAINER'S VIEW

Nicky Henderson on Might Bite "His win at Doncaster was a real confidence-booster that put him bang on course for the festival and when you look back at the Kempton run the performance he was putting up was quite extraordinary, in terms of the horses he was annihilating and the time he was clocking"
Would have recorded a faster time than Thistlecrack did in the King George but for falling at the last at Kempton

Royal Vacation: Feltham win was a fluke but he is improving and has good course form

RSA CHASE RESULTS AND TRENDS

	FORM	WINNER	AGE & WGT	Adj RPR	SP	TRAINER	BEST RPR LAST 12 MONTHS (RUNS SINCE)
16	4F121	**Blaklion** C, D	7 11-4	172-1	8-1	N Twiston-Davies	won Wetherby Gd 2 nov ch (3m) (0)
15	1-211	**Don Poli** C, D	6 11-4	165-2	13-8f	W Mullins (IRE)	won Leopardstown Gd1 nov ch (3m) (0)
14	4-2P1	**O'Faolains Boy** D	7 11-4	160-9	12-1	R Curtis	won Gd2 Reynoldstown Nov Ch (3m) (0)
13	22123	**Lord Windermere**	7 11-4	155-10	8-1	J Culloty (IRE)	3rd Gd1 Dr PJ Moriarty Nov Ch (2m5f) (0)
12	1-132	**Bobs Worth** C, D	7 11-4	172-6	9-2	N Henderson	3rd Gd1 Feltham Nov Ch (3m) (1)
11	21411	**Bostons Angel** D	7 11-4	160-13	16-1	J Harrington (IRE)	won Gd1 Dr PJ Moriarty Nov Ch (2m5f) (0)
10	3F122	**Weapon's Amnesty** C, D	7 11-4	160-15	10-1	C Byrnes (IRE)	2nd Leopardstown Gd1 nov ch (3m) (1)
09	-8131	**Cooldine**	7 11-4	166-3	9-4f	W Mullins (IRE)	won Gd1 Dr PJ Moriarty Nov Ch (2m5f) (0)
08	-1211	**Albertas Run** CD	7 11-4	164-3	4-1f	J O'Neill	won Gd2 Reynoldstown Nov Ch (3m) (0)
07	-1111	**Denman** C, D	7 11-4	170T	6-5f	P Nicholls	won Newbury class 2 nov ch (3m) (0)

WINS-RUNS: 5yo 0-5, 6yo 1-19, 7yo 9-61, 8yo 0-21, 9yo 0-9 **FAVOURITES:** £3.08

TRAINERS IN THIS RACE (w-pl-r): Willie Mullins 2-3-15, Paul Nicholls 1-1-12, Nicky Henderson 1-3-8, Nigel Twiston-Davies 1-1-5, Rebecca Curtis 1-0-1, Alan King 0-1-2, Colin Tizzard 0-0-3, David Pipe 0-0-5, Gordon Elliott 0-1-3, Mouse Morris 0-1-2, Noel Meade 0-1-2, Neil Mulholland 0-0-1, Philip Hobbs 0-1-2, Sandra Hughes 0-0-1, Sue Smith, 0-0-2, Venetia Williams 0-0-2

FATE OF FAVOURITES: 1115544213 **POSITION OF WINNER IN MARKET:** 1115724813

Key trends

🐎 Did not run on the Flat, 10/10

🐎 Adjusted RPR of at least 160, 9/10

🐎 Top-three finish last time out, 10/10

🐎 Contested a Graded chase (eight won, two placed), 10/10

🐎 Six to 12 hurdles and chase runs, 9/10

🐎 Aged seven, 9/10

🐎 Last ran between 24 and 53 days ago, 9/10

🐎 Ran at least three times over fences, 9/10

🐎 Rated within 10lb of RPR top-rated, 8/10

Other factors

🐎 Of the combined 45 chase starts of winners, only last year's scorer Blaklion had finished outside the first three (three had fallen). However, only Denman and Don Poli were unbeaten over fences

🐎 Nine winners had previously run at the festival – five ran in the Albert Bartlett (1P14P), one in the Neptune (2), one in the Martin Pipe (1) and two in the bumper two years previously (07)

🐎 Ten five-year-olds have run in the last 22 years – one won, four placed, three were unplaced and two fell

2.50 Coral Cup (Handicap Hurdle)　　ITV/RUK
🐎2m5f　🐎Grade 3　🐎£95,000

Back the favourite at your peril in this fiercely competitive handicap hurdle – just one outright and one joint-favourite have won the race in its 23-year history. There have been only two winners at single-figure odds since 2004. However, the Gordon Elliott-trained 12-1 shot Diamond King last year became the ninth of the past ten winners who were in the first seven in the betting, so the market is not such a bad guide.

The race has tended to suit younger, less exposed types, with ten of the past 16 winners aged five or six. Just three winners in the last 17 renewals have been aged eight or older. Eight of the last nine victors arrived at Cheltenham with single figures of runs over hurdles.

Ireland has had eight winners and only Xenophon, 4-1 favourite in 2003, was heavily fancied. The other seven Irish winners were returned at between 11-1 and 16-1.

CORAL CUP RESULTS AND TRENDS

	FORM WINNER	AGE & WGT	OR	SP	TRAINER	BEST RPR LAST 12 MONTHS (RUNS SINCE)
16	P-421 **Diamond King**	8 11-3	149^{-5}	12-1	G Elliott (IRE)	won Punchestown hdl (2m4f) (0)
15	1-31 **Aux Ptits Soins**	5 10-7	139^{-4}	9-1	P Nicholls	won Auteuil hdl (2m1½f) (0)
14	-3312 **Whisper** C, D, BF	6 11-6	153^{-4}	14-1	N Henderson	2nd Ffos Las class 2 hcap hdl (2m4f) (0)
13	-2241 **Medinas**	6 11-10	148^{-3}	33-1	A King	won Ffos Las class 2 hcap hdl (2m4f) (0)
12	-9090 **Son Of Flicka**	8 10-6	135^{T}	16-1	D McCain	2nd Martin Pipe Cond Hcp Hdl (2m4½f) (5)
11	2-102 **Carlito Brigante** (2ow)	5 11-0	142^{-10}	16-1	G Elliott (IRE)	2nd Fairyhouse hdl (2m) (0)
10	1-510 **Spirit River** C	5 11-2	141^{-1}	14-1	N Henderson	won Chelt class 3 hcap hdl (2m1f) (1)
09	-4511 **Ninetieth Minute**	6 10-3	140^{T}	14-1	T Taaffe (IRE)	won Thurles Listed hdl (2m) (0)
08	12-71 **Naiad Du Misselot** D	7 10-13	130^{-7}	7-1	F Murphy	won Haydock class 2 hcap hdl (2m4f) (0)
07	23521 **Burntoakboy** D	9 9-12	128^{T}	10-1	R Newland	won Leicester class 3 hcap hdl (2m4½f) (0)

WINS-RUNS: 5yo 3-54, 6yo 3-71, 7yo 1-59, 8yo 2-39, 9yo 1-21, 10yo 0-13, 11yo 0-5, 12yo 0-2　**FAVOURITES:** -£10.00

FATE OF FAVOURITES: 0000020530 **POSITION OF WINNER IN MARKET:** 4266770526

Key trends

🐎Not run for at least 32 days, 10/10

🐎Won a race earlier in the season, 9/10 (six won last time out)

🐎No more than four runs that season, 9/10

🐎Won between 2m2f and 2m6f over hurdles, 8/10

🐎Officially rated 130 to 149, 8/10

🐎No more than nine hurdle runs, 8/10

🐎Aged five to seven, 7/10

🐎Carried no more than 11st 2lb, 7/10

Other factors

🐎The two winners to have had more than nine hurdle runs had 22 and 27 starts

3.30 Betway Queen Mother Champion Chase ITV/RUK
2m *Grade 1* *£350,000*

Just as in his previous nine outings over fences, Douvan is expected to stroll to victory here and become a three-time festival winner following his victories in the 2015 Supreme Novices' Hurdle and 2016 Arkle Chase. The closest any rival has finished behind him in his chasing career was last time when he beat Realt Mor by a comfortable six and a half lengths in the Tied Cottage Chase and he is as surefire a qualifier for 'if he stands up, he wins' status as you will find. The 13 biggest dangers to Douvan are permanently fixed at Cheltenham; if he jumps them, there is little doubt he will leave his rivals standing again. There is just one horse among the entries with the potential to serve it up to Douvan and that is Altior, but he is expected to stick to the novice route in the Arkle. The others – stablemate Un De Sceaux, Colin Tizzard's Fox Norton, 2014 winner Sire De Grugy, God's Own and Special Tiara – will do battle for the minor honours.

Douvan
7 b g; Trainer Willie Mullins
Chase form 111111111, best RPR 178
Left-handed 111111, best RPR 178
Right-handed 111, best RPR 178
Cheltenham form (all) 11, best RPR 165
At the festival 10 Mar 2015 Mid-division, smooth headway after 3 out, shaken up to lead before last, ran on strongly, driven out, won Supreme Novices' Hurdle by four and a half lengths from Shaneshill
15 Mar 2016 With leader, led 3rd, made rest, always travelling strongly, powered clear between last 2, mistake last, ran on well, comfortably, won Racing Post Arkle by seven lengths from Sizing John

Has long been talked up as potentially the best ever horse trained by Willie Mullins and the number of people prepared to argue must be in short supply now. Has won all 13 starts since joining the trainer from France and has been sent off at odds against only once during that time, when 2-1 favourite for the Supreme Novices' Hurdle. No horse has yet got to within three lengths of him in Britain or Ireland and his average winning distance over fences is 12 lengths. If there were any criticisms you could say that he hasn't been a top-class two-miler yet, but there is rarely much depth in the 2m division and with Un De Sceaux in the same yard that was always likely, Douvan could have been asked to take in the Grade 1s in Britain, but Mullins left that to Un De Sceaux, who fairly comfortably held off the best of the home team in the Tingle Creek and Clarence House, but is likely to go for the Ryanair this year. Assuming Altior passes his Arkle test the day will come when Douvan has to take on a horse with as much star potential as him, but until then it's fair to assume he will defeat whatever is put in front of him. Wastes no time in the air, travels like a dream and has a change of gear. Impossible to oppose and not easy to find too many definite runners against him.

Going preference All going comes alike
Star rating ✪✪✪✪✪

Fox Norton
7 b g; Trainer Colin Tizzard
Chase form 1123331112, best RPR 170
Left-handed 233331112, best RPR 170
Right-handed 11, best RPR 147
Cheltenham form 23111, best RPR 170
At the festival 15 Mar 2016 Tracked leaders, pushed along and lost place after 3 out, outpaced after, slightly hampered 2 out, kept on to take 3rd final 75yds, no chance, finished third, beaten 11 lengths in Racing Post Arkle by Douvan

Decent novice who got within 11 lengths of Douvan when third in last season's Arkle and improved out of all recognition afterwards.

He closed the season with an odds-on novice chase win in a four-runner affair at Cheltenham and returned there in October to turn a competitive-looking handicap into a procession, winning by 11 lengths off a mark of 146. Followed that up with a nine-length success from Simply Ned in the Shloer Chase in November following a switch from Neil Mulholland to Colin Tizzard, but suffered minor setback afterwards and not seen until running into crack novice Altior in the Game Spirit at Newbury. With Tizzard's horses seemingly not running as well as earlier in the season there's a fair chance he wasn't quite as his best, but Altior won in a canter by 13 lengths and Fox Norton clearly has his limitations. Obviously goes well at Cheltenham and in pole position for second if on top form.

Going preference Used to be considered a good-ground performer, but best form now on soft
Star rating ✪✪

Un De Sceaux

9 b g; Trainer Willie Mullins
Chase form F1111F12211, best RPR 174
Left-handed 11F21, best RPR 174
Right-handed F11121, best RPR 172
Cheltenham form 121, best RPR 174
At the festival 10 Mar 2015 Raced with zest, made most, shaken up approaching last, quickened clear final 110yds, ran on well, won Racing Post Arkle by six lengths from God's Own 16 Mar 2016 Tracked leader, hit 4th, led after 4 out, ridden when headed before 2 out, soon held by winner, kept on same pace, finished second, beaten three and a half lengths by Sprinter Sacre in Champion Chase

Top-class performer who has won eight of nine hurdles starts and has been beaten only by Sprinter Sacre (twice) in nine completed chase outings. Six-length Arkle winner as novice and went back to Cheltenham last spring as a red-hot 4-6 favourite for Champion Chase glory, but proved no match for Sprinter Sacre after the last, having got into a bit of a battle with Special Tiara from some way out and was then beaten 15 lengths by Nicky

Henderson's superstar at Sandown in April. Back on song this season, though, beating the best of Britain in the Tingle Creek and Clarence House Chase and boasts the best form bar Douvan. However, he is favourite for the Ryanair and while he hasn't run over further than 2m2f over fences, he won very easily over that trip in a Grade 2 hurdle at Auteuil in May and pretty much everyone expects him to be running on the Thursday.

Going preference Very well suited by soft, but can't really quibble with form on faster
Star rating ✪✪✪

God's Own

9 b g; Trainer Tom George
Chase form 242117322F32411233, best RPR 170
Left-handed 24224112, best RPR 167
Right-handed 21173F32133, best RPR 170
Cheltenham form 024, best RPR 166
At the festival 10 Mar 2015 Jumped right a few times, held up, headway 9th, went 2nd before 2 out, about 2 lengths down and trying to challenge when jumped right again last, kept on but unable to go pace of winner final 110yds, finished second, beaten six lengths by Un De Sceaux in Racing Post Arkle
16 Mar 2016 Tracked leader, hit 4th, led after 4 out, ridden when headed before 2 out, soon held by winner, kept on same pace, finished fourth, beaten eight and a half lengths by Sprinter Sacre in Champion Chase

Very decent chaser at his best, but has twice seen the back of Un De Sceaux at the festival, first when a six-length runner up in the Arkle and then when the pair were second and fourth to Sprinter Sacre in this race last year. Seems at least as good this year based on fine weight-carrying second to Third Intention in Old Roan Chase at Aintree in October and then close third to Un De Sceaux at Sandown in December, a track at which he hadn't previous excelled. Trainer always thought he was best on right-handed tracks, but put that to bed a fair while ago and, as he always comes to hand in the spring (has spring festival form figures of 122411) it would not surprise if he went well again. Has Ryanair entry too, but didn't appear to quite get 2m5f at Ascot in November.

Going preference Doesn't want it any worse than good to soft
Star rating ✪✪✪

Special Tiara

10 b g; Trainer Henry de Bromhead
Chase form 12513U3463341314236315, best RPR 170
Left-handed 51U36434335, best RPR 170
Right-handed 1233311261, best RPR 170
Cheltenham form 363335, best RPR 170
At the festival 12 Mar 2014 Led, hit 3rd, blundered and headed 4th, led again before next, headed 6th, stayed pressing leaders until led again after 4 out, headed approaching 3 out, weakened 2 out, finished sixth, beaten 15 and a half lengths by Sire De Grugy in Champion Chase
11 Mar 2015 Led, clear 4th, joined after 3 out, soon ridden, headed on landing last, kept on bravely but no extra final 110yd, finished third, beaten three lengths by Dodging Bullets in Champion Chase
16 Mar 2016 Led, mistake 3rd, headed after 4 out, ridden and every chance after 3 out, held by winner before next but kept pressing for 2nd, stayed on same pace

Really likeable and high-class trailblazer at best who was rated just 124 when springing a massive surprise at Aintree in 2013 and has been running in all the top 2m races since. Got his Grade 1 on the board when beating a below-par Sprinter Sacre in the Celebration Chase at Sandown in April 2015, but otherwise has always come up short. Not been in terrific form this season either, with hard-fought win over Sir Valentino (getting 6lb from horse rated 10lb inferior) at Kempton as good as it's got. That suggests he's on the downgrade at the age of ten and while he may well lead them early, doubtful if he's around at the business end.

Going preference Prefers decent ground
Star rating ✪✪✪

Garde La Victoire

8 b g; Trainer Philip Hobbs
Chase form 111FF21, best RPR 164

Left-handed 11FF best RPR 158
Right-handed 121, best RPR 164
Cheltenham form (all) 20111F, best RPR 152
At the festival 11 Mar 2014 Held up, niggled along and struggling to go pace after 5th, going nowhere when blundered 2 out, never a threat, finished 14th, beaten 18 and a half lengths by Vautour in Supreme Novices' Hurdle
17 Mar 2016 Held up behind leaders, going well enough in close 6th when fell 4 out in JLT Novices' Chase won by Black Hercules

Always been talented and won Greatwood Hurdle off mark of 144 in second season over hurdles. Developed into decent novice chaser last term, too, heading into the JLT as joint favourite on the back of three wins, although his jumping offered cause for concern. It was found out at Cheltenham when he came down four out (hadn't been asked a question) and then he turned in a really shoddy round of jumping before falling at the 13th at Aintree. Has mixed chasing with hurdling this season, winning substandard Welsh Champion in October and the out of his depth against Yanworth at Ascot, and chase form has been better. Ran really well when short-headed by the much improved Sir Valentino in the Haldon Gold Cup and then scored in 2m Sandown handicap off a mark of 154. Obviously needs to find a lot more still and could conceivably run off 158 in Grand Annual, but going the right way.

Going preference Seems happy on most ground
Star rating ✪✪✪

Sir Valentino

8 b g; Trainer Tom George
Chase form F2F5231F51152518152, best RPR 170
Left-handed FF525, best RPR 150
Right-handed 2231F511518152, best RPR 170

Has been chasing since December 2013 and started with handicap mark of just 122, but improved with every season and not far off hitting the big time now. Won Grade 2 Haldon Gold Cup by a short-head from Garde La Victoire in October and while only fifth of six on his first foray into Grade 1 company,

he was beaten only five and a half lengths in the Tingle Creek. Arguably ran an even better race when just failing to run down Special Tiara in 2m contest at Kempton over Christmas when conceding 6lb to rival rated 10lb superior. Winner was probably below par, but connections entitled to think he can get a share of the money the way he is going provided going left-handed is not a bother (form much better the other way round, but last runs just over a year were in keeping with his improvement at the time).

Going preference Doesn't seem to have any issues

Star rating ✪✪✪

OTHERS TO CONSIDER

You could go on for a while given the number of entries, but there comes a stage when it is pointless and we probably reached that not long after Douvan was mentioned. The one glaring omission from the contenders is **Altior**, who does have an entry and would be clear second favourite should he run, but Nicky Henderson is adamant he'll go for the Arkle and you'd have to think he will unless something happens to the favourite.

Uxizandre won the Ryanair so well two years ago you'd have to think he'd have gone close in that year's substandard Champion Chase, and he ran really well when second on his return from a long break in the Clarence House. However, he looks certain to go for another crack at the Ryanair. Vroum Vroum Mag's entry is obviously a wind-up, while Gary Moore's pair **Sire De Grugy** and **Traffic Fluide** are hard to fancy on age and recent form grounds respectively.

VERDICT

There ought to be no stopping DOUVAN (above), whose ante-post odds of 1-3 are likely to look a bargain come raceday. He's in a class of his own. I might take a chance on Garde La Victoire in the without the favourite market, currently 10-1 with a run, because he's getting his act together.

RIDER'S VIEW

Ruby Walsh on Douvan "Deadly, isn't he? He has a huge amount of natural ability – you just have to sit there. You tactically ride the race, the horse does the jumping" *Has recorded RPRs of 176, 171, 178, 178 and 170 on his last five starts without being tested*

CHAMPION CHASE RESULTS AND TRENDS

	FORM WINNER	AGE & WGT	Adj RPR	SP	TRAINER	BEST RPR LAST 12 MONTHS (RUNS SINCE)
16	P2-11 **Sprinter Sacre** CD	10 11-10	177[-1]	5-1	N Henderson	won Kempton Gd2 ch (2m) (0)
15	5-311 **Dodging Bullets** CD	7 11-10	178[-6]	9-2	P Nicholls	won Gd1 Clarence House Ch (2m1f) (0)
14	12111 **Sire De Grugy** D	8 11-10	178[T]	11-4f	G Moore	won Gd1 Clarence House Ch (2m1f) (0)
13	11-11 **Sprinter Sacre** CD	7 11-10	182[T]	1-4f	N Henderson	won Gd1 Victor Chandler Ch (2m1f) (0)
12	21-12 **Finian's Rainbow** D, BF	9 11-10	171[-9]	4-1	N Henderson	2nd Gd1 Victor Chandler Ch (2m1f) (0)
11	3-223 **Sizing Europe** CD	9 11-10	170[-9]	10-1	H de Bromhead (IRE)	3rd Punchestown Gd2 ch (2m) (0)
10	-2141 **Big Zeb** D	9 11-10	171[-19]	10-1	C Murphy (IRE)	won Navan Gd2 ch (2m) (2)
09	12-11 **Master Minded** CD	6 11-10	191[T]	4-11f	P Nicholls	won Gd1 Champion Chase (2m) (3)
08	-2U11 **Master Minded** D	5 11-10	173[-4]	3-1	P Nicholls	won Gd2 Game Spirit Ch (2m1f) (0)
07	2-21U **Voy Por Ustedes** CD	6 11-10	174[-9]	5-1	A King	won Kempton Gd2 ch (2m) (1)

WINS-RUNS: 5yo 1-1, 6yo 2-8, 7yo 2-14, 8yo 1-24, 9yo 3-25, 10yo 1-15, 11yo 0-7, 12yo 0-2, 13yo 0-1 **FAVOURITES:** -£3.64

TRAINERS IN THIS RACE (w-pl-r): Paul Nicholls 3-0-14, Nicky Henderson 3-1-9, Alan King 1-1-3, Gary Moore 1-0-3, Henry de Bromhead 1-4-8, Nicky Richards 0-0-1, Philip Hobbs 0-1-4, Tom George 0-1-3, Willie Mullins 0-1-6, Micky Hammond 0-0-1

FATE OF FAVOURITES: F2140211P2 **POSITION OF WINNER IN MARKET:** 3214521132

Key trends

🐎 Won over at least 2m1f, 10/10

🐎 At least seven runs over fences, 10/10

🐎 No older than nine, 9/10

🐎 Adjusted RPR of at least 170, 10/10

🐎 No more than 9lb off RPR top-rated, 9/10

🐎 Grade 1 chase winner, 9/10

🐎 Won Graded chase last time out, 7/10

Other factors

🐎 Five winners had previously won at the festival

🐎 Six winners were French-bred

🐎 In the past ten years 31 French-breds have run, also yielding three seconds and three thirds

4.10 Glenfarclas Cross Country Chase   ITV/RUK
3m6f   £65,000

This unusual event is in its second year as a conditions race, having previously been a handicap, but there have been some interesting pointers to note over the years.

Ireland has won ten of the 12 runnings, helped largely by the success of Enda Bolger, widely regarded as the cross-country master. He trained four of the first five winners up to 2009 and had 2016 winner Josies Orders, who was awarded the race when the original winner Any Currency was disqualified after a banned substance was detected in a post-race test. Philip Hobbs is the only trainer to have won for Britain, with Balthazar King in 2012 and 2014.

It has paid to back horses at the head of the market, with eight of the 12 winners being returned at 11-2 or shorter. The biggest-priced winner was A New Story at 25-1 in 2010.

An interesting contender is the French-trained Urgent De Gregaine, who caused a 50-1 upset against Cantlow in a handicap at the course in January, albeit in receipt of 15lb.

CROSS COUNTRY RESULTS AND TRENDS

FORM	WINNER	AGE & WGT	OR	SP	TRAINER	BEST RPR LAST 12 MONTHS (RUNS SINCE)
16	18119 **Josies Orders** CD	8 11-4	148-7	15-8f	E Bolger (IRE)	won Chelt cross-country ch (3m6f) (1)
15	4172F **Rivage D'Or**	10 10-10	134-4	16-1	T Martin (IRE)	2nd Kilbeggan hcp ch (3m1f) (2)
14	P-111 **Balthazar King** CD	10 11-12	150-5	4-1	P Hobbs	won Cheltenham cl 2 hcap ch (3m½f) (1)
13	-F742 **Big Shu**	8 10-5	136-10	14-1	P Maher (IRE)	2nd Punchestown cross-country ch (3m) (0)
12	15P00 **Balthazar King** C	8 10-9	139-3	11-2	P Hobbs	won Cheltenham cl 2 hcap ch (3m½f) (4)
11	4-138 **Sizing Australia**	9 10-9	140-7	13-2	H De Bromhead (IRE)	3rd Chelt cross-country ch (3m7f) (0)
10	70454 **A New Story** (4oh)	12 9-7	135-3	25-1	M Hourigan (IRE)	3rd Cork National hcap ch (3m4f) (4)
09	1-421 **Garde Champetre** CD	10 11-12	150-4	7-2	E Bolger (IRE)	won Chelt cross-country ch (3m7f) (0)
08	9-9F1 **Garde Champetre**	9 10-13	129T	4-1	E Bolger (IRE)	won Punchestown cross-country ch (3m) (0)
07	-2341 **Heads Onthe Ground**	10 10-2	126-9	5-2f	E Bolger (IRE)	won Punchestown cross-country ch (3m) (0)

WINS-RUNS: 6yo 0-5, 7yo 0-6, 8yo 3-21, 9yo 2-30, 10yo 4-31, 11yo 0-27, 12yo 1-21, 13yo 0-12, 14yo 0-4, 15yo 0-2

FAVOURITES: -£3.63 **FATE OF FAVOURITES:** 16254P0301 **POSITION OF WINNER IN MARKET:** 1229337271

Key trends

- Won over at least 3m, 10/10

- Trained in Ireland, 8/10

- Officially rated 134-150, 8/10

- Won or placed in a cross-country race at Cheltenham or Punchestown, 8/10 (one exception carried out when set to place)

- Top-four finish in last completed start, 8/10

Other factors

- The inaugural running was in 2005 and JP McManus and Enda Bolger teamed up for four of the first five winners. They also had last year's winner Josies Orders following his promotion on the disqualification of Any Currency

- Two winners had landed the PP Hogan at Punchestown in February, while 2013 winner Big Shu was runner-up in that event

- Only ten British-trained runners have made the first four, although in 2014 the home team had first, second and fourth

- Ireland has had the first four on three occasions and in 2009 had the first nine finishers

4.50 Fred Winter Juvenile Handicap Hurdle RUK
2m½f   Grade 3   £80,000

A fiercely competitive handicap hurdle that has gone to Paul Nicholls in the past two years with Qualando and Diego Du Charmil.

Both were French-breds, who have done extremely well in this juvenile contest with six wins in 12 runnings (a French-bred has finished first or second in the last five renewals).

The big stables are always worth noting. Nicholls has now had three winners, as well as several placed horses, and Nicky Henderson, David Pipe and Gordon Elliott have each celebrated victory.

Eight of the 12 winners had won on one of their last two starts. No winner has carried top weight, with Crack Away Jack (11st 10lb in 2008) the only one to carry more than 11st 4lb. The subsequent eight winners have carried 11st 2lb or less.

It is important to look for runners rated in a certain bracket – 11 of the 12 winners were rated between 124 and 133 (the exception was 2011 winner What A Charm off 115) and three of the first four in 2016 were in that ratings bracket (although it is becoming ever harder to get in off a rating in the 120s).

Claiming jockeys can be significant, with three of the 12 winners having been partnered by conditional or amateur riders, most recently Henderson's Une Artiste in 2012 by then 5lb claimer Jeremiah McGrath.

FRED WINTER HANDICAP HURDLE RESULTS AND TRENDS

FORM	WINNER	AGE & WGT	OR	SP	TRAINER	BEST RPR LAST 12 MONTHS (RUNS SINCE)
16	322	Diego Du Charmil BF	4 11-1	133^{-17}	13-2	P Nicholls	2nd Enghien hdl (2m½f) (0)
15	3-421	Qualando	4 11-0	131^{-9}	25-1	P Nicholls	4th Auteuil Listed hdl (2m1½f) (2)
14	1216	Hawk High D	4 11-1	130^{-12}	33-1	T Easterby	won Warwick class 4 hdl (2m) (1)
13	125	Flaxen Flare D	4 10-8	127^{-5}	25-1	G Elliott (IRE)	5th Leopardstown Gd1 nov hdl (2m) (0)
12	11114	Une Artiste D	4 10-8	127^{-6}	40-1	N Henderson	won Haydock class 2 hdl (2m) (1)
11	757	What A Charm	4 10-6	115^{-3}	9-1	A Moore (IRE)	7th Fairyhouse Gd2 nov hdl (2m) (0)
10	531	Sanctuaire D	4 11-2	127^{-9}	4-1f	P Nicholls	3rd Auteuil hdl (2m2f) (1)
09	52111	Silk Affair (5x)	4 10-4	125^{-12}	11-1	M Quinlan	won Sandown cl 3 nov hcap hdl (2m4f) (1)
08	531	Crack Away Jack D	4 11-10	133^{-22}	14-1	E Lavelle	won Sandown class 3 nov hdl (2m½f) (0)
07	22111	Gaspara (4x) D	4 10-11	130^{T}	9-2jf	D Pipe	won Sandown Listed hcap hdl (2m½f) (0)

FAVOURITES: -£2.25 FATE OF FAVOURITES: 1241430000 POSITION OF WINNER IN MARKET: 1441500002

Key trends

- Officially rated 125 to 133, 9/10
- Top-three finish in at least one of last two starts, 9/10
- Had lost maiden tag over hurdles, 8/10
- Won at least one of last two starts, 7/10
- Beaten in first two starts over hurdles, 7/10
- Sired by a Group 1 winner on the Flat, 7/10

Other factors

- Four of the five winners who had run on the Flat had earned an RPR of at least 87; the other five were unraced on the Flat
- Five winners were French-bred
- Two winners were ridden by conditionals (2005 winner Dabiroun was amateur-ridden)

5.30 Weatherbys Champion Bumper

RUK

🏇 2m½f   🏇 Grade 1   🏇 £75,000

This race used to be dominated by the Irish but Britain had a second consecutive victory last year with Ballyandy, making the score 4-3 in the home team's favour over the past seven years. It is also notable that recent winners have gone on to great success over jumps with the list including Cue Card, Champagne Fever, Moon Racer (a leading fancy for the Supreme Novices' Hurdle this year) and Ballyandy, winner of the Betfair Hurdle last time out. The British upsurge has been one factor in reducing Willie Mullins' previous dominance but he still has the strongest influence on the ante-post market and this year is no exception, with Carter McKay, Ballyward, Next Destination, Come To Me and Redhotfillypeppers all prominent. Gordon Elliott, now a rival to Mullins on every front, has never won this race but has a pair of leading contenders in Samcro and Blow By Blow. Among the British hopes are Daphne Du Clos (Nicky Henderson), Western Ryder (Warren Greatrex) and Cause Toujours (Dan Skelton).

Carter McKay

6 gr g; Trainer Willie Mullins
Bumper form (left-handed) 11, best RPR 130

Normally at this time of year the identity of the favourite is not so clearcut, but bookmakers were falling over themselves to shorten Carter McKay almost quickly as punters were apparently doing so to back him following his impressive win at Naas in February. No bigger than 4-1 with a month to go, he could end up one of the shortest-priced favourites in the race's history, but what is his price based on? The bumper he won featured only four runners and was run on near bottomless ground over 2m3f in a time of 5mins 21.6secs, some 62 seconds outside the Racing Post standard. Carter McKay sure was impressive in beating previous winner West Coast Time, but it showed he is very well at home on bad ground and a strong stayer. The Champion Bumper will ask him different questions as the race will probably take some 90 seconds less to run if the ground isn't bad and he'll have to average something like 12-13 lengths per furlong faster than he did at Naas. Could be a star and he won't be short of backers, but this is the ultimate guessers race at the festival and I won't be one of them at his current price.

Star rating ✪✪✪

Ballyward

5 b g; Trainer Willie Mullins
Bumper form (left-handed) 1, best RPR 124

Second in the betting based on 16-length success at Leopardstown over Christmas (runner-up beaten twice since), but that was over 2m4f. Trainer said he wouldn't have any trouble dropping down in trip provided ground is soft, and stayers have won this.

Star rating ✪✪

Daphne Du Clos

4 b f; Trainer Nicky Henderson
Bumper form (left-handed) 21, best RPR 107

Neck second in Listed 1m6f bumper on debut at Cheltenham in January and duly went one better in often informative Newbury contest on Betfair Hurdle day won last year by Ballyandy. Travelled strongly throughout and took it up on bit, but had to be pushed out to score by three and a quarter lengths from Western Ryder, who was conceding 21lb. It will be 14lb at the festival and that should make things more interesting, but winner returned RPR of only 107 compared to Ballyandy's 137 last year and race does not look up to normal standard.

Star rating ✪✪✪✪

Western Ryder

5 b g; Trainer Warren Greatrex
Bumper form 1212, best RPR 122
Left-handed 12, best RPR 122
Right-handed 21, best RPR 121

Dual winner and second twice for Warren Greatrex, who has an excellent record in bumpers. Probably best form when trying to give 21lb to Daphne Du Clos at Newbury on Betfair Hurdle day, but unless it's a below par year a peak RPR of 122 is around a stone lower than what will be needed at Cheltenham. Given he's had four starts it's hard to see where that is going to come from.

Star rating ✪

West Coast Time

5 b g; Trainer Joseph O'Brien
Bumper form 12, best RPR 121
Left-handed 2, best RPR 117
Right-handed 1, best RPR 121

Impressive enough in seven-runner Cork bumper on debut, although no winners have emerged from it and put in his place by Carter Mckay, who cantered past him at Naas in February. Both runs on bad ground though and dam Refinement, who finished in the first four at four Cheltenham Festivals, including two bumpers, showed all her best form on better going. Sire (Westerner) had three good-ground festival winners too, so every hope he can improve on a better surface.

Star rating ✪✪

Samcro

5 ch g; Trainer Gordon Elliott
Bumper form 11, best RPR 118
Left-handed 1, best RPR 114
Right-handed 1 ,best RPR 118

Point winner who is highly regarded by Gordon Elliott and 2-2 in bumpers, although had to battle to win Listed affair at odds of 1-3 on second start. Best RPR of 118 some way below what is required and long-term prospect who is owned by Gigginstown and therefore surely unlikely to be risked in a race they don't like.

Star rating ✪

Cause Toujours

5 b g; Trainer Dan Skelton
Bumper form (left-handed) 1, best RPR 125

Five-year-old who would have been first or second in sole point had he not unseated his rider at the last and made sparkling bumper debut at Warwick in December. Earned an RPR of 125 for seven-length drubbing of 12 rivals and did it easily, so every chance there is more to come. Half-brother to Analifet, who was fifth in a County Hurdle and makes more appeal than most British contenders providing everything is okay as he hasn't been seen since.

Star rating ✪✪✪

Red Jack

4 b g; Trainer Noel Meade
Bumper form (left-handed) 1, best RPR 110

Won ten-runner bumper at Naas in January at odds of 10-1, but wasn't unexpected by Noel Meade, who said nothing had managed to get him off the bridle at home. Initital RPR of 110 a fair bit lower than some of his rivals, but second beat third next time out and sixth has since won a 20-runner maiden hurdle, so form has some substance. Will get 7lb weight concession for being a four-year-old

Star rating ✪✪

Blow By Blow

6 ch g; Trainer Gordon Elliott
Bumper form 2111, best RPR 136
Left-handed 1, best RPR 129
Right-handed 211, best RPR 136

Already boasts some of the best form having beaten both Death Duty (now favourite for the Albert Bartlett) and Moon Racer (the 2015 Champion Bumper winner) in bumpers last season, the latter in the Grade 1 at Punchestown. However, has not been seen since and is owned by Giggingstown, so strong suspicion double-figure quotes are designed to tempt people into backing a likely non-runner.

Star rating ✪✪

Next Destination

5 b g; Trainer Willie Mullins
Bumper form (right-handed) 1, best RPR 116

Beat five rivals in sole point and four in only bumper start at Fairyhouse on New Year's Day. Odds-on that day, which is nothing unusal for a Willie Mullins bumper horse, but won by only three-quarters of a length from a horse beaten much further next time. Trainer says he handled the soft ground but would be happier on a better surface.

Star rating ✪✪

Come To Me

5 b g; Trainer Willie Mullins
Bumper form (right-handed) 1, best RPR 114

Bit of a cryptic comment from Willie Mullins after this one won at Punchestown in December as he said: "It looks like our bumper horses are better than we thought." The obvious assumption is that he had several better at home, but Come To Me did it well enough and while the placed horses haven't done much for the form, the seventh earned an RPR of 122 when beating the sixth at Leopardstown over Christmas.

Star rating ✪✪

Redhotfillypeppers

5 ch m; Trainer Willie Mullins
Bumper form (right-handed) 1, best RPR 110

Half-sister to staying chaser Wild West Wind, who was set to run in the 4m Eider Chase at the end of February. Stamina looked very much her strong suit, too, when she won a 2m2f mares' bumper at Punchestown. Form nothing special and surprising if she was fast enough on decent ground.

Star rating ✪

Debuchet

4 gr g; Trainer Margaret Mullins
Bumper form (left-handed) 21, best RPR 107

Second to Red Jack on debut at Naas in January and beat third by a similar margin (six and a half lengths) when off the mark at Leopardstown later that month. RPRs

nothing special, but has reportedly also run in schooling hurdles, so will at least have experience of some big fields.

Star rating ✪✪

Paloma Blue

5 b g; Trainer Henry de Bromhead
Bumper form (right-handed) 1, best RPR 115

Described by Henry de Bromhead as "a lovely, lovely horse" who was the standout at the Derby Sale (€160,000). Trainer doesn't rush them and his win at Fairyhouse made him the first first-time-out bumper winner for the yard since Identity Thief scored in 2014.

Star rating ✪✪

Champ

5 b g; Trainer Nicky Henderson
Bumper form (left-handed) 1, best RPR 119

Said to be big and raw by Barry Geraghty after winning bumper at lowly Southwell on debut, but earned a fairly high RPR (119) as he breezed three and a half lengths clear of the runner-up. Clearly much better than bare form (RPR takes that into account, second got 98) and might have been named for a reason, but green enough first time.

Star rating ✪✪

OTHERS TO CONSIDER

I've done my best to stick to the betting market at the time of writing with a few unraced exceptions like **Storm Home**, who had only one quote from a firm who made him joint fourth favourite on the strength of a point run in the spring when he probably would have beaten Getabird (absent with injury but previous favourite) if he hadn't fallen. **Blixt** a three-parts sister to Hurricane Fly, was a talking horse on debut in February but was a well-beaten third at Gowran.

VERDICT

Not a race I take seriously for betting purposes and I won't touch the favourite purely due to the short price. Henry de Bromhead's PALOMA BLUE is the stab if he comes over.

CHAMPION BUMPER RESULTS AND TRENDS

	FORM	WINNER	AGE & WGT	Adj RPR	SP	TRAINER	BEST RPR LAST 12 MONTHS (RUNS SINCE)
16	1121	**Ballyandy** CD	5 11-5	146^T	5-1	N Twiston-Davies	won Newbury Listed bumper (2m½f) **(0)**
15	-11	**Moon Racer** CD	6 11-5	140^{-7}	9-2f	D Pipe	won Cheltenham bumper (2m½f) **(0)**
14	3/2-1	**Silver Concorde** D	6 11-5	132^{-15}	16-1	D Weld (IRE)	won Leopardstown bumper (2m) **(0)**
13	1	**Briar Hill** D	5 11-5	117^{-27}	25-1	W Mullins (IRE)	won Thurles bumper (2m) **(0)**
12	21	**Champagne Fever** D	5 11-5	144^{-1}	16-1	W Mullins (IRE)	won Fairyhouse bumper (2m) **(0)**
11	21	**Cheltenian** D	5 11-5	126^{-13}	14-1	P Hobbs	won Kempton cl 5 mdn bumper (2m) **(0)**
10	1	**Cue Card**	4 10-12	126^{-15}	40-1	C Tizzard	won Fontwell class 6 bumper (1m6f) **(0)**
09	2-11	**Dunguib** D	6 11-5	147^T	9-2	P Fenton (IRE)	won Navan Gd2 bumper (2m) **(0)**
08	1	**Cousin Vinny**	5 11-5	118^{-23}	12-1	W Mullins (IRE)	won Punchestown bumper (2m) **(0)**
07	111	**Cork All Star** CD	5 11-5	145^T	11-2	J Harrington (IRE)	won Cheltenham Lstd bumper (2m½f) **(0)**

WINS-RUNS: 4yo 1-32, 5yo 6-144, 6yo 3-54 **FAVOURITES:** -£4.50

TRAINERS IN THIS RACE (w-pl-r): Willie Mullins 3-4-41, Dermot Weld 1-1-8, Philip Hobbs 1-0-8, David Pipe 1-0-10, Alan King 0-0-3, Donald McCain 0-0-3 **FATE OF FAVOURITES:** 0330622217 **POSITION OF WINNER IN MARKET:** 2520600612

Key trends

🏇Won last time out, 10/10

🏇Aged five or six, 9/10

🏇Adjusted RPR of at least 126, 8/10 (both exceptions were once-raced winners trained by Willie Mullins)

🏇Off the track for at least 32 days, 8/10 (four not seen since Christmas or earlier)

🏇Won a bumper with at least 13 runners, 7/10

🏇Won a bumper worth at least £4,000 or €4,000 to the winner, 7/10

Other factors

🏇Ireland has won six of the last ten and 17 of the 24 runnings

🏇Willie Mullins has the best record with eight victories (three in the last ten years) but is often mob-handed. On four of the occasions he has won it, he saddled just one runner. On the other four, the winner was not his most fancied in the market

🏇The 24 winners have been sired by 24 different stallions. Those are Montelimar, Where To Dance, Strong Gale, Accordion, Welsh Term, Florida Son, Glacial Storm, Mister Lord, River Falls, Broken Hearted, Teenoso, Flemensfirth, Overbury, Shernazar, Fasliyev, Bob Back, Presenting, King's Theatre, Astarabad, Stowaway, Shantou, Dansili, Saffron Walden and Kayf Tara

🏇Five winners were bred in Ireland

Notes

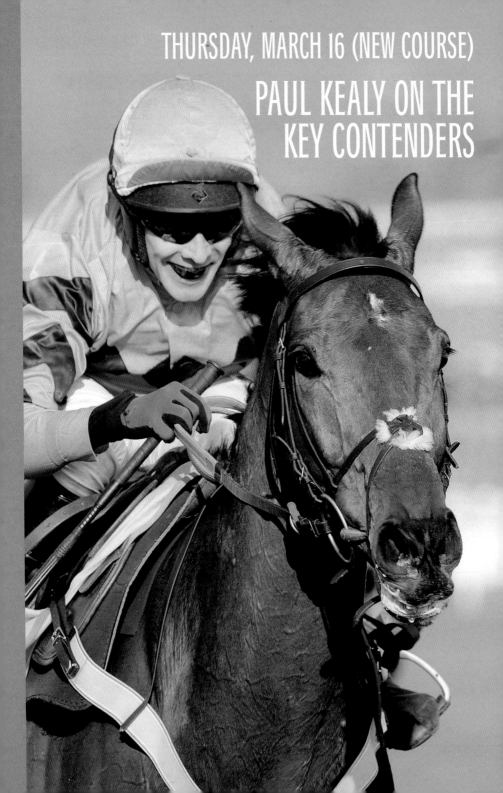

THURSDAY, MARCH 16 (NEW COURSE)

PAUL KEALY ON THE
KEY CONTENDERS

1.30 JLT Novices' Chase — ITV/RUK
2m4f — Grade 1 — £150,000

This has been a good race for Ireland, with five wins in six runnings, and Willie Mullins was victorious for the third time last year with Black Hercules (joining Sir Des Champs and Vautour). The obvious big hope for Mullins this time should be Yorkhill but there are questions hanging over last year's Neptune Novices' Hurdle winner, who has been far from immaculate in his two runs over fences and could yet be switched to the Champion Hurdle. Mullins also has Bellshill to consider, who like Yorkhill is owned by Andrea and Graham Wylie, but the 2m4f trip could be on the short side and he fell last time in the Grade 1 Flogas Novice Chase. The Noel Meade-trained Flogas winner Disko and Eddie Harty's Coney Island are other leading Irish possibles. Nicky Henderson's chief pick from his strong team of novice chasers looks likely to be Top Notch, the Grade 1 Scilly Isles winner, and the other main British challenger is set to be the Paul Nicholls-trained Grade 2 scorer Politologue.

Yorkhill

7 ch g; Trainer Willie Mullins
Chase form 11, best RPR 150
Left-handed 1, best RPR 150
Right-handed 1 ,best RPR 145
Cheltenham form (hurdles) 1, best RPR 158
At the festival 16 Mar 2016 Took keen hold, held up in rear, not fluent 4th and 7th, not much room bend before 3 out, progressed to track leaders 2 out, squeezed through on inner to lead on bend before last, 3 lengths up and fine jump last, edged right and ridden out, won Neptune Investment Management Novices' Hurdle by a length and three-quarters from Yanworth

Excellent winner of last year's Neptune and 2-2 from fences this season, although tendency to jump left-handed has been magnified over the bigger obstacles. Trainer doesn't seem worried by it and Yorkhill will have a left-hand rail to run against if taking up this option, but bare form of those chase wins is nothing special and needed pushing out to beat the 132-rated hurdler Jett at Leopardstown. Reputation is massive, though, and hot favourite for this based on those two efforts and what he did over hurdles. This is probably still the most likely destination for him, although he is favourite with many firms with a run for the Champion Hurdle even though he needs to be supplemented. There is no doubt he is a high-class performer and

Mullins has won three of the six runnings, but wherever he goes his price is going to reflect what people think he can do rather than what he has done. That will be fair enough in the eyes of many, but in early February there were more than 20 horses among the entries who had achieved more on Racing Post Ratings over fences – a few by a fair margin – and quotes ranging from 11-8 to 5-2 are incredibly short.

Going preference Goes on anything, decent ground probably best
Star rating ✪✪✪✪

Top Notch

6 b g; Trainer Nicky Henderson
Chase form 31111, best RPR 160
Left-handed 311, best RPR 154
Right-handed 11, best RPR 160
Cheltenham form (hurdles) 255, best RPR 160
At the festival 13 Mar 2015 In touch, hit 5th, led over 2f out on long run to last, headed final 100yds, continued to challenge and stayed on, always held, finished second, beaten a neck by Peace And Co in Triumph Hurdle
15 Mar 2016 Midfield, headway approaching 3 out, 5th when mistake 2 out, ridden and outpaced before last, stayed on same pace run-in, finished fifth, beaten nine and three-quarter lengths by Annie Power in Champion Hurdle

Neck runner-up in 2015 Triumph Hurdle and

proved just below top class in that sphere last season, finishing fifth in Annie Power's Champion Hurdle. Despite lacking scope for a chaser he has made a good fist of things in his first season, winning four in a row following a debut defeat to the talented Charbel at Uttoxeter. Was particularly impressive at both Plumpton, where he jumped well to beat Romain De Senam comfortably, and Sandown in the Grade 1 Scilly Isles in which he burst clear after the last for an easy win. That is undoubtedly some of the best form on offer, but he isn't very big and, with anything that stays this far likely to avoid Altior in the Arkle, a large field might not suit him. Also has a bit to prove if the surface rides fast as he clearly loves winter soft ground.

Going preference Very much at home when it rides deep
Star rating ✪✪✪

Politologue *(right)*
6 gr g; Trainer Paul Nicholls
Chase form 1121, best RPR 158
Left-handed 12, best RPR 158
Right-handed 11, best RPR 149
Cheltenham form (hurdles) U0, best RPR 137
At the festival 16 Mar 2016 Tracked leaders, challenged from 3 out until weakened quickly soon after 2 out, finished 20th, beaten 20 lengths by Diamond King in Coral Cup

Fair hurdler if somewhat below top class and well thumped in the Coral Cup, but pinpoint jumping has enabled him to become a serious force over fences. Blew the opposition away with a ten-length success at Haydock on debut in November and made all again at Ascot in a Grade 2 before tasting first defeat in this sphere when beaten a length and a quarter by the well-regarded Waiting Patiently. Conceded

3lb to the winner, so came out just best at the weights, but had wasted a lot of energy going down to the start and was keen enough in the race itself, so was a sitting target up the home straight. Showed a good attitude once headed, though, and promises more if connections can keep a lid on his exuberance (has needed two handlers in the parade ring). Seemed to settle a lot better in a first-time hood on his warm-up at Kempton, but with only one rival it was hardly under race conditions and it remains to be seen if it works as well in a big field. Still a highly promising novice, though.

Going preference Well beaten only start on good, handles soft well
Star rating ✪✪✪

Disko
6 gr g; Trainer Noel Meade
Chase form 1331, best RPR 157
Left-handed 31, best RPR 157
Right-handed 13, best RPR 149

Fair novice hurdler but considerably better as a chaser after four starts, winning the two that were run at around the JLT trip. Hard to argue he doesn't stay 3m given he was beaten only a length by Our Duke in the Grade 1 Neville Hotels Novice Chase at Leopardstown over Christmas, but arguably put up best performance in the 2m5½f Flogas Novice Chase at the same track in February, when given his head pretty much from the off. Led after the third fence there and didn't hang around, but still had plenty in reserve to hold off Our Duke by a length and three-quarters. Easy to argue that favourite Bellshill didn't run his race (beaten when fell at the last) but a lot to like about the way Disko went about his task and plenty of 2m4f chases are

TRAINER'S VIEW
Noel Meade on Disko "He jumped so well he got the others in trouble [in the Grade 1 Flogas]. I'd say the usual Cheltenham ground will suit him all right. I'd never think he'd want quick ground. He's still young and there's no reason why he can't improve further"
Recorded RPRs of 156 and 157 in his two Grade 1 chases, on yielding and soft ground

won from the front at Cheltenham. A player if he arrives in good health, but Noel Meade's Cheltenham strike-rate is always a concern and he's still waiting for his first chase winner at the festival.

Going preference Acts on soft and yielding, much faster would be an unknown
Star rating ✪✪✪✪

Coney Island
6 b g; Trainer Edward Harty
Chase form 212, best RPR 156
Left-handed 2, best RPR 156
Right-handed 21, best RPR 150

Dealt with in more detail in the RSA Chase section on Wednesday, but a similar price for this and could easily run here in preference as he is his owner's shortest-priced contender in both. Certainly doesn't lack pace and entitled to be a player.

Going preference Seems to handle any ground
Star rating ✪✪✪

Charbel

6 b g; Trainer Kim Bailey
Chase form 12, best RPR 153
Left-handed 1, best RPR 150
Right-handed 2, best RPR 153
Cheltenham form (hurdles) 5, best RPR 150

At the festival 15 Mar 2016 Led, ridden and headed after 2 out, 4th and held when hit last, lost 4th final strides, finished fifth, beaten 12 and a half lengths by Altior in Supreme Novices' Hurdle

Had some decent form as a novice hurdler, including an 11-length drubbing of Champion Hurdle candidate Brain Power at Musselburgh and fifth in the Supreme, in which he made most of the running and battled on gamely even after a mistake at the last. In appearance he was always more likely to make a chaser, though, and Kim Bailey wasted little time in sending him over fences. Made the perfect start at Uttoxeter in October, jumping boldly from the front and holding off talented pair Le Prezien and Top Notch (this race's second favourite). Ran into a certain Altior in the Grade 1 Henry VIII Novices' Chase at Sandown in December and there was no disgrace in being beaten six lengths. Has looked for a while as though he is crying out for a step up in trip despite his pedigree (by Wokingham winner and July Cup runner-up Iffraaj and no surprise he's his best jumps offspring by a mile) and likely to get it assuming trainer wants to avoid Altior. Interesting contender.

Going preference No evidence of any preference
Star rating ✪✪✪

Whisper

9 b g; Trainer Nicky Henderson
Chase form 211, best RPR 160
Left-handed 11, best RPR 160
Right-handed 2, best RPR 137
Cheltenham form (all) 41315P811, best RPR 160
At the festival 12 Mar 2014 Always in leading group, ridden to lead before last, hard pressed flat, just held on, won Coral Cup by a short head from Get Me Out Of Here
12 Mar 2015 Mid-division, headway when not fluent 2 out, ridden to briefly dispute 2nd before last, soon no extra, finished fifth, beaten ten and a half lengths by Cole Harden in World Hurdle

17 Mar 2016 Held up, mistake 8th, soon pushed along, weakened after 2 out, eased when well beaten before last, finished eighth, beaten 46 lengths by Thistlecrack in World Hurdle

First tried fences two years but turned over at odds of 2-5 and the plan was shelved for a while. Something of a surprise, then, that he took so well to it second time but a two-and-a-half-length success over Baron Alco at Cheltenham was followed by another course success when he beat the well-regarded Clan Des Obeaux by half a length conceding 5lb. Many were of the opinion the runner-up would have won with a better jump at the last, but there's no denying Whisper's guts in a battle and the form looks strong notwithstanding a poor show from Clan Des Obeaux at Sandown next time. Another who is not always the most fluent, though, and a big field could spell danger, although he will have Davy Russell (superb at Cheltenham) doing the steering.

Going preference Has won on all types of going
Star rating ✪✪✪

Le Prezien

6 br g; Trainer Paul Nicholls
Chase form 2113, best RPR 155
Left-handed 21, best RPR 150
Right-handed 13, best RPR 155
Cheltenham form 1, best RPR 152

Decent novice hurdler last season who swerved Cheltenham but ran a below-par Yorkhill to just over two lengths at Aintree. Better as a chaser, following a three-quarter-length second to Charbel at Uttoxeter with wins at Cheltenham and Exeter, while not always jumping fluently. Those jumping flaws were cruelly exposed at Sandown in the Scilly Isles, in which he made a hatful of errors, and it's testament to his raw ability that he was beaten only six and a quarter lengths into third by Top Notch. Might have handicap options off mark of 146 and will be much better than that if cutting out the errors.

Going preference Handles soft well, but one good-ground run hardly disheartening
Star rating ✪✪

JLT NOVICES' CHASE RESULTS

	FORM WINNER	AGE & WGT	Adj RPR	SP	TRAINER	BEST RPR LAST 12 MONTHS (RUNS SINCE)
16	7-11F **Black Hercules** D, BF	7 11-4	169-2	4-1c	W Mullins (IRE)	won Warwick Listed nov ch (3m) **(1)**
15	-1121 **Vautour** C, D	6 11-4	165-10	6-4f	W Mullins (IRE)	won Leop Gd2 nov ch (2m3f) **(0)**
14	11321 **Taquin Du Seuil** C, D	7 11-4	167-6	7-1	J O'Neill	won Haydock Gd2 nov ch (2m5f) **(0)**
13	21241 **Benefficient** D	7 11-4	161-8	20-1	A Martin (IRE)	won Leop Gd1 Arkle nov ch (2m1f) **(0)**
12	1-111 **Sir Des Champs** C, D	6 11-4	161-8	3-1	W Mullins (IRE)	won Limerick Gd2 nov ch (2m3½f) **(1)**
11	4-122 **Noble Prince** D	7 11-4	164-6	4-1	P Nolan (IRE)	2nd Leop Gd1 Arkle nov ch (2m1f) **(0)**

WINS-RUNS: 5yo 0-4, 6yo 2-21, 7yo 4-25, 8yo 0-9, 9yo 0-4 **FAVOURITES:** -£1.84

TRAINERS IN THIS RACE (w-pl-r): Willie Mullins 3-1-11, Alan King 0-1-1, Colin Tizzard 0-0-1, Dan Skelton 0-0-1, David Pipe, 0-1-3, Harry Fry 0-0-1, Henry de Bromhead 0-1-2, Noel Meade 0-1-2, Nicky Henderson 0-1-7, Nigel Twiston-Davies 0-3-5, Paul Nicholls 0-0-7, Philip Hobbs 0-1-4, Venetia Williams 0-0-1

FATE OF FAVOURITES: 202411 **POSITION OF WINNER IN MARKET:** 227411

Key trends

🏇Adjusted RPR of at least 161, 6/6

🏇Rated within 8lb of RPR top-rated, 5/6

🏇Won a Grade 1 or 2 chase, 4/6

🏇Graded winner over hurdles, 4/6

🏇Distance winner, 6/6

🏇Ran over hurdles at a previous festival, 6/6

Other factors

🏇Four winners won last time out – of the two exceptions, one was beaten a short head on their previous start while the other fell when likely to win

🏇Two winners had won over hurdles at a previous festival and both were trained by Willie Mullins (Sir Des Champs and Vautour)

OTHERS TO CONSIDER

Even with Yorkhill in the field this looks incredibly open at this stage – and it will be even more so if he switches to the Champion Hurdle. Paul Nicholls could end up mob-handed as the likes of **Frodon** and **Clan Des Obeaux** are also entered, while Gordon Elliott's **Diamond King** could run here depending on what the handicapper does with his Irish chase rating of 146. He won the Coral Cup over hurdles off 149 last season and could be one for the Plate. **Shantou Village** (*right*) is a bit of a forgotten horse after a heavy fall at Wincanton in November, but he started well enough in the autumn and

it's worth remembering he went off favourite for the Albert Bartlett last year. Looking a long way further down the list, Elliott's **Tiger Roll**, a Triumph Hurdle winner, has one run to his name (among plenty of poorer ones) that would put him right in the mix too.

VERDICT

There are plenty who are not prepared to look much beyond Yorkhill, but this could end up the most competitive of the three Grade 1 novice chases and his jumping – far from convincing in my book – is enough of a worry for me to take him on. I've backed POLITOLOGUE, whose fencing is his chief asset and who could get plenty of them in trouble if taking to the track better than he did in last year's Coral Cup. At the prices Charbel is the other one who interests me most.

2.10 Pertemps Final (Handicap Hurdle)   ITV/RUK
3m   Listed   £95,000

This race has tended to lack the quality of some of the other festival handicaps and Cheltenham has taken steps to rectify that by changing the conditions – as of 2016, horses are eligible to run in the final only if they finished in the first six in one of the 17 qualifiers.

Over the longer term, last-time-out winners have a strong record (11 winners in the past 21 years), although five of the exceptions have been in the past seven years.

Favourites have a poor record, with Fingal Bay in 2014 only the second market leader to have won in the past 19 runnings. Call The Cops at 9-1 in 2015 was the only other winner since 2003 to be sent off less than double-figure odds.

The bottomweight tends to run off a mark around the mid-130s nowadays and the best place to find the winner is from there up to 144 (Mall Dini was rated 139 last year). More specifically, five of the last six winners have been rated between 138 and 142 (the exception was Fingal Bay off 148).

The home team has dominated since the turn of the millennium with 13 of the 16 winners. Oulart (2005), Kadoun (2006) and Mall Dini have been the only Irish-trained winners in that period.

PERTEMPS FINAL RESULTS AND TRENDS

	FORM WINNER	AGE & WGT	OR	SP	TRAINER	BEST RPR LAST 12 MONTHS (RUNS SINCE)
16	31433 Mall Dini	6 10-11	139-7	14-1	P Kelly (IRE)	won Thurles mdn hdl (2m6½f) (3)
15	21-41 Call The Cops (5x) D	6 10-12	138-5	9-1	N Henderson	won Donc class 2 hcap hdl (3m½f) (0)
14	120-1 Fingal Bay C, D	8 11-12	148T	9-2f	P Hobbs	won Exeter class 2 hcap hdl (2m7½f) (0)
13	-2222 Holywell	6 11-4	140-5	25-1	J O'Neill	2nd Warwick class 2 hcap hdl (3m1f) (0)
12	5P504 Cape Tribulation D	8 10-11	142-3	14-1	M Jefferson	5th Haydock Gd3 hcap hdl (3m) (1)
11	28700 Buena Vista CD	10 10-3	138-4	20-1	D Pipe	won Pertemps Final (3m) (6)
10	-8508 Buena Vista	9 10-1	133-1	16-1	D Pipe	5th Haydock Listed hcap hdl (3m1f) (2)
09	26211 Kayf Aramis D	7 10-5	129-7	16-1	V Williams	won Warwick class 3 nov hdl (3m1f) (0)
08	-1271 Ballyfitz D	8 10-8	132-3	18-1	N Twiston-Davies	won Haydock class 2 hcap hdl (3m) (0)
07	2-2F0 Oscar Park	8 10-9	140T	14-1	D Arbuthnot	2nd Newbury class 2 hcap hdl (3m½f) (2)

WINS-RUNS: 5yo 0-16, 6yo 3-51, 7yo 1-64, 8yo 4-50, 9yo 1-23, 10yo 1-16, 11yo 0-12, 12yo 0-1, 13yo 0-2 **FAVOURITES:** -£4.50

FATE OF FAVOURITES: 0200000100 **POSITION OF WINNER IN MARKET:** 7005960136

Key trends

- Winning form between 2m4f and 2m6f, 9/10
- Carried no more than 11st 4lb, 9/10
- Aged six to eight, 8/10
- Officially rated 132 to 142, 8/10
- Six to ten runs over hurdles, 8/10 (exceptions 22-plus)
- Won a Class 2 or higher, 7/10
- Off track between 20 and 48 days, 7/10
- Won over at least 3m, 6/10

Other factors

- Creon in 2004 was the last winner from out of the handicap (2lb wrong)
- Five winners had run at the festival before, including a dual winner (Buena Vista) who recorded a top-two finish in this race the previous year
- Pragada in 1988 is the only winning five-year-old in the race's 42-year history, while Buena Vista in 2011 was the first horse aged older than nine to oblige since 1981

2.50 Ryanair Chase
2m5f Grade 1 £300,000

ITV/RUK

Vautour was a somewhat controversial supersub for Willie Mullins when taking last year's Ryanair and Ireland's champion trainer again has the favourite with Un De Sceaux, beaten at odds-on by Sprinter Sacre in last year's Champion Chase. Un De Sceaux has won the Grade 1 Tingle Creek and Clarence House over 2m on his two starts this season but Mullins indicated he would step up in distance for the Ryanair. While Un De Sceaux has won over the 2m5f trip, that form was over hurdles in France and his jumping is not bombproof. Alan King's Uxizandre, winner of this race in 2015, was having his first outing since then when a five-length runner-up in the Clarence House and is set to reoppose over this more suitable trip. Other Irish possibles include Sizing John and Empire Of Dirt, first and second in the Irish Gold Cup last time, and Sub Lieutenant. Nicky Henderson, twice successful in this race, has an interesting challenger in Peterborough Chase winner Josses Hill, who has got his act together over fences this season.

Un De Sceaux
9 b g; Trainer Willie Mullins
Chase form F1111F12211, best RPR 174
Left-handed 11F21, best RPR 174
Right-handed F11121, best RPR 172
Cheltenham form 12, best RPR 170
At the festival 10 Mar 2015 Raced with zest, made most, shaken up approaching last, quickened clear final 110yds, ran on well, won Racing Post Arkle by six lengths from God's Own 16 Mar 2016 Tracked leader, hit 4th, led after 4 out, ridden when headed before 2 out, soon held by winner, kept on same pace, finished second, beaten three and a half lengths by Sprinter Sacre in Champion Chase

Has the Champion Chase as an option and hasn't tried this trip over fences yet, but stayed it well over hurdles and you'd have to think it is his most likely target with stablemate Douvan such a hot favourite on the Wednesday. It will certainly take a good one to beat him as the only horse who has when he has stood up over fences is Sprinter Sacre in last season's Champion Chase and again at Sandown. Sometimes throws in the odd scrappy jump but has largely been excellent this year and beat the best of the British in the 2m Tingle Creek and Clarence House Chases, being particularly impressive in the latter. That confirmed he is still as good as ever at the age of nine and the 2015 Arkle winner is a worthy favourite, especially now he seems more amenable to restraint. We will have to see if that is the case going up in trip but there is unlikely to be much hanging around.

Going preference Goes very well on soft but does act on good
Star rating ✪✪✪✪

Uxizandre
9 ch g; Trainer Alan King
Chase form (all left-handed) 11521418U12, best RPR 174
Cheltenham form 2112, best RPR 174
At the festival 13 Mar 2014 Held up in rear, jumped slowly 4th and 12th, headway to track leaders after 4 out, driven to dispute close 2nd 2 out, challenged last and stayed upsides until led under pressure final 75yds, stayed on well, finished second, beaten three-quarters of a length by Taquin Du Seuil in JLT Novices' Chase 12 Mar 2015 Made all, steadily went clear from 8th, reduced advantage 4 out, jumped left 3 out, found extra approaching last and about 3 lengths up, ran on well, in command final 100yds, won Ryanair Chase by five lengths from Ma Filleule

High-class chaser who is very much a spring horse having won at both the Cheltenham and Aintree festivals in his time. Finished second in the 2014 JLT as a novice having tried to

make all. Having run poorly in the Game Spirit in his prep for the 2015 Ryanair, he was sent off at 16-1 but left his Newbury form well behind with a string of prodigious leaps from the front and this time had more than enough in hand after the last to get the job done by five lengths from Ma Filleule, with subsequent Gold Cup winner Don Cossack back in third. Unfortunately an injury meant he missed all of last season and he wasn't seen again on the track until the rescheduled Clarence House Chase at Cheltenham in January, when he exceeded Alan King's wildest dreams by rattling home for a five-length second to Un De Sceaux having looked to be going nowhere at halfway. There's a chance he was slightly flattered with the pace looking fairly strong, but nevertheless it was an excellent return for a horse considered very much in need of the outing. Clearly loves Cheltenham and will be happier on better ground, and so as long as he doesn't recoil from that return he must have a fair shot again.

Going preference Handles soft but very much at home on a decent surface
Star rating ✪✪✪✪

TRAINER'S VIEW

Alan King on Uxizandre "I couldn't have been more pleased with Uxizandre if I'd been standing in the winner's enclosure [after his comeback second at Cheltenham]. He took a right old blow after the race and will come on an awful lot for what was his first race for almost two years" *RPR of 168 in the Clarence House was a career best over 2m, exceeded only by his 174 for winning the 2m5f Ryanair Chase in 2015*

Sizing John *(above)*

7 b g; Trainer Jessica Harrington
Chase form 112233211, best RPR 168
Left-handed 22321, best RPR 168
Right-handed 1131, best RPR 166
Cheltenham form (all) 32, best RPR 156
At the festival 10 Mar 2015 Tracked leader, led 2 out, soon ridden, headed before last, kept on but no extra when lost 2nd run-in, finished third, beaten seven lengths by Douvan in Supreme Novices' Hurdle
15 Mar 2016 Led, headed 3rd, remained in close 2nd place until before 3 out, outpaced on bend before hampered and left 2nd 2 out, stayed on run-in but no chance with winner, finished second, beaten seven lengths by Douvan in Racing Post Arkle

Had spent much of the previous two seasons staring at Douvan's backside over two miles, and it was the same again over Christmas when he was second in the Paddy Power Chase at Leopardstown, but step up in trip has worked wonders with wins over 2m4f and then 3m in the Irish Gold Cup. Entitled to be a player here, but given owners' desire for Gold looks more likely to be running on Friday and dealt with in more detail in that section.

Going preference Handles soft but always considered better on a decent surface
Star rating ✪✪✪✪

Josses Hill

9 b g; Trainer Nicky Henderson
Chase form 21234F18115, best RPR 165
Left-handed 1348, best RPR 161
Right-handed 22F1115, best RPR 165
Cheltenham form (all) 238, best RPR 161
At the festival 11 Mar 2014 In touch, pushed along to challenge for places approaching last, stayed on to take 2nd final 110yds, no chance with winner, finished second, beaten six lengths by Vautour in Neptune Investment Management Novices' Hurdle
10 Mar 2015 In touch, not fluent 5th, dropped to midfield 6th, mistake 8th, effort to chase leaders approaching 3 out where not fluent, stayed on same pace under pressure from last,

finished third, beaten eight lengths by Douvan in Racing Post Arkle
17 Mar 2016 Chased leaders, not fluent 12th, soon pushed along, outpaced after 3 out, weakened last, finished eighth, beaten 22 lengths by Vautour in Ryanair Chase

High-class performer but a slow learner over fences due to his seeming inability to arch his back properly. That didn't stop him showing decent form, though, as when third in the Arkle as a novice, but he took a crashing fall in the 2015 Tingle Creek and after beating God's Own at Kempton (where he goes so well) he made no show in the Ryanair last season. However, his jumping seems to have become much more fluent this season and a win in a two-runner conditions chase at Kempton was followed by his best run in the Peterborough Chase, which he won by six lengths from Tea For Two. Seemingly got outpaced about a mile from home when stepped up to 3m for the King George and, while he attempted to rally entering the straight, he didn't quite see the trip out, finishing last of five, although beaten only seven lengths. This is the right race for him, but it remains to be seen whether it's the right track as he does seem best suited by going right-handed.

Going preference Acts on any
Star rating ✪✪

Sub Lieutenant

8 b g; Trainer Henry de Bromhead
Chase form 342341P31132, best RPR 164
Left-handed 3341, best RPR 147
Right-handed 42P31132, best RPR 164

Grade 3 novice chase winner at Naas last year who is enjoying his best season. Began campaign with two clear-cut wins at Limerick and in a Grade 2 at Down Royal, where he was particularly impressive in seeing off subsequent Irish Lexus Chase winner Outlander, although he did have the benefit of a run. Comparable form on next two starts, although defeats by Djakadam and Sizing John reveal his limitations. Also in the Gold Cup and was tried in the 3m5f Irish National last season, but clear best form at 2m4f and

owner sure to have at least one runner in race he sponsors.
Going preference Acts well on soft, but sole good-ground run among his best
Star rating ✪✪

Black Hercules

8 b g; Trainer Willie Mullins
Chase form 11F1543, best RPR 164
Left-handed 11F14, best RPR 164
Right-handed 53, best RPR 156
Cheltenham form (all) 471, best RPR 164
At the festival 12 Mar 2014 Led at good pace, driven and headed over 1f out, one pace after, finished fourth, beaten three and three-quarter lengths by Silver Concorde in Champion Bumper
13 Mar 2015 Held up, headway approaching 2 out where 7th, no impression on leaders and beaten after, finished seventh, beaten 35 lengths by Martello Tower in Albert Bartlett Novices' Hurdle
17 Mar 2016 Led until after 2nd, tracked leader, upsides from 9th, hit 3 out, ridden in 1 length 2nd when hampered next, led narrowly last, stayed on well to draw clear in JLT Novices' Chase, beating Bristol De Mai by three lengths

Took really well to fences last season and would have been unbeaten in four runs had he not fallen at the last when well in command at Navan in February. Did not let that affect his confidence when jumping really well and winning what looked a strong JLT by three lengths from Bristol De Mai (now rated 166), so it's a bit of a mystery what has gone wrong so far this season. Could not really have been expected to beat Djakadam or Douvan on first two starts, but was beaten a long way in both and wasn't much better when third to Sizing John at Thurles. Always a chance he could bounce back but unlikely to have Ruby Walsh in the saddle assuming Un De Sceaux runs, so not a likely shortener in the run-up.

Going preference Handles any
Star rating ✪

Empire Of Dirt

10 b g; Trainer Gordon Elliott
Chase form 4F32F1FF2P1112, best RPR 167
Left-handed 431FP1112, best RPR 167
Right-handed F2FF2, best RPR 144
Cheltenham form 1, best RPR 154

At the festival 17 Mar 2016 Held up behind, badly hampered 3rd, steady progress from 11th, led approaching 2 out, soon ridden, wandered run-in but well in command, readily, won Plate handicap chase by four lengths from Tango De Juilley

A slow-burner whose progress was checked at least in part by a tendency to clout the odd fence. Was rated only 123 two years ago and fell three times in four starts, but started to get his act together last season for Colm Murphy and hasn't looked back since winning the Leopardstown Handicap Chase off 133 in January last year. Rocked up at the festival for the Plate and travelled supremely well off a 9lb higher mark to win by four lengths and then repeated that margin of success stepped back up to 3m on his return in the Troytown, winning pretty much as he liked on his first run for Gordon Elliott. First foray into Grade 1 company was pretty good too as he went down by just three-quarters of a length to Sizing John in the Irish Gold Cup. No doubt that he stays 3m, but trainer believes Gold Cup trip and tempo of the race will stretch him and reckons the Ryanair is the right race given the way he travels. Would need to step up again, but has done so in leaps and bounds on every run for a year, so despite being a ten-year-old it's not impossible.

Going preference Has stepped up on soft ground this season but last year's festival win was on good
Star rating ✪✪✪✪

Zabana
8 ch g; Trainer Andrew Lynch
Chase form 14U1417, best RPR 158
Left-handed 14U7, best RPR 157
Right-handed 141, best RPR 158
Cheltenham form (all) 2U, best RPR 150
At the festival 11 Mar 2015 Led, pressed when mistake 3 out, driven and headed last, rallied well flat, just held, finished second, beaten a neck by Aux Ptits Soins in Coral Cup
17 Mar 2016 Sideways on when shied at tapes and unseated rider start in JLT Novices' Chase won by Black Hercules

Eight-time winner who acts on any ground,

but does a lot of his best running when it dries out and put up a career best at the time over hurdles when second in the 2015 Coral Cup. Returned to the festival as a novice chaser last year and had been backed into 8-1 from much longer odds for the JLT, but was unable to show what he could do because he was sideways on when the starter let them go and he unseated, with jockey Davy Russell quite rightly fuming. Compensation awaited, though, as Zabana lowered the colours of Outlander in the 3m1f Grade 1 Champion Novice Chase at Punchestown. Probably at least as good in three starts this season, though didn't seem to see out the 3m trip so well on yielding ground in the Lexus when 16 lengths behind winner Outlander and was pulled out of the Irish Gold Cup due to the very soft ground. Also in the Gold Cup but doubtful stayer and needs to find plenty of improvement to be competitive in either race.

Going preference Prefers better ground
Star rating ✪✪

Taquin Du Seuil
10 b/br g; Trainer Jonjo O'Neill
Chase form 11321132P4916515, best RPR 166
Left-handed 1121132P4916515, best RPR 166
Right-handed 3, best RPR 152
Cheltenham form (all) 6121961, best RPR 166
At the festival 13 Mar 2013 Chased leaders from 3rd, went 2nd briefly 2 out, weakened under pressure before last, finished sixth, beaten 17 lengths by The New One in Neptune Investment Management Novices' Hurdle
13 Mar 2014 Held up in rear, jumped slowly 4th and 12th, headway to track leaders after 4 out, driven to dispute close 2nd 2 out, challenged last and stayed upsides until led under pressure final 75yds, stayed on well, won JLT Novices' Chase by three-quarters of a length from Uxizandre
12 Mar 2015 Held up, hit 10th, steady headway into midfield when blundered 4 out, struggling when mistake 3 out, well beaten after, finished ninth, beaten 38 lengths by Uxizandre in Ryanair Chase
17 Mar 2016 Held up, mistake 4 out, some headway next, soon ridden, hit last, stayed on run-in, never threatened leaders, finished sixth, beaten 13 and a quarter lengths by Vautour in Ryanair Chase

Has had a bit of a chequered career but always been very talented especially when the mud is flying. Showed he didn't always need it bottomless when winning the JLT from Uxizandre as a seven-year-old three years ago, and went into summer quarters considered a live contender for the next season's Gold Cup. However, things didn't pan out and he endured a difficult season, only to remind people how good he could be when bolting up in a soft-ground handicap on his return last February. Could manage only sixth in last year's Ryanair on better ground, though, and does seem more surface-dependent now. Was certainly helped by the deteriorating ground conditions in the BetVictor Gold Cup in November, in which he was a battling winner from course specialist Village Vic off a mark of 156. Hard to say he didn't stay when fifth in the Lexus as he was plugging on, but it wasn't quite his form. Only Al Ferof has won the BetVictor off a higher mark and deep ground would have to give him a fair shot of being in the shake-up. Best left alone given normal spring conditions, though.

Going preference Has some form on good but loves the mud
Star rating ✪✪

Fox Norton

7 b g; Trainer Colin Tizzard
Chase form 11233331112, best RPR 170
Left-handed 233331112, best RPR 170
Right-handed 11, best RPR 147
Cheltenham form 23111, best RPR 170
At the festival 15 Mar 2016 Tracked leaders, pushed along and lost place after 3 out, outpaced after, slightly hampered 2 out, kept on to take 3rd final 75yds, no chance, finished third, beaten 11 lengths in Racing Post Arkle by Douvan

Dealt with in more detail for the Champion Chase in Wednesday's section, but if Sizing John goes for the Gold Cup there's always a chance he'll come here instead of banging his head against the brick wall that is Douvan. Trainer said he has suspects he's a 2m4f horse really, but has yet to race over such a trip.

Going preference Used to be considered a good-ground performer but best form now on soft
Star rating ✪✪

OTHERS TO CONSIDER

Cue Card has been deliberately left out of calculations despite being joint-favourite as his owners have confirmed him on target for another crack at the Gold Cup. He's a former winner who would have a clear chance, but shapes more and more like an out-and-out stayer these days. It's also hard to believe **Vroum Vroum Mag** will be asked to run in her first chase for nearly two years (she'd need to improve a stone on her chase form anyway and quotes of 5-1 with a run are laughable). **Bristol De Mai** is now much shorter for this than he is for the Gold Cup after his tame (and lame) performance in the Denman Chase, but Nigel Twiston-Davies is still looking towards the Gold Cup if he can get him back in time, while connections of **Champagne West** are also leaning towards gold after his Thyestes Chase romp. **Champagne Fever** might turn up but isn't good enough any more, while **Village Vic** needs it soft and **Vaniteux** has largely been disappointing. **Traffic Fluide** has the form if he stays and comes on dramatically for his run in the Game Spirit (too free on first start for a year). **God's Own** doesn't appear to quite stay the trip.

VERDICT

It is hard to quibble with Un De Sceaux's position as favourite, but the competition is arguably deeper at this trip than it is at 2m and he'll have plenty of different rivals to face. Uxizandre has been there and done it before, but it's not absolutely guaranteed he'll come on for his return in the Clarence House as he had a hard race there and could recoil. EMPIRE OF DIRT is a strong traveller who just seems to get better and better and might well appreciate dropping back in trip, so he just gets the each-way vote at double-figure odds.

RYANAIR CHASE RESULTS AND TRENDS

	FORM WINNER	AGE & WGT	Adj RPR	SP	TRAINER	BEST RPR LAST 12 MONTHS (RUNS SINCE)
16	11-12 **Vautour** CD	7 11-10	184^T	Evensf	W Mullins (IRE)	2nd Gd1 King George Chase (3m) (0)
15	-418U **Uxizandre** C	7 11-10	170^{-5}	16-1	A King	Won Cheltenham Listed chase (2m) (2)
14	21-25 **Dynaste** C, D, BF	8 11-10	179^T	3-1f	D Pipe	2nd Gd1 Betfair Chase (3m1f) (1)
13	2-151 **Cue Card** C, D	7 11-10	174^{-2}	7-2	C Tizzard	won Gd1 Ascot Chase (2m5½f) (0)
12	121-1 **Riverside Theatre** D	8 11-10	176^T	7-2f	N Henderson	won Gd1 Ascot Chase (2m5½f) (0)
11	1-4FP **Albertas Run** CD	10 11-10	176^{-1}	6-1	J O'Neill	won Gd1 Melling Chase (2m4f) (3)
10	P1362 **Albertas Run** C, D	9 11-10	171^{-3}	14-1	J O'Neill	won Ascot Gd2 chase (2m3f) (3)
09	14-16 **Imperial Commander** C, D	8 11-10	165^{-19}	6-1	N Twiston-Davies	won Paddy Power Gold Cup (2m4½f) (1)
08	23-22 **Our Vic** CD, BF	10 11-10	176^{-2}	4-1	D Pipe	2nd Gd1 King George VI Chase (3m) (1)
07	-1F31 **Taranis** CD	6 11-0	169^{-13}	9-2	P Nicholls	3rd Gd3 Boylesports Gold Cup (2m5f) (0)

WINS-RUNS: 6yo 1-4, 7yo 3-18, 8yo 3-39, 9yo 1-29, 10yo 2-12, 11yo 0-7, 12yo 0-3 **FAVOURITES:** £0.50

TRAINERS IN THIS Jonjo O'Neill 2-1-7, Alan King 1-2-7, Colin Tizzard 1-0-3, Nicky Henderson 1-2-12, Nigel Twiston-Davies 1-0-3, Paul Nicholls 1-2-12, Willie Mullins 1-2-9, Gordon Elliott 0-1-1, Mouse Morris 0-1-2, Noel Meade 0-1-1, Philip Hobbs 0-0-7, Dan Skelton 0-0-1, Tom George 0-0-1, Evan Williams 0-0-1, Henry de Bromhead 0-0-1, Jessica Harrington 0-0-3

FATE OF FAVOURITES: 4522412131 **POSITION OF WINNER IN MARKET:** 3228212181

Key trends

🐎Adjusted RPR of at least 165, 10/10

🐎Course winner, 9/10

🐎No more than four runs since October, 9/10

🐎At least seven runs over fences, 8/10

🐎Top-two finish in at least one of last two starts, 8/10

🐎From the first three in the market, 8/10

Other factors

🐎Four of the seven beaten favourites had won a Grade 1 chase last time out

🐎Five winners had recorded a top-four finish in a Grade 1 or 2 chase over 3m-plus (four of the other five achieved that subsequently)

🐎The first five winners (2005-2009) had either won or been placed in the BetVictor Gold Cup or Caspian Caviar Gold Cup, but none of the last seven had run in either

Notes

3.30 Sun Bets Stayers' Hurdle
ITV/RUK

3m   Grade 1   £300,000

At last year's festival Unowhatimeanharry completed a remarkable rise through the ranks with victory in the Albert Bartlett Novices' Hurdle and he has gone even higher this season, capturing three of the most important staying races to take his winning run to eight under the guidance of Harry Fry. In that period he has risen 44lb to a mark of 167 and is a worthy favourite here. The chief danger could be the 2014 Champion Hurdle winner Jezki, if he is given the go-ahead to take on Unowhatimeanharry in the same JP McManus colours. Willie Mullins has plenty of options, with Vroum Vroum Mag, Shaneshill, Nichols Canyon and Clondaw Warrior all possibles. Another leading British hope is 2015 winner Cole Harden, beaten just under two lengths when runner-up to Unowhatimeanharry in the Cleeve Hurdle last time.

Unowhatimeanharry
9 b g; Trainer Harry Fry
Hurdles form 3335334237P11111111, best RPR 167
Left-handed 33534111111, best RPR 167
Right-handed 3237P11, best RPR 167
Cheltenham form 1111, best RPR 167
At the festival 18 Mar 2016 Held up, hampered 8th, headway after 3 out, pushed along after 2 out, switched left before last where carried left, mistake and led, soon hung right, kept on well towards finish, won Albert Bartlett Hurdle by a length and a quarter from Fagan

Did not get off the mark over hurdles until his 12th start two years after the first, but that coincided with a move from Helen Nelmes to Harry Fry and it's fair to say he hasn't looked back since. Went through last season unbeaten and was a battling winner of the Albert Bartlett at the festival on his final start. However, many were under the impression it was a substandard renewal and, having gone into the race on a mark of 152, he came out of it on 149. The horse certainly didn't know, though, as he reappeared in the Grade 2 Long Distance Hurdle at Newbury and proceeded to bolt up by six lengths from Ballyoptic. Two more wins have followed, with a four-and-a-half-length success from Lil Rockerfeller in the Long Walk at Ascot (Ballyoptic had probably just been mastered when coming down at the last) and his Trials Day success in the Cleeve from 2015

winner Cole Harden under an 8lb penalty. Certainly knows how to battle when the chips are down and hard to knock a horse who keeps winning, so he goes there with a solid favourite's chance.

Going preference Goes very well on soft, but seems versatile
Star rating ✪✪✪✪

Jezki
9 b g; Trainer Jessica Harrington
Hurdles form 1111311124112234111, best RPR 171
Left-handed 1113241234111, best RPR 171
Right-handed 1111121, best RPR 168
Cheltenham form 314, best RPR 171
At the festival 12 Mar 2013 Midfield, headway to track leaders 3 out, effort and switched left when mistake last, stayed on same pace final 75yds, finished third, beaten two and three-quarter lengths by Champagne Fever in Supreme Novices' Hurdle
11 Mar 2014 Took keen hold, tracked leaders, not fluent 4 out, slight lead 2 out, edged left and ridden approaching last, stayed on well under pressure run-in, all out, won Champion Hurdle by a neck from My Tent Or Yours
10 Mar 2015 Raced keenly, upsides and in 2nd place from 3 out, ridden and not quicken approaching last where mistake and lost 2nd, stayed on same pace run-in, finished fourth, beaten eight and a quarter lengths by Faugheen in Champion Hurdle

The 2014 Champion Hurdle winner is rated

the same as ownermate Unowhatimeanharry and has been a better horse in his prime. Appeared to have lost a bit of his speed the year after his big win and could manage only fourth to the brilliant Faugheen in his defence, but won 2m4f Aintree Hurdle afterwards and then made successful step up to 3m in the World Series Hurdle at Punchestown. Whether that was just a case of beating the non-staying Hurricane Fly and a lot of substandard rivals is hard to tell, but unfortunately Jezki suffered an injury and wasn't seen again until reappearing over 2m at Navan in January. He won very nicely there but was getting 6lb from a horse rated 18lb inferior. Ran on heavy ground in the Red Mills Trial Hurdle at Gowran after that but beaten by Navan third Tombstone and took big walk in market for this and Champion Hurdle. Trainer Jessica Harrington wasn't unduly concerned, though, reasoning that he'd been beaten on heavy ground several times before. Decision over festival target is still apparently some way off, but no doubt he'll enjoy better ground wherever he goes.

Going preference Acts on any but always considered best on decent going
Star rating ✪✪✪

Nichols Canyon *(below)*
7 b g; Trainer Willie Mullins
Hurdles form 11U131111333312F, best RPR 166
Left-handed U131133332F, best RPR 166
Right-handed 11111, best RPR 166
Cheltenham form 33, best RPR 166
At the festival 11 Mar 2015 Took keen hold, held up in midfield, closed 3 out, challenged and mistake 2 out, stayed on same pace before last, finished third, beaten five lengths by Windsor Park in Neptune Investment Management Novices' Hurdle
15 Mar 2016 Always prominent, not fluent 3rd, ridden and not quicken between last

2, blundered last, stayed on under pressure run-in and challenging for 2nd near finish, no chance with winner, finished third, beaten four and three-quarter lengths by Annie Power in Champion Hurdle

Group-class performer on the Flat in his younger days and capable of very high-class hurdles form on his day. Pick of his efforts include a defeat of Faugheen at Punchestown (taking his record right-handed to 4-4, now 5-5) and third place in last season's Champion Hurdle. Returned looking as good as ever at Punchestown in November when slamming Jer's Girl by 12 lengths, but wheels have come off somewhat since. Proved no match for Petit Mouchoir when sent off 2-5 for the Ryanair Hurdle at Leopardstown over Christmas and went down by seven lengths – and a similar beating was in the offing in the Irish Champion Hurdle until he fell at the last. That leaves him with questions to answer over any trip and he didn't quite convince with his staying effort in the 2m5f Neptune in March 2015 and was tailed off over 2m4f on soft at Aintree last year. Got a lot closer in 3m Iroquois Hurdle in America in May, but RPR of 144 tells you all you need to know about the quality.

Going preference Acts on any
Star rating ✪✪

Vroum Vroum Mag

8 b m; Trainer Willie Mullins
Hurdles form 121111211, best RPR 157
Left-handed 12111, best RPR 155
Right-handed 1112, best RPR 157
Cheltenham form 1, best RPR 146
At the festival 15 Mar 2016 Towards rear of midfield, smooth headway from 4 out, tracked leaders 2 out, led before last, ran on well, ridden out, won OLBG Mares' Hurdle by two and three-quarter lengths from Rock On The Moor

Won 3m Christmas Hurdle on first attempt at the trip at Leopardstown over Christmas but was pretty much all out to beat the 155-rated Clondaw Warrior by a length and a quarter and probably only just stayed. Would need to run a career best to win this, but the Stayers' is far more plausible than the Champion

Hurdle, especially given her lacklustre win back at 2m at Doncaster last time. Hard to believe she's going anywhere other than the Mares' Hurdle, though.

Going preference Acts on any
Star rating ✪✪

Shaneshill

8 b g; Trainer Willie Mullins
Hurdles form 122132F233F1, best RPR 159
Left-handed 22223F, best RPR 159
Right-handed 113F31, best RPR 155
Cheltenham form (all) 222, best RPR 162
At the festival 12 Mar 2014 Well placed behind leaders, closed 3f out on inner, ridden to lead over 1f out, headed just inside final furlong, stayed on but held after, finished second, beaten a length and a half by Silver Concorde in Champion Bumper
10 Mar 2015 Tracked leaders, ridden to chase leader after 2 out, stayed on run-in but not going pace of winner, finished second, beaten four and a half lengths by Douvan in Supreme Novices' Hurdle
16 Mar 2016 Held up, hit 2nd and 11th, headway after 3 out, challenged next, ridden between last 2, jumped slightly left last, led very briefly soon after, stayed on well with every chance, held towards finish, finished second, beaten half a length by Blaklion in RSA Chase

Super-consistent performer at a range of distances who has tended to save his best for the festival, finishing runner-up three times on the spin. Showed his versatility by finishing second to Blaklion in the RSA and then occupying the same spot behind Thistlecrack back over hurdles at Aintree. Has since been kept to the smaller obstacles and seems as good as ever. Had just been headed but was battling on when falling at the last in the Christmas Hurdle won by Vroum Vroum Mag at Leopardstown and warmed up with a Grade 2 win from Snow Falcon on soft ground at Gowran. Needs more to challenge the favourite, but not that much and you have to respect his Cheltenham record.

Going preference Happiest on decent ground
Star rating ✪✪✪

Cole Harden

8 b g; Trainer Warren Greatrex
Hurdles form 41127212341233432, best RPR 168
Left-handed 4117212341233432, best RPR 168
Right-handed 2, best RPR 129
Cheltenham form 73413432, best RPR 168
At the festival 12 Mar 2014 Led, jumped left 1st, blundered 7th, headed 3 out, steadily weakened before last, finished seventh, beaten 15 lengths by Faugheen in Neptune Investment Management Novices' Hurdle
12 Mar 2015 Jumped slightly left at times, made all, clear 5th, hit 7th and next where reduced advantage, ridden 3 lengths clear again approaching last, stayed on strongly, won World Hurdle by three and a quarter lengths from Saphir Du Rheu
17 Mar 2016 Led, ridden and headed just before 2 out, outpaced by front pair between last 2, well held and lost 3rd run-in, finished fourth, beaten 31 lengths by Thistlecrack in World Hurdle

Brave and convincing winner of 2015 running from the front, but seemed slightly below par last season and managed only three outings during the campaign. Would not have beaten Thistlecrack even on his best form in last year's renewal but 31-length defeat was not him and things did not look too rosy when he was sent over fences at Wetherby and finished a well-beaten second at odds-on, having never really taken a cut at the bigger obstacles. Was a shade better back over hurdles with cheekpieces added to his usual tongue-tie on New Year's Day when third over an inadequate 2m4f and then hinted there may be even better days ahead when second to Unowhatimeanharry in the Cleeve, beaten just under two lengths. It's true he was receiving 8lb, but that run represented not far off his best form when the ground is soft and in normal spring conditions he will be a lot happier. A year younger than the favourite, so a long way from a spent force in the staying hurdle game, and could be a major player if ground is right.

Going preference Best form on decent surface
Star rating ✪✪✪

Clondaw Warrior

10 br g; Trainer Willie Mullins
Hurdles form 135609237B23121123, best RPR 159
Left-handed 3B32, best RPR 159
Right-handed 135602723111, best RPR 156
Cheltenham form (bumper) 1, best RPR 120

Excellent dual-purpose performer who enjoyed his best year in 2016, finishing third in the Scottish Champion Hurdle and the Queen Alexandra Stakes at Royal Ascot before landing the Galway Hurdle off a mark of 142 by half a length from Hidden Cyclone. He even went to America to run in the American St Leger, in which he finished second, and closed the year with an excellent second to Vroum Vroum Mag in the Christmas Hurdle at Leopardstown, coming off best at the weights. Sent off favourite but not quite at his best in small-field Galmoy Hurdle at Gowran in January, finishing only third to Shaneshill, who is likely to reoppose. Will need a career best at the age of ten to play a hand – the last winner older than nine was Crimson Embers in 1986 – but he is a big-field specialist who has won eight times in races of 12 or more runners. Easy to see him bang in contention going well at the top of the hill, less easy to see him storming home in front.

Going preference Record suggests all ground comes alike
Star rating ✪✪

Snow Falcon

7 b g; Trainer Noel Meade
Hurdles form 22156315F111F32, best RPR 157
Left-handed 221531F11F3, best RPR 157
Right-handed 6512, best RPR 156
Cheltenham form 5, best RPR 145
At the festival 11 Mar 2015 Patiently ridden in last trio, closed and in touch 3 out, asked for effort after 2 out, ridden and stayed on same pace before last, finished fifth, beaten five and a half lengths by Windsor Park in Neptune Investment Management Novices' Hurdle

Decent performer who looked to be improving in 2016 when winning three on the spin, including a pair of Grade 2s at Navan.

Certainly appeared to be carrying that improvement over to Britain when he ran in the Long Distance Hurdle at Newbury and appeared to be going better than most heading to three out only to fall in the race that marked Unowhatimeanharry's winning return. How much he would have found at the business end must be open to question, though, as two runs since haven't seen any further improvement, the first when beaten by Vroum Vroum Mag in the Christmas Hurdle and then when second to Shaneshill at Gowran. Staying-on fifth in Neptune as a five-year-old confirms Cheltenham holds no fears, but needs to find a fair bit to be competitive.

Going preference Acts well on soft but trainer used to think he wanted better ground
Star rating ✪✪

Ballyoptic

7 b g; Trainer Nigel Twiston-Davies
Hurdles form 1111F2F4, best RPR 162
Left-handed 1111F24, best RPR 158
Right-handed F, best RPR 162
Cheltenham form 4, best RPR 153

Didn't make hurdles debut until February last year but soon made up for lost time and was a Grade 1 winner on his third start when edging out Bellshill at Aintree. Continued on an upward curve when scoring in handicap company over just short of 2m4f at Chepstow on his return – a fair effort considering he was already looking an out-and-out stayer. Has suffered his share of misfortune since as he was cutting down the leaders when falling after the last in the West Yorkshire Hurdle and looked like getting closer to Unowhatimeanharry than he had in the Long Walk at Ascot. He had just been headed at the time, but has a reputation for being a battler and could have pulled out more. However, he did not cover himself in glory on his next crack at Harry Fry's favourite as he was beaten nine and three-quarter lengths into fourth in receipt of 4lb. Better than that, but now needs to show he can produce it at Cheltenham.

Going preference Acts well on soft, but best good-ground form comparable
Star rating ✪✪

Lil Rockerfeller

6 ch g; Trainer Neil King
Hurdles form 33241133123173224, best RPR 162
Left-handed 324321734, best RPR 162
Right-handed 31131322, best RPR 162
Cheltenham form 3274, best RPR 156
At the festival 15 Mar 2016 Midfield, ridden along from after 2nd, weakened before 2 out, finished seventh, beaten 20 lengths by Annie Power in Champion Hurdle

Really admirable six-year-old who has a well- deserved reputation for being a trier and has finished out of the first four only once in a hurdle, when seventh in last year's Champion Hurdle. Has always preferred a bit further than the minimum trip, though, and proved he stays 3m when third in the West Yorkshire Hurdle on return and second to Unowhatimeanharry in the Long Walk at Ascot (probably would have been third had Ballyoptic stood up). Cheltenham form is patchy as well-beaten second and fourth in last two runnings of the Relkeel on soft/ heavy ground. However, wasn't far off best at the track on a better surface earlier in career and balance of form says he probably wants it no worse than good to soft, although he'll try his heart out on anything. Boasts better form and higher rating than some of those ahead of him in the market and very likely to run his race.

Going preference Most ground fine, but arguably doesn't want it too soft
Star rating ✪✪✪

OTHERS TO CONSIDER

Apple's Jade has got stayer written all over her but connections are probably wisely going to stick to the Mares' Hurdle at this stage of her career, while the likes of **Yanworth** and **The New One** are Champion Hurdle-bound. Plenty are keen to see The New One tried over 3m, but with big guns Faugheen and Annie

Power out of the Champion the temptation will surely be too much to resist. Thistlecrack's half-brother **West Approach** has taken on the big guns twice already this season, but also has the Albert Bartlett as an option and he's obviously much shorter for that. **Ptit Zig** was a Grade 1 winner over 3m at Auteuil in June but hasn't come close to matching the form since, while stablemate **Zarkandar**, a former Triumph winner and second in this two years ago, has disappointed since a promising return (unseated when going well). Another former festival winner, **Wicklow Brave**, could be more interesting if given the go-ahead. The 2015 County Hurdle winner made no show in the Melbourne Cup in November, but it's only two starts ago that he beat Order Of St George in the Irish St Leger and he's very talented when on song.

VERDICT

The right favourite is clearly Unowhatimeanharry, who has yet to suffer defeat since moving to Harry Fry and has plenty of heart for a battle. He clearly acts very well on a soft surface but did win a good-ground Albert Bartlett, so is very hard to knock. However, there was enough promise from COLE HARDEN (right) when second in the Cleeve Hurdle to think he might be able to narrow the gap considerably should we get much quicker conditions in the spring. He was not right last year but won the 2015 running in commanding fashion and that form is as good, if not better, than any of the likely runners can offer. The stayers' crown has been regained on a couple of occasions and at double-figure odds he looks fair value each-way.

TRAINER'S VIEW

Harry Fry on Unowhatimeanharry "It was encouraging to see Barry Geraghty looking full of confidence on him coming down the hill [in the Cleeve Hurdle] and it wasn't misplaced. The horse eased to the front before, as usual, thinking he had done enough. Given that he was conceding 4lb to his principal rivals and always keeps a bit in reserve, it was a perfect warm-up for the Stayers' Hurdle" *Recorded an RPR of 167 in the Cleeve, identical to the mark of his two previous wins this season*

	FORM	WINNER	AGE & WGT	Adj RPR	SP	TRAINER	BEST RPR LAST 12 MONTHS (RUNS SINCE)
16	-2111	**Thistlecrack** CD	8 11-10	176^T	Evensf	C Tizzard	won Gd2 Cleeve Hurdle (3m) (0)
15	-1234	**Cole Harden**	6 11-10	162^{-7}	14-1	W Greatrex	2nd Newbury Gd2 hdl (3m½f) (2)
14	1-111	**More Of That** C	6 11-10	165^{-14}	15-2	J O'Neill	won Gd2 Relkeel Hdl (2m4½f) (0)
13	22/21	**Solwhit**	9 11-10	169^{-5}	17-2	C Byrnes (IRE)	2nd Punchestown Hurdle (2m4f) (1)
12	1-111	**Big Buck's** CD	9 11-10	182^T	5-6f	P Nicholls	won Gd1 Liverpool Hurdle (3m½f) (3)
11	11-11	**Big Buck's** CD	8 11-10	180^T	10-11f	P Nicholls	won Gd1 World Hurdle (3m) (3)
10	11-11	**Big Buck's** CD	7 11-10	180^T	5-6f	P Nicholls	won Gd1 Liverpool Hurdle (3m½f) (2)
09	1-U11	**Big Buck's** CD	6 11-10	170^{-7}	6-1	P Nicholls	won Gd2 Cleeve Hurdle (3m) (0)
08	13-11	**Inglis Drever** C, D	9 11-10	174^T	11-8f	H Johnson	won Newb Gd2 Long Dist Hdl (3m½f) (1)
07	1F-12	**Inglis Drever** CD	8 11-10	171^{-2}	5-1	H Johnson	2nd Gd2 Cleeve Hurdle (3m) (0)

WINS-RUNS: 5yo 0-7, 6yo 3-32, 7yo 1-36, 8yo 3-31, 9yo 3-15, 10yo 0-6, 11yo 0-5, 13yo 0-2 **FAVOURITES:** -£0.05

TRAINERS IN THIS RACE (w-pl-r): Paul Nicholls 4-3-17, Warren Greatrex 1-0-1, Alan King 0-3-9, Gordon Elliott 0-0-1, Mouse Morris 0-0-2, Nicky Henderson 0-2-13, Noel Meade 0-0-2, Rebecca Curtis 0-1-3, Willie Mullins 0-2-14, Jessica Harrington 0-0-1, Philip Hobbs 0-0-2, Nigel Twiston-Davies 0-0-2, Nick Williams 0-0-4

FATE OF FAVOURITES: F14111P221 **POSITION OF WINNER IN MARKET:** 3131114361

Key trends

🐎 Aged six to nine, 10/10

🐎 Ran no more than four times since August, 10/10

🐎 Top-two finish last time out, 9/10

🐎 Adjusted RPR of at least 165, 9/10

🐎 Previously ran at the festival, 8/10

🐎 Not out of the first two in all hurdle starts that season, 8/10

🐎 Won a Graded hurdle over at least 3m, 8/10

🐎 Ran between nine and 20 times over hurdles, 7/10

Other factors

🐎 A five-year-old has never won. However, two of the seven to have run in the past ten seasons were placed

🐎 Four of the five Irish winners since the mid-1980s prepped in the Boyne Hurdle at Navan (the other, Solwhit in 2013, prepped in the Grade 3 Limestone Lad at Navan)

🐎 The record of Cleeve Hurdle winners is 311721421

Notes

4.10 Brown Advisory & Merriebelle Plate   ITV/RUK
2m5f handicap chase   Grade 3   £105,000

Overall this race (established in 1951 and traditionally known as the Mildmay of Flete) has been the biggest graveyard for favourites at the festival with just four winning, and it was a familiar story in 2016 when 16-1 shot Empire Of Dirt came home in front.

The only two successful favourites in recent years both came from the Pipe stable – Majadou (trained by Martin) in 1999 and Salut Flo (trained by David) in 2012. The Pipe stable has won the race seven times in the past 19 runnings and is always to be respected. Apart from the Pipe favourites, no other winner since 1998 has gone off shorter than 12-1.

Empire Of Dirt became only the second winner in the last 13 years rated higher than 140 and was the second Irish winner in the race's long history.

Some of the bigger stables struggle to get runners at the lower end of the handicap and Paul Nicholls has not won in 27 attempts (second and fourth are his best showings).

Nicky Henderson has been more successful, with two winners, a third and a fourth from his last 15 runners. Venetia Williams is another trainer to note, having won three times in the last ten runnings.

BROWN ADVISORY & MERRIEBELLE STABLE PLATE RESULTS AND TRENDS

	FORM	WINNER	AGE & WGT	OR	SP	TRAINER	BEST RPR LAST 12 MONTHS (RUNS SINCE)
16	-F2P1	Empire Of Dirt D	9 10-11	142-13	16-1	C Murphy (IRE)	2nd Punchestown hcp ch (2m6f) (2)
15	7/157	Darna D	9 10-11	140-6	33-1	K Bailey	won Sedgefield class 3 hcp ch (2m3½f) (2)
14	P18-P	Ballynagour D	8 10-9	140-1	12-1	D Pipe	8th Cheltenham Gd3 hcap ch (2m5f) (1)
13	4P61P	Carrickboy	9 10-5	136-13	50-1	V Williams	won Chepstow class 2 hcap ch (2m3½f) (1)
12	112/0	Salut Flo	7 10-10	137-5	9-2f	D Pipe	12th Atlantic4 Gold Cup hcap ch (2m5f) (0)
11	152F1	Holmwood Legend (5x) D	10 10-6	130-5	25-1	P Rodford	won Sandown class 3 hcap ch (2m4½f) (0)
10	-3144	Great Endeavour D	6 10-1	135-11	18-1	D Pipe	4th Fontwell class 3 nov ch (2m6f) (1)
09	20272	Something Wells	8 10-7	139-1	33-1	V Williams	2nd Ascot class 2 hcap ch (2m5½f) (2)
08	547U5	Mister McGoldrick D	11 11-7	145-6	66-1	S Smith	4th Wetherby class 2 hcap ch (2m½f) (2)
07	6-134	Idole First C, D	8 10-7	136T	12-1	V Williams	won Kempton class 3 hcap ch (2m4½f) (2)

WINS-RUNS: 5yo 0-3, 6yo 1-19, 7yo 1-36, 8yo 3-61, 9yo 3-47, 10yo 1-35, 11yo 1-16, 12yo 0-5, 13yo 0-2 **FAVOURITES:** -£4.50

FATE OF FAVOURITES: 0F2231022P **POSITION OF WINNER IN MARKET:** 5000010608

Key trends

🐎 Won a Class 3 or higher, 10/10

🐎 Won between 2m3f and 2m5f, 10/10

🐎 Officially rated 135 to 142, 9/10

🐎 Carried no more than 10st 11lb, 9/10

🐎 Ran no more than 12 times over fences, 8/10

Other factors

🐎 None of the last ten winners had been placed in one of the big 2m4f-2m5f handicaps run at Cheltenham that season. Last year, Empire Of Dirt became Ireland's first winner since Double-U-Again in 1982

🐎 Salut Flo in 2012 was the first winning favourite since Majadou (1999)

🐎 Four of the last five winners had been well beaten on their previous start (two pulled up, two unplaced)

🐎 Two winners were trained by David Pipe and had not run since the turn of the year

4.50 Trull House Stud Mares Novices' Hurdle — RUK
2m1f — Grade 2 — £80,000

This race was run for the first time last year and, as expected, it became another showcase for Willie Mullins' tremendous strength in depth in the mares' division with odds-on Limini scoring easily by four and a half lengths. Unlike the Mares' Hurdle, which he has won for eight consecutive years, Mullins will have to keep unearthing new talent to keep hold of this prize but that does not look a problem for him and he has the ante-post favourite in Grade 1 Royal Bond winner Airlie Beach, as well as main market rival Let's Dance *(below)*, Augusta Kate and Asthuria. A leading British hope is the Warren Greatrex-trained La Bague Au Roi, whose Listed victory at Newbury in November came at the expense of Dusky Legend (last year's runner-up) by only around a length less than Limini's winning margin.

5.30 Fulke Walwyn Kim Muir Handicap Chase   RUK
3m2f   Amateur riders   £70,000

The best amateur jockeys are always in demand for this contest and Jamie Codd is the main man, having landed his fourth win in the last eight runnings with last year's victory aboard the Gordon Elliott-trained Cause Of Causes. Non-claiming riders have the edge in quality and others to note include Sam Waley-Cohen, Patrick Mullins and Derek O'Connor.

With little between most of the runners nowadays (only 9lb covered the field in 2016), the higher-rated runners have started to do well and the last eight winners carried 11st 4lb or more (including topweights Character Building and Ballabriggs).

A number of the larger stables target this race and their runners always merit respect. Eight of the past 15 winners have come from the Pipe stable, Nicky Henderson and Donald McCain. David Pipe, whose father Martin won this race on three occasions, had the first two in 2011 and landed the spoils again in 2015, while Henderson has had three successes, including a couple of one-twos, and McCain has had two winners and a runner-up.

Only three aged older than nine (eight- and nine-year-olds do best) have won this in the last 24 runnings, while Cause Of Causes continued the trend of Kim Muir winners bouncing back from disappointing efforts (11 of the past 16 winners were unplaced last time out).

KIM MUIR HANDICAP CHASE RESULTS AND TRENDS

	FORM WINNER	AGE & WGT	OR	SP	TRAINER	BEST RPR LAST 12 MONTHS (RUNS SINCE)
16	8-005 **Cause Of Causes** C	8 11-9	142-6	9-2	G Elliott (IRE)	5th Naas Gd2 ch (2m) (0)
15	30-6P **The Package** CD	12 11-4	137T	9-1	D Pipe	6th Cheltenham Gd3 hcap ch (3m3½f) (1)
14	13280 **Spring Heeled** (2ow)	7 11-8	140-5	12-1	J Culloty (IRE)	2nd Limerick hcap ch (3m) (2)
13	34136 **Same Difference**	7 11-0	137-2	16-1	N Twiston-Davies	3rd Newbury class 2 nov ch (3m) (1)
12	-37P9 **Sunnyhillboy** C	9 11-11	142-1	13-2f	J O'Neill	3rd Irish Grand National (3m5f) (3)
11	31-32 **Junior**	8 11-6	134-4	10-3f	D Pipe	3rd Cheltenham Gd3 hcap ch (3m3½f) (0)
10	0-311 **Ballabriggs** D	9 11-12	140T	9-1	D McCain	won Ayr class 2 hcap ch (3m1f) (0)
09	14339 **Character Building** D	9 11-12	139-10	16-1	J Quinn	3rd Cheltenham cl 2 hcap ch (3m2½f) (1)
08	1-43P **High Chimes**	9 10-10	127-7	14-1	E Williams	3rd Haydock class 2 hcap ch (3m) (1)
07	36120 **Cloudy Lane** D, BF	7 10-11	124T	15-2f	D McCain	2nd Newcastle class 3 nov ch (3m) (1)

WINS-RUNS: 6yo 0-13, 7yo 3-46, 8yo 2-59, 9yo 4-55, 10yo 0-33, 11yo 0-16, 12yo 1-11, 13yo 0-3 **FAVOURITES:** £10.33

FATE OF FAVOURITES: 1U0311200U **POSITION OF WINNER IN MARKET:** 1853110632

Key trends
- Ran over at least 3m last time out, 9/10
- Rated within 7lb of RPR top-rated, 9/10
- Aged seven to nine, 9/10
- Won over at least 3m, 9/10
- No more than 11 runs over fences, 8/10
- Officially rated 134 to 142, 8/10 (the last eight)
- Finished in first three in either or both of last two starts, 6/10
- Won a handicap chase, 6/10

Other factors
- Ireland have won two of the last three runnings (Spring Heeled in 2014 and Cause Of Causes in 2016). The last Irish-trained winner before them was Greasepaint in 1983
- Six winners had run at a previous festival
- Five winners had run within the past 33 days, the other five had been off for at least 58

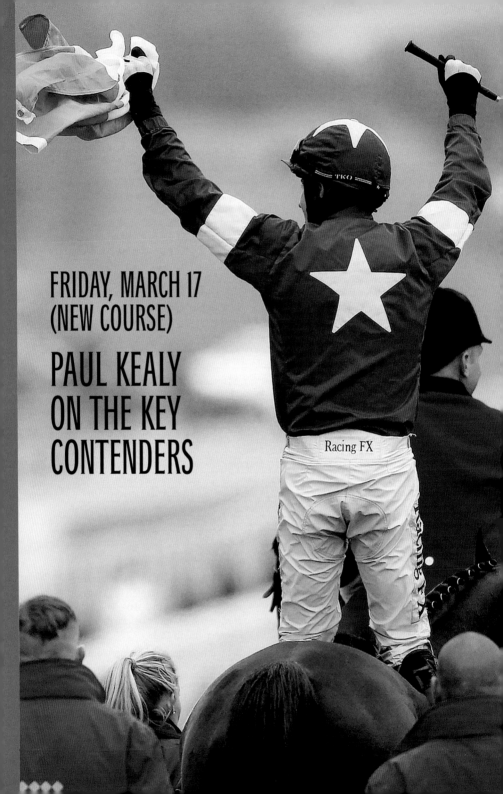

FRIDAY, MARCH 17
(NEW COURSE)

PAUL KEALY
ON THE KEY
CONTENDERS

1.30 JCB Triumph Hurdle

🏇 2m1f   🏇 Grade 1   🏇 £125,000   **ITV/RUK**

Barry Geraghty has ridden the winner for the past two years, and five times in all since 2003, and JP McManus's retained rider can choose from a pair of leading fancies this time. Defi Du Seuil has been the long-time ante-post favourite, having compiled a five-race winning streak for trainer Philip Hobbs, and McManus has another highly regarded French import in Charli Parcs, who started his career under Nicky Henderson with an eight-length success at Kempton's Christmas meeting. The Supreme is an option if the McManus team want to keep them apart. The main market opposition comes from the Irish pair Mega Fortune (trained by Gordon Elliott) and Bapaume (Willie Mullins), first and second in the Grade 1 Spring Juvenile Hurdle in February – a reversal of form from Leopardstown's Christmas meeting. Elliott also has the filly Dinaria Des Obeaux, who was third in the Spring, while Joseph O'Brien has a shot at a second consecutive Triumph (this time officially in his own name) with Landofhopeandglory.

Defi Du Seuil

4 b g; Trainer Philip Hobbs
Hurdles form (all left-handed) 11111, best RPR 150
Cheltenham form 111, best RPR 136

Clear standard-bearer at the time of writing having won all five starts over hurdles since joining Philip Hobbs after running in two AQPS bumpers in France. Did not have much to beat in first three starts, but won all of them without any effort and then pulverised the 144-rated filly Evening Hush in the Finale Junior Hurdle at Chepstow by 13 lengths. The runner-up did make a blunder four out in the soft ground, but it was nowhere near enough to make a difference to the result and Defi Du Seuil has since sauntered home in the Triumph Trial at Cheltenham at odds of 1-5, again with not much to beat once his original market rival Charli Parcs was taken out. His Chepstow win represents his one standout piece of form as it's hard to rate any of the others too highly and there's just the worry he's a proper soft-ground performer who might get found out on a quicker surface. The Finale is not known for producing Triumph winners as the conditions in which each race is run tend to be very different and the last to bag both was Mysilv in 1993. That said, Hobbs will not have seen too much to worry him and his star does boast standout credentials on the book.

Going preference Won on good and soft, but clearly handles soft very well
Star rating ✪✪✪✪

Charli Parcs

4 b g; Trainer Nicky Henderson
Hurdles form (all left-handed) 11, best RPR 139

Joined Nicky Henderson with a huge reputation and lived up to it when sauntering home on Kempton debut, giving 5lb and an eight-length beating to a horse now rated 132. Is clearly very useful and price for Triumph is based on the assumption – possibly dangerous if you're an ante-post punter – that JP McManus will not run all his quality juveniles (he has enough of them) in the same contest. That was the case when Charli Parcs was taken out of the Triumph Trial at Cheltenham in January, but he had been odds-on against Defi Du Seuil and Barry Geraghty was booked to ride him rather than the Hobbs contender. We are likely to see him one more time, probably in the Adonis at Kempton.

Going preference Too soon to say
Star rating ✪✪✪

Mega Fortune

4 b g; Trainer Gordon Elliott
Hurdles form F1331, best RPR 143
Left-handed 31, best RPR 143
Right-handed F13, best RPR 132

Had peak official rating of 80 on the Flat and achieved it after sluicing through bottomless ground in a 1m2½f handicap at Sligo last May. Inauspicious first start over hurdles when fell after being hampered at the second flight at Thurles (odds-on) but then won weak race at Down Royal in fine style before stepping up in class. Both his Grade 3 third to Landofhopeandglory at Fairyhouse and Grade 2 second to Baupaume represented further steps forward but they did also hint at limitations. However, the return to very soft conditions brought about another chunk of improvement in the Spring Juvenile Hurdle at Leopardstown in February as he took up the running from an early stage and stayed in the first two throughout. He raced keenly but still had plenty in the tank to reverse form with the pace-pressing Bapaume and win by three and a half lengths. On that evidence you have to think a soft-ground festival will give him a shot, but otherwise he'll be vulnerable.

Going preference Loves the mud
Star rating ✪✪✪

Bapaume

4 b g; Trainer Willie Mullins
Hurdles form 61212, best RPR 140
Left-handed 6112, best RPR 140
Right-handed 2, best RPR 133

Won second of two hurdles starts in France and first run for Willie Mullins was full of promise as he was second to high-class Flat performer Landofhopeandglory at Fairyhouse. Duly reversed that form (well backed to do so) despite 1lb worse terms at Leopardstown by a length and three-quarters, with Mega Fortune a short head back in third. On the strength of that he was made favourite for the Spring Juvenile Hurdle back at Leopardstown in February, but this time had no answer to Mega Fortune's finishing kick in the straight and was beaten three

and a half lengths into second. That was on very soft ground which he handled in France (at a much lower level), but there must be a chance he can reverse placings on a better surface that will not suit the winner so well. Form probably some way behind Defi Du Seuil, though.

Going preference Too early to say for sure but doesn't seem ground dependent
Star rating ✪✪

Landofhopeandglory

4 b g; Trainer Joseph O'Brien
Hurdles form 1112, best RPR 138
Left-handed 2, best RPR 138
Right-handed 111, best RPR 138

Decent on the Flat, but not without his quirks and, despite earning a peak official mark of 103, had only a maiden win to his name in ten starts. Got the winning habit to start with over hurdles, though, easily taking first two starts in minor events at Fairyhouse and Punchestown and battling on well for a length success over Bapaume – who was making his debut for Willie Mullins – in a Grade 3, also at Fairyhouse. Runner-up turned that form around in the Knight Frank Juvenile Hurdle at Leopardstown over Christmas, though, and not been seen since. Chances are he doesn't want winter ground and his Flat form entitles him to respect, but gives the impression he'll fold when push comes to shove.

Going preference Handles decent ground well
Star rating ✪✪

Dinaria Des Obeaux

4 b f; Trainer Gordon Elliott
Hurdles form 13, best RPR 130
Left-handed 3, best RPR 130
Right-handed 1, best RPR 128

AQPS bumper winner in France over 1m4f in April and spreadeagled her field in three-year-old maiden hurdle at Cork in December on debut for Gordon Elliott at 6-1, reportedly surprising connections with ease of win. Was not seen again until the Spring Juvenile Hurdle at Leopardstown in February and, although well backed second favourite was beaten just over ten lengths into third. However, that only tells half the story as she was moving up in third place before making a right hash of the second-last, nearly falling and losing all momentum. It would be bold to say she'd have won given the distance beaten, but no doubt she's considerably better than the form suggests and that was only her second start over hurdles. By same sire as the likes of Bristol De Mai, Alpha Des Obeaux and Apple's Jade, so chances are she's going to want a test, but the Triumph does provide one. As a filly, though, she will also have the option of the mares' novice and a weight concession for her age.

Going preference Early to say but obviously handles soft well enough
Star rating ✪✪✪✪

Cliffs Of Dover
4 b g; Trainer Paul Nicholls
Hurdles form 1311111, best RPR 138
Left-handed 1111, best RPR 138
Right-handed 31, best RPR 118
Cheltenham form 1, best RPR 125

Six starts on the Flat for Charlie Hills, but ended rated only 64, so nothing special in that sphere. All change for Paul Nicholls, though, winning five out of six, the only defeat coming on his second outing, form of which has been well left behind since. Wasn't really considered anything special to start with, hence being sent handicapping with a mark of 121 and getting all the weight allowances, but steadily progressed and nine-length win in Listed Wensleydale Hurdle at Wetherby from Nietzsche, who was getting 8lb and has won three times since, was impressive. Got job done in tidy fashion in Grade 2 at Doncaster in December as well and deliberately put away for the winter. However, still a suspicion he was beating up relatively soft early-season opposition, so will have it to prove in better company in spring, provided he gets over a setback that has reportedly made him a doubt.

Going preference Goes very well on fast ground
Star rating ✪✪

Meri Devie
4 ch f; Trainer Willie Mullins
Hurdles form (left-handed) 14, best RPR 123

Listed-placed in France, ran in Group 1 Prix Saint-Alary (seventh of nine) and very well backed to beat Housesofparliament on hurdles debut for Willie Mullins at Leopardstown in December. She did so by five lengths, quickening nicely, and may have found much softer ground, which she does handle, too testing when beaten 13 lengths into fourth in the Spring Juvenile Hurdle. No other reason why she should beat third-placed Dinaria Des Obeaux – who she passed when that one made a mistake but lost third to on the run-in – let alone the front two, and will also have the mares' novice as a potential target.

Going preference Won on heavy in France but fair form on better surface too
Star rating ✪

Most Celebrated
4 b g; Trainer Neil Mulholland
Hurdles form 1 (left-handed), best RPR 122

Rating 84 from four starts for Godolphin on the Flat, winning a maiden on second outing. Made sparkling jumps debut when romping home by 28 lengths at Wetherby in late January, although race had no depth. Jumping was excellent, and we should learn a lot more if seen out again before the Triumph.

Going preference Flat and hurdles wins on good to soft
Star rating ✪✪

Duca De Thaix
4 b g; Trainer Gordon Elliott
Hurdles form (left-handed) 1, best RPR 124

Ran four times for Guy Cherel in France, winning a bumper on third start and then getting off the mark over hurdles by a neck at Auteuil. Anyone's guess what the form amounts to but purchased by Gigginstown and given an entry in the Supreme as well.

Going preference Wins on good to soft and soft
Star rating ✪

Cosmeapolitan

4 b g; Trainer Alan King
Hurdles form (left-handed) 1, best RPR 106

With Alan King for two-season Flat campaign and most progressive as a three-year-old, taking handicap mark up from 82 to 95. Made debut over hurdles at Newbury in December and duly won by seven lengths at odds of 1-3, but rivals ranged from moderate to useless and form can't be rated at all highly. He also made a mistake at nearly every hurdle, including a particularly bad one two out. Needs more experience, but definitely has some class between the obstacles and it will help that there are only two of them in the last mile, providing he doesn't mess up the first six.

Going preference Progressive on all surfaces on the Flat
Star rating ✪✪

Coeur De Lion

4 b g; Trainer Alan King
Hurdles form 1221, best RPR 128
Left-handed 12, best RPR 125
Right-handed 21, best RPR 128

Rated 73 on the Flat after five starts and fair juvenile hurdler after a further four. Scored by a neck on debut from Forth Bridge (now rated 139) at Wetherby in November and beaten only a length and three-quarters by Defi Du Seuil at Cheltenham on next start, although margin of victory greatly flatters the runner-up. Turned over at odds of 1-3 at Sandown next time – but winner Don Bersy is promising and has won again – and completed Cheltenham preparations with head success over Rather Be. Trainer says he has four or five who could run in the Fred Winter so might head for the Triumph with this one, although you expect he'd have a much better chance in the handicap off 133.

Going preference Two wins on soft and heavy, but best Flat run on good
Star rating ✪✪

Forth Bridge

4 b g; Trainer Charlie Longsdon
Hurdles form 211, best RPR 130
Left-handed 2, best RPR 111
Right-handed 11, best RPR 130

Trained by Michael Bell for the Queen on the Flat and had a peak rating of 89. Good start over hurdles when going down by only a neck to Coeur De Lion at Wetherby in November and the ratings suggest he has moved ahead of that one in two starts since. Beat Warp Factor by only a neck at 30-100 at Musselburgh on next start in December, but confirmed that superiority on 8lb worse terms when beating

the same rival in the Scottish Triumph Hurdle Trial at the same track in February. Trainer thinks he might be handicapped out of the Fred Winter on a mark of 139, but if that's the case it hardly bodes well for him in this.

Going preference Seems to like decent ground
Star rating ✪✪

OTHERS TO CONSIDER

Project Bluebook is another to race in the JP McManus colours and he shaped as though a stiffer stamina test would be right up his alley when third to Forth Bridge in the Scottish Triumph Trial. However, he was dropped 3lb to 138 for that and, having already run in and won a handicap, he may well be a candidate for the Fred Winter. **Domperignon Du Lys** almost certainly didn't give his running when well beaten by Defi Du Seuil at Cheltenham, but he has won well either side of that and could be a contender, although a mark of 133 looks very fair too.

VERDICT

In a season in which very few juveniles have set the world alight, it is probably going to take a big performance for anything to beat DEFI DU SEUIL or Charli Parcs. The difference in price between the two – 3-1 and 8-1 at the time of writing – is only because everyone seems to think the latter with contest the Supreme, for which he is a slightly shorter price. That may well be the case but for ante-post purposes it's a dangerous game as if the ground looked like being softer earlier in the week and drier later they could easily switch places, or they could both end up running. Defi Du Seuil has the best form in the book, but if I was going to back one to upset the McManus pair it would be Dinaria Des Obeaux (pictured winning below), who hasn't been given the credit for her recovery from a shocking error two out in the Spring. She's not an ante-post proposition either, though, as the mares' novice must be under consideration.

RIDER'S VIEW

Barry Geraghty on Defi Du Seuil "He's very happy on good to soft and easier, but he travels and jumps and I wouldn't be worried about a bigger field. He has loads of experience and loads of bottle" *Yet to race in a field of more than nine runners and four of his five wins have been against no more than four rivals*

	FORM	WINNER	AGE & WGT	Adj RPR	SP	TRAINER	BEST RPR LAST 12 MONTHS (RUNS SINCE)
16	14	**Ivanovich Gorbatov** D, BF	4 11-0	149^{-5}	9-2f	A O'Brien (IRE)	won Leopardstown maiden hdl (2m) **(1)**
15	111	**Peace And Co** CD	4 11-0	159^{T}	2-1f	N Henderson	2nd Doncaster Gd2 hdl (2m½f) **(1)**
14	12	**Tiger Roll** D	4 11-0	150^{-2}	10-1	G Elliott (IRE)	2nd Gd1 Leopardstown nov hdl (2m) **(0)**
13	111	**Our Conor**	4 11-0	160^{-3}	4-1	D Hughes (IRE)	won Gd1 Leopardstown nov hdl (2m) **(0)**
12	12123	**Countrywide Flame** D	4 11-0	151^{-6}	33-1	J Quinn	2nd Gd1 Finale Hurdle (2m½f) **(1)**
11	1	**Zarkandar**	4 11-0	155^{-2}	13-2	P Nicholls	won Gd2 Adonis Nov Hdl (2m) **(0)**
10	4211	**Soldatino** D	4 11-0	150^{-6}	6-1	N Henderson	won Gd2 Adonis Nov Hdl (2m) **(0)**
09	11	**Zaynar** D	4 11-0	152^{-6}	11-2	N Henderson	won Newb class 4 nov hdl (2m½f) **(1)**
08	12	**Celestial Halo** D, BF	4 11-0	145^{-11}	5-1	P Nicholls	won Newb class 3 nov hdl (2m½f) **(1)**
07	12111	**Katchit** CD	4 11-0	150^{-10}	11-2	A King	2nd Wetherby Listed nov hdl (2m) **(3)**

FAVOURITES: -£1.50

TRAINERS IN THIS RACE (w-pl-r): Nicky Henderson 3-4-14, Paul Nicholls 2-2-19, Alan King 1-3-15, Gordon Elliott 1-0-5, John Quinn 1-0-6, Philip Hobbs 0-1-2, Tony Martin 0-0-1, Alan Fleming 0-0-1, David Pipe 0-0-6, Charlie Longsdon 0-0-2, Nick Williams 0-0-2, Willie Mullins 0-3-16, Evan Williams 0-1-3, Venetia Williams 0-0-3, Warren Greatrex 0-0-1, Ian Williams 0-0-2, John Ryan 0-0-3

FATE OF FAVOURITES: 0224436411 **POSITION OF WINNER IN MARKET:** 2233302611

Key trends

🐎Last ran between 19 and 55 days ago, 10/10

🐎Won at least 50 per cent of hurdle races, 10/10

🐎Top-three finish last time out, 9/10 (six won)

🐎Adjusted RPR of at least 150, 8/10

🐎By a Group 1-winning sire, 8/10

🐎Ran two or three times over hurdles, 7/10

Other factors

🐎Zarkandar is the only once-raced hurdler to win in the past 30 years

🐎Five winners were undefeated over hurdles

🐎Five winners had landed Graded events (two had won the Adonis at Kempton in February)

🐎Five winners had raced on the Flat in Britain and Ireland and all had recorded an RPR of at least 83

🐎Since the introduction of the Fred Winter Hurdle in 2005, 11 of the 12 winners have had an SP of 10-1 or shorter

Notes

2.10 Randox Health County H'cap Hurdle   ITV/RUK
⚐2m1f ⚐Grade 3 ⚐£95,000

Ireland has accounted for seven of the last ten winners, with five of them trained by a Mullins. Willie Mullins had his first festival handicap victory in this race with Thousand Stars in 2010, followed up in 2011 with Final Approach and confirmed his liking for the race with 25-1 winner Wicklow Brave in 2015 (he didn't have a runner in 2012 but had the runner-up in 2013 and 2014 and four of the first six in 2015).

Paul Nicholls has done best of the British trainers, winning four times in the last 13 runnings. Superb Story won in 2016 to give Dan Skelton (a former Nicholls assistant) his first festival success.

The last 11 winners have been rated in the 130s and Superb Story continued the excellent record of second-season hurdlers, who have won 13 of the last 16 runnings. Since 1970 just seven winners have carried more than 11st, which is a clear sign that a well-treated runner fits the bill. Only one horse older than six (Alderwood in 2012) has won in the last nine runnings.

The Betfair Hurdle and the Coral.ie Hurdle (formerly the BoyleSports) have been key pointers – nine of the past 16 winners had run in one of those hot contests.

COUNTY HURDLE RESULTS AND TRENDS

	FORM WINNER	AGE & WGT	OR	SP	TRAINER	BEST RPR LAST 12 MONTHS (RUNS SINCE)
16	44-12 **Superb Story** D	5 10-12	138T	8-1	D Skelton	2nd Cheltenham Gd3 hcap hdl (2m½f) **(0)**
15	F580P **Wicklow Brave** D	6 11-4	138-1	25-1	W Mullins (IRE)	11th Newbury Gd3 hcap hdl (2m½f) **(1)**
14	8-141 **Lac Fontana** CD	5 10-11	139-3	11-1	P Nicholls	won Chelt class 2 hcap hdl (2m1f) **(0)**
13	31923 **Ted Veale**	6 10-6	134-2	10-1	A Martin (IRE)	3rd Boylesports Hcap Hurdle (2m) **(0)**
12	10120 **Alderwood** D	8 11-1	139-3	20-1	T Mullins (IRE)	won Killarney hcap hdl (2m6f) **(2)**
11	13-51 **Final Approach**	5 10-12	139-8	10-1	W Mullins (IRE)	won MCR Hcap Hurdle (2m) **(0)**
10	40110 **Thousand Stars** D	6 10-5	134-5	20-1	W Mullins (IRE)	14th MCR Hcap Hurdle (2m) **(0)**
09	1349 **American Trilogy** D	5 11-0	135-7	20-1	P Nicholls	3rd Cheltenham Gd2 nov hdl (2m½f) **(2)**
08	22233 **Silver Jaro** BF	5 10-13	132-11	50-1	T Hogan (IRE)	3rd Pierse Hcap Hurdle (2m) **(1)**
07	-1713 **Pedrobob**	9 10-0	135-10	12-1	A Mullins (IRE)	3rd Gd3 Tote Trophy Hcap Hdl (2m½f) **(0)**

WINS-RUNS: 5yo 5-65, 6yo 3-77, 7yo 0-62, 8yo 1-28, 9yo 1-20, 10yo 0-9, 11yo 0-2 **FAVOURITES:** -£10.00

FATE OF FAVOURITES: 0260000P04 **POSITION OF WINNER IN MARKET:** 4070403503

Key trends

⚐Achieved career-best RPR of at least 129 on a left-handed track, 10/10

⚐Officially rated between 132 and 139, 10/10

⚐Carried no more than 11st 1lb, 9/10

⚐Ran no more than 12 times over hurdles, 9/10

⚐No previous festival form, 8/10

⚐Aged five or six, 8/10

Other factors

⚐There have been five winning novices since 1996

⚐Two winners ran in the Betfair Hurdle, finishing 30

⚐Four ran in the (now) Coral.ie Hurdle, finishing 3013

⚐Paul Nicholls has had four winners, two seconds and a fourth since 2004

⚐Ireland has won seven of the last ten, including three for Willie Mullins

2.50 Albert Bartlett Novices' Hurdle　ITV/RUK
*3m　*Grade 1　*£125,000*

Gordon Elliott says Death Duty is the best hurdler he has had and the six-year-old has lived up to the hype this season with a four-race winning streak capped by a nine-length success in the Grade 1 Lawlor's Hotel Novice Hurdle at Naas in early January. Death Duty has yet to try 3m, even as a point-to-pointer, but his performances over 2m4f give every indication stamina will not be a problem and the betting indicates he is more likely to run here than in the Neptune. The main British opponents look set to be the Colin Tizzard-trained West Approach, 11th in this race last year as a 66-1 shot but strongly fancied this time after finishing third in the Cleeve Hurdle on Trials Day, and Nigel Twiston-Davies's three-time Cheltenham winner Wholestone. Willie Mullins, yet to win the race, has a number of possibles as usual, including Augusta Kate, Let's Dance and Bacardys.

Death Duty
6 b g; Trainer Gordon Elliott
Hurdles form 1111, best RPR 150
Left-handed 111, best RPR 150
Right-handed 1, best RPR 140

Extremely well regarded by Gordon Elliott, who said after his Naas win in January: "At this stage, of all the good horses I have had, none of them were as good over hurdles." That's high praise indeed and hasn't done anything for his Cheltenham odds, but in fairness he has won all four starts over hurdles, showing progressively better form on every start. He has been brought along very slowly, running in four bumpers from April 2015 to March last year and winning two – including one against Grade 1 chase winner Our Duke – and finding only Blow By Blow (beat Moon Racer at Punchestown next time) too good on his final outing in that sphere. Made short work of his maiden opposition when he finally tackled hurdles for the first time in October and then took step up in class in his stride with a very easy win in a Grade 3 at Navan. He had to work a little bit harder up another notch at the same track next time, but was ultimately well on top of Monalee (beat Champion Bumper runner-up Battleford next time out) at the end, winning by three and three-quarter lengths. His final start, in the Grade 1 Lawlor's Hotel Novice

Hurdle at Naas, resulted in a nine-length win from Turcagua, but that tells only half the story as Augusta Kate was trading at odds-on in running approaching the last, where she fell. Death Duty did look very strong at the end, though, and it would be a brave call to suggest he'd have been beaten. Looks sure to stay 3m, but hasn't run over the trip yet and hasn't run on anything faster than soft. It might not be an issue, but in a race that usually attracts a big field he's a short price without that form in the book.

Going preference Only raced on soft/heavy
Star rating ✪✪✪✪

West Approach
7 b g; Trainer Colin Tizzard
Hurdles form 935201235U3, best RPR 157
Left-handed 935012353, best RPR 157
Right-handed 2U, best RPR 152
Cheltenham form 3502353, best RPR 157
At the festival 18 Mar 2016 Midfield until weakened 3 out, finished 11th, beaten 50 lengths by Unowhatimeanharry in Albert Bartlett Novices' Hurdle

Second-season novice and half-brother to Thistlecrack who doesn't exactly boast form figures to make him a confident pick for a race like this. However, those figures mask the fact he has actually been progressing at a rate of knots because his last two starts have come in open company and he has excelled himself both times. He looked booked for fourth behind Stayers' Hurdle favourite Unowhatimeanharry when unseating at the last in the Grade 1 Long Walk Hurdle at Ascot and bettered that form in the Cleeve when third to Harry Fry's nine-year-old, beaten only a three and a quarter lengths. Yes, he was receiving 6lb and it's possible he was flattered by being held up in a race run at fair clip, but the Racing Post Rating (157) he earned there would have been good enough to win all bar one of the previous 11 runnings of this race and none of those previous runners had recorded quite as high a figure before the festival. He's in the Stayers' Hurdle, too, but back in novice company he must have a serious chance and he'll certainly run a lot better than when a 66-1 shot in the race last year.

Going preference Doesn't seem to mind
Star rating ✪✪✪✪

Wholestone
6 b g; Trainer Nigel Twiston-Davies
Hurdles form (left-handed) 3F11211, best RPR 147
Cheltenham form 1211, best RPR 147

Won sole bumper in September 2015 and, like West Approach, is a second-season novice, although he ran only twice in first season, a fall at Newcastle on his second outing ending his campaign. Had clearly improved for the time off and was backed from 11-8 to 8-11 for his October return at Warwick and duly dotted up by ten lengths. After that followed four runs at Cheltenham and in the first he beat West Approach by half a length, albeit in receipt of 3lb. Confirmed that form in Grade 2 in November on worse terms, although finished only second behind Peregrine Run, but stepped up again when a Grade 2 winner at the December meeting, scoring by a length from Ami Debois (subsequent handicap winner off 137) with the stumbling West Approach again behind. Probably better still back to 2m4½f at the trial meeting when three-length winner from William Henry. Sire

Craigsteel's best offspring was Cross Kennon, a real tough battler who finished fourth in a World Hurdle, and this one is in the same mould. West Approach is now rated 12lb higher than him, but doubt there's anywhere near that much between them and this one is a proven winner.

Going preference Has won on good and soft
Star rating ✪✪✪

Bacardys
6 b g; Trainer Willie Mullins
Hurdles form F11, best RPR 147
Left-handed 11, best RPR 147
Right-handed F, best RPR 129
Cheltenham form (bumper) 3
At the festival 16 Mar 2016 Held up in midfield, progress over 4f out to track leaders 3f out, ridden and no impression 2f out, stayed on final furlong to take 3rd last 100yds, finished third, beaten two lengths by Ballyandy in Champion Bumper

Has yet to run beyond 2m2f over hurdles but did win a soft-ground point, and victory in the Deloitte showed he was all about stamina. Is a similar price for the Neptune (dealt with in more detail in that section) and, like many of the Mullins novices, has entries in all three Grade 1s. But Patrick Mullins said 3m might end up being his best trip after getting off him at Leopardstown and would be a major player here if showing up.

Going preference Handles soft well, but third on good ground at last year's festival
Star rating ✪✪

Augusta Kate
6 b m; Trainer Willie Mullins
Hurdles form 1F, best RPR 139
Left-handed 1, bestRPR 127
Right-handed F, best RPR 139
Cheltenham form (bumper) 5, best RPR 121
At the festival 16 Mar 2016 Well in touch behind leaders, close up over 2f out, ridden well over 1f out, no extra, finished fifth, beaten five lengths by Ballandy in Champion Bumper

Really good and tough bumper mare who finished fifth in the Champion Bumper at the festival when sent off 7-2 favourite, then finished second and first in the mares' equivalents at the Aintree and Punchestown festivals. Had looked all about stamina then and began hurdles career over 2m7f at Thurles, winning easily against her own sex at odds of 2-9. Was set a much stiffer task and wasn't unbacked in the Grade 1 Lawlor's Hotel Novice Hurdle at Naas in January and looked to be running a huge race until falling at the last. Indeed, she had touched odds-on on Betfair just before coming down as she matched strides with this race's favourite Death Duty. The winner did stay on really strongly after the last, so it would be a very bold call to say she'd have won, but it's doubtful if the current price discrepancy between them will be the same should she line up. That's the problem as she'll obviously have other mares' options, but that's true of plenty of her stablemates and her proven stamina could see her sent here.

Going preference No apparent issues
Star rating ✪✪✪

Monalee

6 b g; Trainer Henry de Bromhead
Hurdles form 121, best RPR 145
Left-handed 2, best RPR 142
Right-handed 11, best RPR 145

Fair bumper horse who won nicely on maiden hurdle debut over 2m6f at Punchestown in November, but was then put in his place by Death Duty in the Grade 2 2m4f Navan Novice Hurdle, going down by just under four lengths in receipt of 3lb. However, he improved again upped to 3m when easily accounting for Champion Bumper runner-up Battleford and staying does appear to be his game. Has done most of his running on soft or heavy ground but trainer adamant he won't have a problem with faster, and sire Milan, who had the one-two in this race in 2015 with Martello Tower and Milsean (albeit on soft ground), does get plenty who like a decent surface, including last year's Pertemps winner Mall Dini.

Going preference Clearly acts well on soft
Star rating ✪✪✪

Willoughby Court

6 br g; Trainer Ben Pauling
Hurdles form 211, best RPR 147
Left-handed 11, best RPR 147
Right-handed 2, best RPR 121

Also in the Neptune and yet to run over further than 2m5f, so dealt with in more detail in Wednesday's section, but certainly shapes like a stayer. Does act particularly well on soft though and questions to answer on normal Cheltenham ground.

Going preference Very well suited by soft
Star rating ✪✪

Baltazar D'Allier

6 br g; Trainer Gordon Elliott
Hurdles form (left-handed) 12, best RPR 144

Very lightly raced six-year-old who won 23-runner Naas maiden on his debut in November and was shipped by Gordon Elliott to Britain to contest the Grade 1 Challow Hurdle. Didn't have any answer to Messire Des Obeaux on that occasion, going down by two lengths, but stayed on nicely at the end. However, is considered by trainer to still be a bit weak and he said it was doubtful we'd see much more of him this season. Has to be a doubt about him travelling.

Going preference Too soon to tell
Star rating ✪

Invitation Only

6 b g; Trainer Willie Mullins
Hurdles form 13, best RPR 141
Left-handed 3, best RPR 141
Right-handed 1, best RPR 132

Big reputation and won opening maiden hurdle at odds of 1-4 following successes in a point and bumper. Sent off at evens favourite against Death Duty in the Navan Novice Hurdle on next start, but appeared to have no excuses when beaten five and a quarter lengths into third (would have been fourth but for Augusta Kate's fall). Far too soon to dismiss, though, and also has Neptune entry.

Going preference Won on a range of going
Star rating ✪✪

Constantine Bay

6 b g; Trainer Nicky Henderson
Hurdles form (left-handed) 111, best RPR 147

Unbeaten in three starts since joining Nicky Henderson after winning a point, the first two over around 2m3f. Showed improved form upped to 3m for the first time in the River Don at Doncaster when all out to win by a head from No Hassle Hoff, the pair having pulled 13 lengths clear of the third. That was a good effort and showed his willingness for a battle and there could be more to come. Although connections reckoned the ground was much too fast for him, he handled it well enough.

Going preference Best form on good, but not for long if connections are right
Star rating ✪✪

Penhill

6 b g; Trainer Willie Mullins
Hurdles form 1611141, best RPR 148
Left-handed 61, best RPR 140
Right-handed 11141, best RPR 148

Has more experience than most, having run 18 times on the Flat, something that would make him a most unusual winner of this. Used to race too keenly on the level and on occasions looked a bit soft, but apart from one lamentable effort at Killarney in July he has been very progressive over hurdles, winning five out of seven. An easy seven-length win of a Grade 2 at Limerick earned him an RPR of 148, which puts him up with the best of these bar clear form horse West Approach, but it would be disappointing if a proper NH bred wasn't able to put him in his place.

Going preference Liked a bit of cut on the Flat, but no real problem with faster
Star rating ✪

OTHERS TO CONSIDER

Possible the most interesting of those at much bigger odds is Harry Fry's **Any Drama**, but only if there is plenty of rain and the going is soft. He sluiced through the mud to win a bumper at Thurles by 22 lengths in January 2016 and after suffering defeat on his hurdles debut ay Newbury, won by a country mile at Market Rasen. The competition was probably nothing special, but he earned an RPR of 150 for that, which puts him on the same level as Death Duty if it can be believed. He will stay and only has the Albert Bartlett entry.

Ami Debois was only a length behind Wholestone at Cheltenham in December and has progressed again since. He's another really stout stayer who could probably do with it being a testing festival. **Let's Dance** is the one major omission from those further up the lists, but it seems apparent she will be racing in the mares' novice. Willie Mullins has more obvious contenders than **Battleford**, who has ground to make up with Monalee on Clonmel running, but he does have festival form having come within a nose of winning the Champion Bumper and he deserves respect on that score alone. Nigel Twiston-Davies, who has a strong contender in Wholestone, also has Ballymalin among the entries, but he qualified for the Pertemps at Exeter in February and is rated high enough to get in there.

VERDICT

If you listen to some fans of Death Duty he only has to turn up to win, but he has yet to race on ground faster than soft or over the trip. The latter won't be a problem but the former might and as this race regularly features a big field he looks short enough. I backed WEST APPROACH straight after he ran third to Unowhatimeanharry in the Cleeve Hurdle and he undoubtedly has the best form, although that may only be because he's the only one to have run in open company. He is a half-brother to Thistlecrack and does seem to be improving at a rate of knots. Of those at slightly bigger prices Monalee is of interest, being by a sire who has had a couple of 3m hurdle winners at the meeting. He has solid enough form as it is but just might prove a different proposition again given some better ground. Conversely, Any Drama would make plenty of each-way appeal if we get a wet festival.

	FORM WINNER	AGE & WGT	Adj RPR	SP	TRAINER	BEST RPR LAST 12 MONTHS (RUNS SINCE)
16	-1111 **Unowhatimeanharry** CD	8 11-5	154-9	11-1	H Fry	won Exeter class 2 hcap hdl (2m7f) **(0)**
15	11F12 **Martello Tower** D	7 11-7	151-6	14-1	M Mullins (IRE)	2nd Leopardstown Gd2 nov hdl (2m4f) **(0)**
14	-1253 **Very Wood**	5 11-7	143-18	33-1	N Meade (IRE)	3rd Naas Gd2 nov hdl (2m4f) **(0)**
13	-1111 **At Fishers Cross** CD	6 11-7	161T	11-8f	R Curtis	won Cheltenham Gd2 nov hdl (2m5f) **(0)**
12	2111 **Brindisi Breeze** D	6 11-7	157-6	7-1	L Russell	won Haydock Gd2 nov hdl (3m) **(0)**
11	1-111 **Bobs Worth** C	6 11-7	160T	15-8f	N Henderson	won Cheltenham Gd2 nov hdl (2m4½f) **(0)**
10	12F34 **Berties Dream**	7 11-7	155-3	33-1	P Gilligan (IRE)	3rd Cheltenham Gd2 nov hdl (2m5f) **(1)**
09	-5112 **Weapon's Amnesty** D, BF	6 11-7	150-12	8-1	C Byrnes (IRE)	2nd Leopardstown Gd2 nov hdl (2m4f) **(0)**
08	1-212 **Nenuphar Collonges** CD	7 11-7	146-12	9-1	A King	2nd Warwick Gd2 nov hdl (2m5f) **(0)**
07	-1211 **Wichita Lineman** C	6 11-7	161T	11-8f	J O'Neill	won Gd1 Challow Hurdle (2m5f) **(1)**

WINS-RUNS: 5yo 1-38, 6yo 5-84, 7yo 3-41, 8yo 1-16, 9yo 0-2 **FAVOURITES:** -£2.38

TRAINERS IN THIS RACE (w-pl-r): Alan King 1-1-8, Harry Fry 1-0-2, Nicky Henderson 1-1-7, Jonjo O'Neill 1-0-1, Noel Meade 1-0-5, Rebecca Curtis 1-0-8, Ben Pauling 0-0-1, Charlie Longsdon 0-0-3, Charlie Mann 0-1-2, Colin Tizzard 0-1-6, David Pipe 0-1-6, Dan Skelton 0-0-1, Mouse Morris 0-0-2, Jessica Harrington 0-0-2, Nigel Twiston-Davies 0-1-7, Paul Nicholls 0-3-9, Philip Hobbs 0-0-4, Evan Williams 0-0-2, Gordon Elliott 0-2-3, Willie Mullins 0-4-18

FATE OF FAVOURITES: 132P121F0P **POSITION OF WINNER IN MARKET:** 1540121976

Key trends

🏇At least three runs over hurdles, 10/10

🏇Adjusted RPR of at least 146, 9/10

🏇Won over at least 2m5f, 9/10

🏇Top-three finish in a Graded hurdle last time out, 8/10 (four won)

🏇Aged six or seven, 8/10

🏇Rated within 9lb of RPR top-rated, 7/10

Other factors

🏇Seven winners had won a Graded hurdle

🏇Five winners had raced at least twice at Cheltenham (all had won at the course)

Notes

3.30 Timico Cheltenham Gold Cup   ITV/RUK
3m2½f *Grade 1* *£575,000*

In 2015 Coneygree became the first novice to land the Gold Cup since Captain Christy in 1974 but the wait for another first-season chaser to repeat the feat may take considerably less time, with Thistlecrack heading the market having already taken the King George VI Chase for Colin Tizzard. Last year's spectacular World Hurdle winner lost his unbeaten record over fences to the ill-fated Many Clouds on Cheltenham's Festival Trials Day but still leads Tizzard's strong team alongside Native River and Cue Card, who might have won 12 months ago but for falling three out. Djakadam, runner-up for the past two years, is the only one who can break the Tizzard stranglehold on the top of the market, while Lexus winner Outlander and Irish Gold Cup one-two Sizing John and Empire Of Dirt are next in the ante-post betting.

Thistlecrack

9 b g; Trainer Colin Tizzard
Chase form 11112, best RPR 178
Left-handed 1112, best RPR 174
Right-handed 1, best RPR 178
Cheltenham form (all) 71112, best RPR 174
At the festival 17 Mar 2016 Midfield, headway approaching 7th, went 2nd before 3 out, led on bit just before 2 out, always travelling strongly, effortlessly went clear run-in, impressive, won World Hurdle by seven lengths from Alpha Des Obeaux

Superstar staying hurdler last season who totally dominated his division, winning all five starts and sauntering to victory in the World Hurdle and its equivalent at Aintree three weeks later, a Racing Post Rating of 178 for his Cheltenham victory being every bit as good as Big Buck's ever managed. He undoubtedly could have had that division at his mercy for as long as he stayed sound, but connections were keen to press on with a chase career and, as he was already eight last season, they made no bones about the fact they would be chasing Gold Cup glory rather than the novice championships. The bookmakers took note and made him favourite before he'd even jumped a fence and while most pundits thought that a ludicrous position to take – this one included – he soon proved them all wrong. First three novice chases were won in a hack canter and while

there was the odd blip – he almost landed on top of the fifth fence at Cheltenham after taking off miles too early on his second start – his jumping was often bold and sometimes spectacular. Thrown into the deep end on his next start in the King George at Kempton, he raced in second early, stood out outside the wings of the first open ditch, took it up just after the last on the first circuit, turned up the tempo down the back and had them all cooked turning for home, Tom Scudamore able to ease down after the last and pass the line standing up in the saddle. It was a breathtaking performance, but hard-nosed form students could find reason to crab the value of it as main rival and defending King George hero Cue Card jumped terribly and is miles better than the other three who finished right on his heels, three and a half lengths off the winner (could have been twice that). Never mind, it elevated Thistlecrack to the

TRAINER'S VIEW

Colin Tizzard on Thistlecrack "With hindsight he might be better on spring ground. We've all seen what he did on better ground at Kempton. He got there to win it [in the Cotswold Chase] but was outstayed up the hill" *Best RPR is 178 over both hurdles (in last year's World Hurdle) and fences (King George) – both on good ground and at least 4lb better than he has achieved on softer*

top of the chasing tree, with odds-on Gold Cup quotes the norm and some wondering what was going to turn up against him at Cheltenham. Then came the race that typifies the sport's ability to warm the heart one minute and break it the next. A red-hot 4-9 favourite to make it ten wins on the spin in the Cotsworld Chase on trials day, Thistlecrack lost out in a pulsating home-straight duel with 2015 Grand National winner Many Clouds, who so sadly collapsed and died shortly afterwards. Pinpoint accurate jumping and heart of a lion won it for Many Clouds and while you couldn't crab Thistlecrack in the latter department, his jumping did not come up to scratch. There were probably only three minor errors in reality, but on both starts at Cheltenham he has seemed to have to put a lot of effort into his jumping and he certainly wasn't as quick through the air as he had been at Kempton. Better ground might help, but any mistakes are likely to be punished in a big field and, at Cheltenham at least, he's nowhere near as sure-footed as Coneygree was in 2015. There's a reason Coneygree was the first novice to score in 40 years – you simply have to get everything right. That said, Thistlecrack is undoubtedly the class act and the right favourite, although with that defeat his aura of invincibility has disappeared and he won't be short of rivals to take him on.

Going preference No issues but better ground will help jumping
Star rating ✪✪✪✪

Native River *(right)*

7 ch g; Trainer Colin Tizzard
Chase form 3113321111, best RPR 171
Left-handed 31321111, best RPR 171
Right-handed 13, best RPR 155
Cheltenham form (all) F92, best RPR 160
At the festival 13 Mar 2015 Prominent, blundered 6th and lost place, weakened after 3 out, finished ninth, beaten 53 lengths by Martello Tower in Albert Bartlett Novices' Hurdle
15 Mar 2016 In touch, blundered 13th, chased winner 19th (water), lost 2nd and ridden after 4 out, outpaced after 3 out, rallied run-in and hung left, went 2nd final 120yds, stayed on to close on winner near finish, finished second, beaten one and a quarter lengths by Minella Rocco in National Hunt Chase

Terrific old-fashioned staying chaser who has surprised a few with his continued progress this season and is unbeaten over fences since running second to Minella Rocco in the National Hunt Chase last year. Warmed up for the new campaign with a fair second over hurdles at Wetherby in October and was then a very heavily backed favourite for the Hennessy at Newbury and, although off the bridle a long way from home, he had shot clear jumping the last and was never really in danger of being caught by the closing Carole's Destrier. That race has hardly worked out with, at the time of writing, not a single finisher winning another race since except, of course, Native River, who won in similar style in the Welsh National off the same mark of 155. This time he burst clear a lot further before being closed down to a length and three-quarters by the exposed 11-year-old Raz De Maree, but once again he was never in danger. Native River warmed up by winning the three-runner Denman Chase at Newbury, but it's hard to say he achieved much as market rival Bristol De Mai was way below form and runner-up Le Mercurey was beaten only just over three lengths in receipt of 1lb despite being officially 17lb inferior. Trainer has always considered him better on a Flat track and he did appear to get badly outpaced at the top of the hill in the four-miler (roared home after the last) at Cheltenham, which makes you wonder what he'll be like in a good-ground Gold Cup, but it's hard to knock a horse with the winning habit and he does find plenty when asked.

Going preference Goes on any but could probably do with some ease in a Gold Cup
Star rating ✪✪✪

Djakadam

8 b g; Trainer Willie Mullins
Chase form 11F81221F23213, best RPR 177
Left-handed 11F82F233, best RPR 177
Right-handed 12121, best RPR 175
Cheltenham form F2F2, best RPR 177

At the festival 13 Mar 2014 Chased leaders, not fluent 3rd, hit 9th, disputing 3 lengths 2nd and going okay when fell 4 out in JLT Novices' Chase won by Taquin Du Seuil

13 Mar 2015 Mid-division, smooth headway 16th, tracked leaders travelling well 18th, ridden in close 3rd approaching 2 out, hit last, stayed on to go 2nd run-in, held when drifted right final 70yds, finished second, beaten one and a half lengths by Coneygree in Gold Cup

18 Mar 2016 In touch, tracked leaders 10th, upsides after 16th, narrow lead after next, ridden and headed after 3 out, not fluent next, stayed on from last but no impression on winner, finished second, beaten four and a half lengths by Don Cossack in Gold Cup

Has run four times at Cheltenham and fallen twice, his tendency to land a bit steeply on occasions finding him out in the 2014 JLT and last season's Cotswold Chase. However, he has also finished second in the last two Gold Cups and a return to that sort of form would make him a huge contender. After finishing second to Don Cossack last year he ran at Aintree, finishing a distant third to Cue Card, and Punchestown, where Carlingford Lough proved too hot for him, and the question remains whether he is still capable of matching his previous peak of as he hasn't quite scaled those heights in two starts this season. That said, he has hardly run badly as he beat Outlander in the Grade 1 John Durkan Memorial at Punchestown over 2m4f and then finished a two-and-a-half-length third to the same horse in the Lexus Chase at Leopardstown over Christmas. He was 5-4 favourite that day and it wasn't his best form, but those two runs came within 17 days of each other and he was reportedly looking well short of full fitness for the first and had to work hard to win – so it could have left its mark. His Lexus run was still a better Gold Cup prep than his one the year before when

he fell at Cheltenham and suffered a cut, and he has gone well fresh, so the absence ought not be a worry. There are plenty who doubt his stamina and would like to see him in the Ryanair, but he was ten lengths clear of strong stayer Don Poli two out in last year's Gold Cup and still that far ahead at the line – he just got beat by a very good winner.

Going preference No preference
Star rating ✪✪✪

Cue Card (left)

11 b g; Trainer Colin Tizzard
Chase form 1U2121511231244524111F143121, best RPR 180
Left-handed 1U2121214211F131, best RPR 180
Right-handed 151324541421, best RPR 180
Cheltenham form (all) 1124U21F, best RPR 180
At the festival 17 Mar 2010 Took keen hold, held up well in rear, scythed through field from 5f out, tracked leader over 2f out and still cruising, led over 1f out, hung left briefly but romped clear, won Champion Bumper by eight lengths from Al Ferof
15 Mar 2011 Took keen hold, held up in midfield, progress before 3 out, joined leader 2 out, ridden soon after, hanging and not quicken before last, faded, finished fourth, beaten six and a half lengths by Al Ferof in Supreme Novices' Hurdle
13 Mar 2012 Led until mistake and headed 9th, chased winner from 4 out, stayed on well to try to close on winner after 2 out and 4 lengths down soon after, readily outpaced from last but stayed on well for clear 2nd, finished second, beaten seven lengths by Sprinter Sacre in Racing Post Arkle
14 Mar 2013 Made all, not fluent 3rd, reached for 8th, asserted approaching last, soon clear, ran on well and in command after, won Ryanair Chase by nine lengths from First Lieutenant
18 Mar 2016 In touch, hit 9th, tracked leaders 14th, disputing lead and travelling well when fell 3 out in Gold Cup won by Don Cossack

One of the most popular horses in training and it's easy to see why as he has been top class since the day he first set foot on a racecourse at the age of four and has overcome some major problems in his time. Indeed, it's amazing to consider that he will be contesting his sixth Cheltenham Festival at the age of 11 despite having missed two of the last three. Eight-length winner of the Champion Bumper, fourth in a Supreme Novices' Hurdle, second in an Arkle and a nine-length winner of the Ryanair, he has pretty much done it all apart from land a Gold Cup – and he would surely have gone close to doing so if he hadn't hit the deck last year. At the end of the 2014-15 season it looked as if Cue Card's troubles had got the better of him as he was beaten a combined 82 lengths in five starts, but instead he enjoyed his best campaign the following season, winning the Charlie Hall, Betfair Chase and King George, the last two races setting him up for a £1 million bonus if he could grab gold at Cheltenham. Unfortunately he came down when joining issue with Don Cossack and Djakadam at the third-last. All three were still going well then, so it's hard to say what would have happened and the winner is a class act, but you have to think he'd have gone close. It hasn't been plain sailing this season, with below-par runs in the Charlie Hall and King George, but he has also landed two Grade 1s by wide margins, the Betfair Chase by 15 lengths from Coneygree and the Ascot Chase over 2m5f by the same margin from Shantou Flyer. It's just a shame that the real Cue Card didn't turn up in the King George inbetween and, while he was beaten only three and a quarter lengths by an eased-down Thistlecrack, the rest of the field were on his heels and he's miles better than them. Still, connections think they know the reason and in any case we can allow him the odd blowout at his age. Age is a problem, though, as no horse older than ten has won the Gold Cup since 1969. His two best pieces of form this season say he's as good as ever, though, and if Cheltenham isn't Thistlecrack's track he has as good a chance as any of being the one to take advantage.

Going preference Seems to like it soft these days but never used to have a problem on faster
Star rating ✪✪✪✪

Outlander

9 b g; Trainer Gordon Elliott
Chase form 111F222F21, best RPR 170
Left-handed 1F1, best RPR 170
Right-handed 11222F2, best RPR 164
Cheltenham form (all) 6F, best RPR 147
At the festival 11 Mar 2015 Held up in midfield, not fluent 2nd, blundered 7th, progress to chase leaders 3 out, ridden next, one pace before last, finished sixth, beaten six lengths by Windsor Park in Neptune Investment Management Novices' Hurdle
17 Mar 2016 Hampered start, tracking leaders by 3rd, went right 11th, going well enough in close 4th when fell 4 out in JLT Novices' Chase won by Black Hercules

Nine-year-old who has progressed slowly but steadily with every season and as a result is now not far from the top of the tree. A Grade 1 winner for Willie Mullins as a novice over 2m5½f, he didn't attempt a trip in excess of 3m over fences until Punchestown in April when getting it well enough to finished second to Zabana. Switched to Gordon Elliott for this season he has been better than ever, running a respectable second in a Grade 2 at Down Royal on his return and then having the race at his mercy when coming down at the last in the Clonmel Oil Chase on his next start. He gave the odds-on Djakadam a fright in the John Durkan next time and then reversed form just over two weeks later when scoring the biggest win of his career in the Lexus Chase by two and a half lengths from Don Poli, with Djakadam a head back in third. That form is still a few pounds shy of what is going to be needed at Cheltenham and he does have to prove himself over another couple of furlongs. But he keeps improving and has only finished out of the first two in a chase when falling, and he'd have won one of those and was still going well in the other (JLT last year).

Going preference Has won on all types of ground
Star rating ✪✪

Sizing John

7 b g; Trainer Jessica Harrington
Chase form 112233211, best RPR 168
Left-handed 22321, best RPR 168
Right-handed 1131, best RPR 166
Cheltenham form (all) 32, best RPR 162
At the festival 10 Mar 2015 Tracked leader, led 2 out, soon ridden, headed before last, kept on but no extra when lost 2nd run-in, finished third, beaten seven lengths by Douvan in Supreme Novices' Hurdle
15 Mar 2016 Led, headed 3rd, remained in close 2nd place until before 3 out, outpaced on bend before hampered and left 2nd 2 out, stayed on run-in but no chance with winner, finished second, beaten seven lengths by Douvan in Racing Post Arkle

Quality performer who would have won a lot more races than he has were it not for a certain Douvan, whose backside he has got to know quite well over the years. Although he was switched to Jessica Harrington from Henry de Bromhead for the start of this season it looked like business as usual on his return in the Paddy Power Chase at Leopardstown over Christmas as he was second to Douvan for the sixth time in seven meetings (was third in the other). But Harrington then moved him up to 2m4f for only the second time in the Kinloch Brae at Thurles and he stayed on really strongly to beat Sub Lieutenant by two and half lengths with last year's JLT winner Black Hercules 12 lengths back in third. Following that race rider Robbie Power declared Sizing John had become so laid back he'd stay any trip and connections decided to roll the dice by running him in the Irish Gold Cup over 3m. It proved an inspired decision as, despite racing keenly off a steady early gallop, he was always going well and, produced to lead over the last, he had enough in reserve to hold off Empire Of Dirt by three-quarters of a length with Don Poli the same distance back in third. Harrington has confirmed the Gold Cup rather than the Ryanair is now the target and, while he is another who is going to have to improve again and prove himself over the extra yardage at Cheltenham, he'll go into the race having run three career bests on RPRs. He has also saved his best for the festival for the last two years and that latest 3m win gives him almost the perfect profile.

Going preference Goes on any but likes good ground
Star rating ✪✪✪

Champagne West

9 b g; Trainer Henry de Bromhead
Chase form 112F2PFP311, best RPR 170
Left-handed 1122PP, best RPR 162
Right-handed FF311, best RPR 170
Cheltenham form (all) 41122PP, best RPR 162
At the festival 14 Mar 2014 Held up, not fluent 5th, steady headway 8th, chased leaders 3 out, ridden after 2 out, one pace before last, no impression after, finished fourth, beaten nine and a half lengths by Very Wood in Albert Bartlett Novices' Hurdle
17 Mar 2016 Always outpaced in rear, tailed off when pulled up before 11th in Ryanair Chase won by Vautour

Yet another who has switched trainers for this season, this one having changed nationality too, as he joined Henry de Bromhead from Philip Hobbs. Always talented for Hobbs, he was unfortunately equally clumsy and his jumping had fallen apart by the end of last season, his final three form figures reading PFP. Those frailties seem to have been mostly ironed out by De Bromhead, though, as after running a respectable third to Zabana on his stable debut at Gowran in November, he won his next two starts in impressive fashion. The first was in a Listed chase at Tramore on New Year's Day when he slammed Roi Des Francs by 12 lengths and he then rocked up under top weight in the Thyestes Chase at Gowran, where he made all despite one bad mistake and never looked like getting

beaten. That gives him a similar profile to On His Own (2014) and Djakadam (2015), who both scored under big weights in the Thyestes before running second in the Gold Cup, and if Champagne West can hold his jumping together he's not out of it. Whether he can on fast ground is another matter and he won't get an easy time up front.

Going preference Almost all best form on soft ground
Star rating ✪✪

Don Poli *(below)*

8 b g; Trainer Gordon Elliott
Chase form 111511323P23, best RPR 168
Left-handed 111113223, best RPR 168
Right-handed 153P, best RPR 164
Cheltenham form (all) 113, best RPR 168
At the festival 14 Mar 2014 Held up in rear, headway 3 out, driven to challenge after 2 out, slight lead last, driven clear final 110yds, won Martin Pipe Conditional Jockeys' Handicap Hurdle by four and a half lengths from Thomas Crapper
11 Mar 2015 Tracked leaders, nudged along from 13th, good jump to draw upsides 4 out, led travelling best approaching 2 out, stayed on strongly to draw clear run-in, won RSA Chase by six lengths from Southfield Theatre
18 Mar 2016 Held up in last pair well off pace, headway 3 out, went 3rd 2 out, stayed on but never any threat to front pair, finished third, beaten 14 and a half lengths by Don Cossack in Gold Cup

Dour stayer with an excellent Cheltenham Festival record having won twice and finished third in last season's Gold Cup. Was well fancied in many quarters for last year's renewal having beaten Many Clouds at Aintree and then won the Lexus, although was all out to beat the previously (and subsequently) regressive veteran First Lieutenant and the form actually gave him several pounds to find with the main protagonists. He couldn't find them when it mattered and, while some were not happy with the ride he was given out the back by Davy Russell, in reality he looked on occasions as though he was struggling to keep up and he was closer to the winner and second at the top of the hill than he was at the line. Defeats followed to Cue Card and Carlingford Lough at Aintree and Punchestown and it looked as though he'd simply found his level – which is just a little way below Gold Cup class in a good year. After a lamentable first effort for Gordon Elliott this season, it seems the same is true this season, for while he has travelled more kindly following a spell hunting, he hasn't been able to turn better track position into victory, with a Lexus second and Irish Gold Cup third producing very similar figures to last season's best. He needs to find more to be a major player and it's hard to see where it's going to come from, although with this year's race looking likely to turn into a more searching test of stamina than last year's, he could stay on into a place and beat a few more fancied rivals.

Going preference There are plenty who seem to think he wants soft ground, but his three best RPRs are on good, yielding and good to soft
Star rating ✪✪

Bristol De Mai

6 gr g; Trainer Nigel Twiston-Davies
Chase form 212111222213, best RPR 173
Left-handed 21122213, best RPR 173
Right-handed 2112, best RPR 158
Cheltenham form 2, best RPR 161
At the festival 17 Mar 2016 Led after 2nd, awkward 3rd, hit 3 out, ridden and headed before next, disputing 3-length 4th jumping last, stayed on into 2nd towards finish but no threat to winner, finished second, beaten three lengths by Black Hercules in JLT Novices' Chase

Youngest horse in the race and very talented at best, but in danger of earning an 'unreliable' tag. He has not finished out of the first three

in any race since joining Nigel Twiston-Davies from France, but that tells only half the story as he has actually finished last (of two and three) on two of his four starts this season. The first was when he was beaten 12 lengths by sole rival Seeyouatmidnight at odds of 2-5 at Carlisle in October and then when backed down to favouritism against Native River in the Denman Chase at Newbury in February. Each time he was held up and he gives the impression he sulks when not allowed to join the heat of battle, which is what he did when running his two better races this season. Although beaten by Otago Trail in the Rehearsal Chase at Newcastle, he had everything in trouble before getting tired approaching the second-last and, following a wind operation, he destroyed that rival, a winner next time, by 22 lengths in the Peter Marsh at Haydock. That earned him a Racing Post Rating of 173, which is the third-best of any horse among the Gold Cup entries this season, but it's also the second time he has looked a superstar at Haydock, where the easy fences and soft ground seem to suit so well. He did finish second in last year's JLT, though, and despite racing too keenly and belting a few he rallied really well when looking booked for fourth at the last, so he can act at Cheltenham.

Going preference Handles soft ground well
Star rating ✪✪

Minella Rocco

7 b g; Trainer Jonjo O'Neill
Chase form 3P6213FU, best RPR 162
Left-handed 3P613FU, best RPR 162
Right-handed 2, best RPR 151
Cheltenham form P613, best RPR 162
At the festival 15 Mar 2016 Held up, reminder after 8th, headway 4 out, upsides 2 out, led just before last, stayed on well and edged right run-in, kept up to work towards finish, won National Hunt Chase by a length and a quarter from Native River

Beat Native River in last season's National Hunt Chase and that's something nothing else has managed to do over fences since.

Unfortunately nothing has gone right for him since a pleasing enough third under a big weight back at Cheltenham in November as he took a heavy fall at the last when challenging Many Clouds at Aintree (held, but form looks better now) and then unseated at the fifth in the Irish Gold Cup. That hardly gives him the form to be seriously considered, but Jonjo O'Neill intends to run and he has seriously ability when he puts it altogether. Perhaps Cheltenham and some better ground is what he needs.

Going preference No real preference
Star rating ✪✪✪✪

More Of That

9 b g; Trainer Jonjo O'Neill
Chase form 113P36U, best RPR 162
Left-handed 113P6U, best RPR 162
Right-handed 3, best RPR 151
Cheltenham form (all) 11113P, best RPR 172
At the festival 13 Mar 2014 Held up, headway approaching 2 out, soon tracked leaders, disputed lead before last where took narrow advantage, ridden run-in, stayed on well and in command final 75yds, won World Hurdle by a length and a half from Annie Power
16 Mar 2016 Held up in last pair, little slow 5th, nudged along after 15th, short of room when taking closer order before 3 out, ridden and every chance 2 out, close 3rd and still decent chance when squeezed up last, no extra (broke blood vessel), finished third, beaten eight and a half lengths by Blaklion in RSA Chase

The only horse to beat Annie Power when she has stayed on her feet, the 2014 World Hurdle winner has had something of a chequered career since sent chasing and, after breaking a blood vessel when 6-4 favourite in last season's RSA Chase (third), this term has been little short of a disaster. A breathing operation was supposed to have sorted him out and he was sent off favourite for the BetVictor Gold Cup on his return, but he never travelled and was pulled up – and a third in the Peterborough Chase was still some way short of his peak form. He then finished sixth in the Lexus, beaten 11 and a half lengths, and looked anything like a Gold Cup contender. However,

while he fell at the last on his latest start in the Irish Gold Cup, he was coming with a late run and would not have been far away from winner Sizing John had he stood up. Apparently a second breathing operation has worked and he could well be set for a big run if allowed to take his chance. That's not certain, though, because he's been given a handy weight for the Grand National and trainer Jonjo O'Neill has admitted he's tempted but doesn't want to run in both.

Going preference Handles any ground
Star rating ✪✪

OTHERS TO CONSIDER

Zabana is at least a Grade 1 winner over 3m1f and likes good ground, so he wouldn't be totally out of it, but last season's RSA winner **Blaklion** hasn't come up to scratch this season and looks likely to head to the Grand National after finishing second in the trial at Haydock in February, while the rest have either had their day or just aren't good enough.

VERDICT

The market has the right favourite in Thistlecrack, but he worries me with how much he puts into his jumping and I have a feeling this is much more open than his odds of 7-4 suggest. Native River is admirable, but there has to be a question mark about him holding his position if the ground rides fast, while history suggests Cue Card is surely too old, as much as we'd all like to see him win. I can't see what's wrong with DJAKADAM, who has been second in two good Gold Cups and, as he's only eight now, should still be in his prime. It's true he hasn't quite shown the same sparkle this season, but Willie Mullins will have had his eye on only one target and there's no Don Cossack to beat. Of those at slightly bigger odds, it would not be wise to underestimate Sizing John, who has stamina to prove but will likely travel well and still be in contention two out if the ground rides no worse than good to soft. As a young horse who has just won a 3m Grade 1, he has a fair profile.

GOLD CUP RESULTS AND TRENDS

	FORM WINNER	AGE & WGT	Adj RPR	SP	TRAINER	BEST RPR LAST 12 MONTHS (RUNS SINCE)
16	111F1 **Don Cossack**	9 11-10	185^T	9-4f	G Elliott (IRE)	won Gd1 Punchestown Gold Cup (3m1f) **(4)**
15	3/111 **Coneygree** C	8 11-10	173^{-9}	7-1	M Bradstock	won Newbury Gd2 chase (2m7½f) **(0)**
14	1-876 **Lord Windermere** C	8 11-10	161^{-24}	20-1	J Culloty (IRE)	7th Gd1 Lexus Chase (3m) **(1)**
13	321-1 **Bobs Worth** C, D	8 11-10	178^{-6}	11-4f	N Henderson	won Gd3 Hennessy Gold Cup (3m2½f) **(0)**
12	-P731 **Synchronised**	9 11-10	175^{-12}	8-1	J O'Neill	won Gd1 Lexus Chase (3m) **(0)**
11	13-31 **Long Run**	6 11-10	184^{-2}	7-2f	N Henderson	won Gd1 King George VI Chase (3m) **(0)**
10	1-P25 **Imperial Commander** C	9 11-10	181^{-15}	7-1	N Twiston-Davies	2nd Gd1 Betfair Chase (3m) **(1)**
09	2-1U1 **Kauto Star** CD	9 11-10	188^{-1}	7-4f	P Nicholls	won Gd1 King George VI Chase (3m) **(0)**
08	1-111 **Denman** C, D	8 11-10	184^{-5}	9-4	P Nicholls	won Gd3 Hennessy Gold Cup (3m2½f) **(2)**
07	11111 **Kauto Star**	7 11-10	188^T	5-4f	P Nicholls	won Gd1 Betfair Chase (3m) **(3)**

WINS-RUNS: 6yo 1-4, 7yo 1-23, 8yo 4-40, 9yo 4-40, 10yo 0-22, 11yo 0-9, 12yo 0-3 **FAVOURITES:** £6.50

TRAINERS IN THIS RACE (w-pl-r): Paul Nicholls 3-6-25, Nicky Henderson 2-2-9, Gordon Elliott 1-0-1, Jim Culloty 1-0-2, Jonjo O'Neill 1-2-6, Nigel Twiston-Davies 1-0-4, Alan King 0-0-5, Colin Tizzard 0-0-2, Noel Meade 0-1-3, Oliver Sherwood 0-0-1, Philip Hobbs 0-0-2, Rebecca Curtis 0-0-3, Willie Mullins 0-5-11, Henry de Bromhead 0-0-1, Nick Williams 0-0-1

FATE OF FAVOURITES: 121F131501 **POSITION OF WINNER IN MARKET:** 1213131721

Key trends

🏇Grade 1 chase winner, 10/10

🏇Aged between seven and nine, 9/10

🏇Two to five runs that season, 9/10

🏇Adjusted RPR of at least 173, 9/10

🏇Won over at least 3m, 9/10

🏇Won a Graded chase that season, 8/10

🏇Ran between five and ten times over fences, 7/10

🏇Won or placed previously at the festival, 7/10

🏇Within 9lb of RPR top-rated, 7/10

Other factors

🏇In 2015, Coneygree became the first winner not to have run at a previous festival since Imperial Call in 1996. He was also the first novice to win since Captain Christy in 1974

🏇The most popular reappearance race among the last ten winners was the Hennessy, with three victors making their seasonal debut in the Newbury handicap. Two won (Denman and Bobs Worth) and the other finished eighth (Lord Windermere)

🏇Bobs Worth and Coneygree were the only two of the last ten winners not to have run in the King George or Lexus that season

Notes

4.10 St James's Place Foxhunter Chase   ITV/RUK
3m2½f   Amateur riders   £45,000

Enda Bolger's On The Fringe joined a select group last year when he became the eighth dual winner since the second world war and only the fourth to achieve the feat in consecutive years. The 12-year-old returns with a favourite's chance of completing the hat-trick, having already bucked the age trend by becoming only the fourth from the double-figure age bracket in the past quarter of a century to score a first win in the race (although he was the fourth to score again at the age of ten or older).

Since the first Irish-trained victory in 1983 there have been ten subsequent wins, including in each of the last six years.

The Leopardstown Inn Hunters Chase (formerly known as the Raymond Smith Memorial) in early February is the best Irish trial. Three of the last five winners have gone on to victory here, although On The Fringe was only second and seventh in that race before winning here. He was runner-up again this time behind Foxrock, who is not eligible for this race.

FOXHUNTER CHASE RESULTS AND TRENDS

	FORM	WINNER	AGE & WGT	Adj RPR	SP	TRAINER	BEST RPR LAST 12 MONTHS (RUNS SINCE)
16	11-17	**On The Fringe** CD, BF	11 12-0	148^T	13-8f	E Bolger (IRE)	won Aintree Fox Hunters ch (2m5f) (2)
15	-1122	**On The Fringe**	10 12-0	144^T	6-1	E Bolger (IRE)	1st Punchestown hunt ch (2m7f) (4)
14	-6213	**Tammys Hill** BF	9 12-0	139-9	15-2	L Lennon (IRE)	2nd Down Royal hunt ch (2m7f) (2)
13	-1221	**Salsify** CD	8 12-0	143-6	2-1f	R Sweeney (IRE)	won Foxhunter Chase (3m2½f) (5)
12	-11P1	**Salsify**	7 12-0	132-14	7-1	R Sweeney (IRE)	won Leopardstown hunt ch (3m) (0)
11	44-21	**Zemsky**	8 12-0	125-23	33-1	I Ferguson (IRE)	won Musselburgh cl 6 hunt ch (3m½f) (0)
10	2-121	**Baby Run**	10 12-0	144-7	9-2jf	N Twiston-Davies	won Warwick class 6 hunt ch (3m½) (0)
09	11	**Cappa Bleu**	7 12-0	130-14	11-2	S Crow	won Chaddesley Corbett open (3m) (0)
08	-P211	**Amicelli**	9 12-0	128-6	33-1	C Coward	won Brocklesby Park open (3m) (1)
07	19F0-	**Drombeag**	9 12-0	119-17	20-1	J O'Neill	9th Foxhunter Chase (3m2½f) (2)

WINS-RUNS: 6yo 0-1, 7yo 2-17, 8yo 2-39, 9yo 3-44, 10yo 2-48, 11yo 1-44, 12yo 0-28, 13yo 0-11, 14yo 0-2 **FAVOURITES:** £-0.13

TRAINERS IN THIS RACE (w-pl-r): Enda Bolger 2-1-4, Rodger Sweeney 2-0-2, Jonjo O'Neill 1-0-5, Paul Nicholls 0-0-9, Alan Hill 0-2-5, Brian Hamilton 0-0-1, Colin McBratney 0-2-3, Gordon Elliott 0-0-3, James Joseph Mangan 0-2-4, Rebecca Curtis 0-0-3, Willie Mullins 0-0-1

FATE OF FAVOURITES: 2P01421531 **POSITION OF WINNER IN MARKET:** 8021031421

Key trends

- Won over at least 3m, 10/10
- Ran between 20 and 41 days ago, 9/10 (exception was having first start in nearly a year)
- Adjusted RPR of at least 125, 9/10
- Top-three finish last time out, 8/10
- Aged seven to nine, 7/10

Other factors

- Record of previous year's winner is 204U11

- Salsify (2012-13) and On The Fringe (2015-16) were back-to-back winners. The last one before them was Double Silk in 1993-94
- Four winners had competed at the festival before and all had finished in the first four
- Four winners were former handicap chasers and six had come from points
- Those aged 12 or older are winless in the last ten years. The 13-year-old Earthmover (2004) is the only winner from this category since 1990

Willie Mullins and Paul Nicholls have dominated this handicap hurdle, winning five times between them in the last six years. Although Mullins is the only Irish trainer to have won the race, his compatriots have been competitive too and Ireland had the first four in 2015 (although nothing better than fourth last year).

The Mullins winners have had the shortest SPs (9-2 favourite, 7-1 and 12-1) with the others sent off at 14-1 or bigger.

Mullins has several possibles again this year, including last year's Champion Bumper runner-up Battleford and Chacun Pour Soi, while Nicholls contenders might include Lac Fontana (already a festival winner in the 2014 County) and Brio Conti.

Although the race is open to four-year-olds and upwards, only five- and six-year-olds have been successful. They have also been placed 14 times.

The lowest-rated runner in 2016 ran off a mark of 135, while seven of the eight winners were within 7lb of the top-rated. Runners rated between 133 and 139 have won six of the eight runnings.

David Pipe has yet to win the race named in honour of his father, having had the beaten favourite three times and two unplaced second favourites.

Another to watch is No Comment (trained by Philip Hobbs and owned by JP McManus), who is open to further improvement and looks the type to be suited by a big field with a strong pace.

MARTIN PIPE HANDICAP HURDLE RESULTS

	FORM	WINNER	AGE & WGT	OR	SP	TRAINER	BEST RPR LAST 12 MONTHS (RUNS SINCE)
16	4-235	**Ibis Du Rheu**	5 11-7	139-4	14-1	P Nicholls	3rd Lanzarote hcap hdl (2m5f) (1)
15	-5123	**Killultagh Vic** D	6 11-1	135-5	7-1	W Mullins (IRE)	3rd Leop Gd2 nov hdl (2m4f) (0)
14	2-211	**Don Poli**	5 11-5	143-4	12-1	W Mullins (IRE)	won Clonmel Gd3 nov hdl (3m) (0)
13	-4251	**Salubrious** D	6 11-5	141-9	16-1	P Nicholls	won Musselburgh cl 3 hcap hdl (2m4f) (0)
12	135P1	**Attaglance**	6 11-3	139T	20-1	M Jefferson	won M Rasen class 3 hcap hdl (2m3f) (0)
11	1-1	**Sir Des Champs**	5 11-3	134T	9-2f	W Mullins (IRE)	won Navan hdl (2m) (0)
10	-445U	**Pause And Clause** D	6 11-10	137-3	14-1	E Lavelle	4th Haydock Listed hcap hdl (3m1f) (2)
09	-4134	**Andytown** C, D	6 11-2	133-6	25-1	N Henderson	won Chelt class 3 cond hcap hdl (2m5f) (1)

WINS-RUNS: 4yo 0-1, 5yo 3-49, 6yo 5-62, 7yo 0-41, 8yo 0-19, 9yo 0-8, 10yo 0-5, 12yo 0-1 **FAVOURITES:** -£2.50

FATE OF FAVOURITES: 3010P030 **POSITION OF WINNER IN MARKET:** 06108626

Key trends

🐎 Officially rated 133-143, 8/8

🐎 Aged five or six, 8/8

🐎 Top-three finish in at least one of last two starts, 7/8

🐎 Rated within 6lb of RPR top-rated, 7/8

🐎 No more than eight hurdle runs, 7/8

🐎 Had won that season, 6/8

Other factors

🐎 Willie Mullins accounts for all three Irish-trained winners. Two were owned by Gigginstown and went on to be top class over fences

🐎 All 74 runners aged seven or older have been beaten

🐎 Six of the eight winners carried between 11st 1lb and 11st 5lb

5.30 Grand Annual Handicap Chase　　　RUK
2m½f　Grade 3　£105,000

Solar Impulse became the longest-priced winner of last year's festival with his 28-1 victory in this race, emphasising yet again that this is a difficult 'getting out stakes' for punters. Alderwood in 2013 is the only successful favourite since 2004 and eight of the last 11 winners were sent off 12-1 or bigger.

Victory went to runners rated 129-134 in nine out of ten runnings up to 2010 but, as with the other festival handicaps, the threshold is moving upwards and five of the last six winners have been in the 140s. The last three winners, Savello (11st 5lb), Next Sensation (11st 2lb) and Solar Impulse (11st), have ended a 14-year run where no winner carried more than 10st 13lb.

A strong recent trend is that four of the last eight winners were officially novices. This has been a good race for novices with 12 winners, rated from 129 to 140, since 1983.

The 2008 winner Tiger Cry is the only winner aged over nine in the past 15 years, while Palarshan (2003) is the only five-year-old to win in the past 50 years.

The race's title has commemorated Nicky Henderson's father Johnny since 2005 and the trainer won the following year with Greenhope and again in 2012 with Bellvano (both 20-1 shots). He has also had four runner-ups and two thirds from a total of 35 runners.

Solar Impulse was a third winner in the past 13 runnings for Paul Nicholls (the previous two carried 10st 1lb and 10st 11lb), although he has also had four beaten favourites.

Ireland has won six of the last 17 runnings, including twice in the past four years, and three of them prepped over hurdles – two of the exceptions were the novices Fota Island and Alderwood.

Seven of the last ten British-trained winners had won at Cheltenham before.

*Rock The World (left):
prominent in the
ante-post market*

	FORM	WINNER	AGE & WGT	OR	SP	TRAINER	BEST RPR LAST 12 MONTHS (RUNS SINCE)
16	63-3P	**Solar Impulse** D	6 11-0	140^{-8}	28-1	P Nicholls	3rd Haydock class 2 ch (2m½f) (1)
15	5-604	**Next Sensation** D	8 11-2	143^{-5}	16-1	M Scudamore	4th Newbury class 2 hcap ch (2m½f) (0)
14	-3439	**Savello** D	8 11-5	147^{-2}	16-1	A Martin (IRE)	3rd Leopardstown hcap ch (2m1f) (1)
13	-S312	**Alderwood** C, D	9 10-11	140^{T}	3-1f	T Mullins (IRE)	2nd Punchestown hcap ch (2m) (0)
12	-1621	**Bellvano** D	8 10-2	138^{T}	20-1	N Henderson	won Kelso class 2 nov ch (2m1f) (0)
11	U6483	**Oiseau De Nuit** CD	9 10-13	145^{-3}	40-1	C Tizzard	3rd Newbury Gd2 ch (2m1f) (0)
10	222F5	**Pigeon Island** C, D	7 10-1	129^{T}	16-1	N Twiston-Davies	2nd Cheltenham Gd2 nov ch (2m5f) (2)
09	423F2	**Oh Crick** (1oh) C, D	6 10-0	130^{-13}	7-1	A King	2nd Hereford class 3 nov ch (2m3f) (0)
08	4P-36	**Tiger Cry** D	10 10-6	134^{-1}	15-2	A Moore (IRE)	3rd Ascot class 2 hcap ch (2m1f) (0)
07	3-333	**Andreas** CD, BF	7 10-11	143^{-1}	12-1	P Nicholls	3rd Sandown Gd3 hcap ch (2m) (0)

WINS-RUNS: 5yo 0-5, 6yo 2-25, 7yo 2-44, 8yo 3-57, 9yo 2-40, 10yo 1-29, 11yo 0-10, 12yo 0-1 **FAVOURITES:** -£6.00

FATE OF FAVOURITES: 620P001243 **POSITION OF WINNER IN MARKET:** 4228001970

Key trends

🏇Distance winner, 10/10

🏇No more than 12 runs over fences, 9/10

🏇Aged nine or under, 9/10

🏇Top-three finish on at least one of last two starts, 8/10

🏇Carried no more than 11st, 8/10

🏇Officially rated 129 to 143, 8/10

🏇Yet to win that season, 8/10

🏇Had run at a previous festival, 7/10

🏇No more than four runs since August, 6/10

Other factors

🏇Five winners had won at the course – three of the exceptions had placed in this race previously

🏇There have been four winning novices

🏇Since 2005, when the race was renamed in honour of his father, Nicky Henderson's runners have finished 346, 180P, 800, 20, 3P, 20P, 60, 1240PF, 2589PF, 590, 0 (no runner in 2015 when the race was named after AP McCoy)

🏇The record of the previous year's winner is 045B0

Notes